Varqá and Rúhu'lláh

101 Stories of Bravery on the Move

Boris Handal

Published: Second Edition July 2025
Boris Handal

Varqá and Rúhu'lláh: 101 Stories of Bravery on the Move
ISBN: 978-0-6489014-5-7 (print)

Varqá and Rúhu'lláh: 101 Stories of Bravery on the Move
ISBN: 978-0-6489014-6-4 (e-book)

"O friends, now indeed is the time, the time of service,
the time for acquiring divine bounty, the time of victory."
Rúḥu'lláh Varqá

To the Bahá'ís of Iran

Foreword

Journeys are a pervasive theme in Bahá'í literature, no less so in *Varqá and Rúḥu'lláh: 101 Stories of Bravery on the Move* by Dr. Boris Handal. As the title suggests, this volume invites the reader to accompany two heroic souls as they scale the rugged mountains on their approach to their Beloved: the father, Mírzá 'Alí-Muḥammad, surnamed "Varqá" (Dove) by Bahá'u'lláh, and his young son, Rúḥu'lláh (meaning the "Spirit of God"). Both individuals figure prominently in Bahá'í history: Varqá, a Hand of the Cause of God, and a renowned teacher, poet and physician and in 'Abdu'l-Bahá's words, an "incomparable person, a jewel of kindness"; and Rúḥu'lláh, a prodigy who was referred to as Jináb-i-Mubaligh (the Honourable Religious Teacher) by Bahá'u'lláh. They were both inhumanly put to death in prison in Tehran in 1896; their only "crime" – being Bahá'ís.

In this volume, the reader is taken on a journey of transformation and discovery. Transported to distant lands, whether on the uplifting and awe-inspiring journeys to pilgrimage in the Holy Land or on the long and perilous journey on horseback from Zanján to Tehran, in chains and fetters and in the bitter cold, the author employs the resources of language and imagery to depict the backdrop of the literal and metaphorical journey: "For days the prisoners kept moving through the rocky road flanked on the left by the ruggy slopes of the Alborz ranges and on the right by the vastness of the Iranian plateau". As we marvel at Varqá's and Rúḥu'lláh's endurance and the bravery of their exploits, we are prompted to consider afresh the condition and purpose of our own inner lives and spiritual journeys.

The author has assembled many luminous gems to captivate and inspire the reader, amongst them a detailed account of Varqá's integral role in communicating with Bahá'u'lláh in respect to the treasured portrait of the Báb (painted by artist Áqá Balá Bayg of Shishavan); and a story about the endearing relationship between Rúḥu'lláh and the revered Umm-i-Ashraf (Mother of Ashraf) who showered love and hospitality upon the young Rúḥu'lláh in Zanján in 1882. Also notable is Rúḥu'lláh's affection and high regard for his aunt Bíbí Túbá (Varqá's only sister) whom he refers to in glowing terms: "my exalted aunt" and "the esteemed and respected aunt", a regard rarely accorded to women in Persia in those days. Further, there is a graphic description of the brutal Anbár prison which "epitomised the miseries of Qajar society" where Varqá, Rúḥu'lláh and their two companions, Mírzá Ḥusayn and Ḥájí Ímám, were incarcerated and where Varqá and Rúḥu'lláh were later martyred. It was here that we see the fraternal feeling between Rúḥu'lláh (then aged 12 years) and his older brother, the valiant Azízu'lláh (aged 15 years) who despite the very real danger posed for his own safety (as Varqá himself had cautioned) managed to gain access to that hellish place to be of assistance to his father and brother.

We cannot fail to mention the stirring extracts from Varqá's and Rúḥu'lláh's poetry on the mystical themes of love, sacrifice and the mysteries of martyrdom which beckon the reader to search out more. And while Rúḥu'lláh possessed a maturity well beyond his age, his poetry has an evocative quality of the spirit of idealism and service so characteristic of his own age of junior youth:

> Hoisting the flags of guidance, march
> Towards the world, O lovers of Bahá,
>
> That these intoxicated creatures may awaken
> And move away from fancies and doubts,
>
> And the light of God may enlighten their eyes,
> And the thorns of their hearts may become roses.

The concluding stories are devoted to the lives of Varqá's third son, Mr Valíyu'lláh Varqá and grandson, Dr. 'Alí-Muḥammad Varqá who were both Hands of the Cause of God and Trustees of the Institution of Ḥuqúqu'lláh. How remarkable that Varqá's lineage should have such a deep association with the law of Ḥuqúqu'lláh! – a law, Bahá'u'lláh tells us, in which "there are benefits and wisdoms beyond the ken of anyone but God, the Omniscient, the All-Informed".[1] Apt then, is the inclusion of an Appendix with a talk by Dr. Varqá on Ḥuqúqu'lláh given at the Sixth International Convention in Haifa in 1988.

At its closure, the author offers some final reflections which include a welcome recognition of the often hidden yet indispensable role of women in this historical account, at a time when "referring to women's names was forbidden by common laws" and "houses did not even have windows opening upon the outside world". Women used to talk to visitors at home behind curtains and cover their faces in public. While we look back askance at such severe oppression and can take some heart at progress being made in relation to gender equality, the author is at pains to remind us of the systematic oppression of the Bahá'ís in Iran which distressingly continues to the present day.

This foreword would be incomplete without a note on illustrations. Widely sourced, and accompanied by the author's rich descriptive narrative, they provide fascinating insights to illuminate the context, dating back to early Persia.

One of the stories in this volume concerns a recollection of Varqá upon attaining the honour of meeting Bahá'u'lláh while on his first pilgrimage in 1878. On this occasion, Bahá'u'lláh emphasised the importance of writing: "the Blessed Tongue repeated the Command of the 'First Point,' which was that the believers should each one write books demonstrating the truth of 'He whom God shall manifest.'" It is hoped that the publication of Varqá and Rúḥu'lláh: 101 Stories of Bravery on the Move will inspire other individuals to similarly arise and put pen to paper and heed Rúḥu'lláh's admonition to "Make an effort, O my friends! The time to serve hath come!"

Dr Felicity Rawlings-Sanaei
Sydney, Australia
September, 2020

---

[1] Bahá'u'lláh. The Kitáb-i-Aqdas, Bahá'í Reference Library available at: www.bahai.org/r/443108496

Preface

I first met the Hand of the Cause of God Dr 'Alí-Muḥammad Varqá, member of the illustrious Varqá family, in 1985. An international Bahá'í youth conference was held in Lima, Peru, and Dr Varqá was the special speaker at the invitation of the National Spiritual Assembly of Peru. Youth from almost all of Latin America were interested in coming. However, those were difficult times due to political instability and insecurity because of the threat of armed groups.

At that time, months after the Iranian Islamic revolution Dr Varqá was residing in Canada. He was not feeling well but when invited over the phone his immediate response was: "If that is for the youth I will be there". With a group of friends, I went to receive him at the airport late at night to take him to his hotel. At one of the sessions, I sat next to him and spoke about an article that I had written about his grandfather Varqá and his uncle Rúḥu'lláh. Dr Varqá was impressed by my modest thirty-page article written in the Spanish language and was very encouraging about its publication. For my delight, he signed the book cover. I remember him becoming very interested about the sources of my work with a gentleness of which I will treasure forever.

Dr Varqá spoke about the Covenant and how the Universal House of Justice was elected in 1963. He referred to the year 1957 when suddenly Shoghi Effendi died leaving the Hands of the Cause in a leadership role to the Bahá'í world. Given the empty space left by the Guardian's passing, the Hands studied together the Writings of Bahá'u'lláh, 'Abdu'l-Bahá and Shoghi Effendi to find guidance on what they could do to move the Faith forward. Finally, the Hands decided to continue advancing the Ten Year Crusade and at its conclusion arranged for the election of the first Universal House of Justice. The point that Dr Varqá made was that whatever a problem is, we should always find the solution in the Writings of our Faith.

The conference was a total success and people came to see the Hand of the Cause. Five-hundred youth from eighteen countries in Latin America, North America and four native groups congregated together around Dr Varqá to celebrate the International Year of the Youth announced by the United Nations. The youth were able to interact personally with the Hand of the Cause at all times. "His presence and his words inspired hundreds of young people from almost twenty Latin American countries", a conference organiser wrote. "Dr Varqá's visit to Lima turned a crisis into a great victory, lighting the flame of the spirit of more than five hundred young people".[2]

I later learned that Dr Varqá's father, the Hand of the Cause Valíyu'lláh Varqá, had come to Lima in the first week of August 1953 in the midst of an intense winter on an exhausting teaching tour taking him to Panama, Quito, Guayaquil, Lima, Santiago, Montevideo and Brazil.[3] He came by sea and was received at the main port by a group of eleven believers of the nascent Peruvian Bahá'í community. At that time, only two Spiritual Assemblies were formed in the country. Several meetings were held for Bahá'ís and their friends. The compact local shop functioning as a Bahá'í centre proved not enough to accommodate everyone and therefore talks were held at his Euro Hotel in the Miraflores part of the city next to the sea. For these believers, it was the first time that they were meeting a designated Hand of the Cause of God and they still recall his evident dignity and courtesy. Both Hands visited eight Hispano-American countries during their lifetimes.

The next time I saw Dr Varqá was when I went on pilgrimage in 1996. We shook hands again in Bahjí and he signed my prayer book which I still treasure much. Although, Dr Varqá looked frailer as he was in his eighty-fifth year, yet he was ceaselessly interacting with the dozens of pilgrims. I remember our pilgrim guide taking us to the Office of Ḥuqúqu'lláh to get a glimpse of Dr Varqá in his work environment as the Chief Trustee. I had the impression that his desk

---

[2] Enrique Sanchez Jr, personal communication to the author.
[3] Boris Handal, Eve Nicklin: She of the Brave Heart (Charleston, South Carolina: CreateSpace, 2011).

had been placed next to his door so that he could see the passing of the pilgrim groups. As pilgrims, we also heard him speak at the building of the International Teaching Centre for the pilgrims.

In a calm but resonant voice, Dr Varqá spoke about the existence of over 10,000 Local Spiritual Assemblies worldwide, and also about the need for personal teaching plans when we return back home. He radiated much kindness throughout his talk and summoned the friends to a greater level of courage and hard work. He spoke with a wonderful spirit from beginning to end, and that spirit stayed with the audience even when he left the auditorium. In a subsequent pilgrimage, I saw Dr Varqá sitting in a small white car at Collins Gate in Bahjí in deep reflection about the Shrine of Bahá'u'lláh from a distance, the place where his grandfather Varqá had stood in 1893, solemnly contemplating and grieving the ascension of the Blessed Beauty that took place the year after his second pilgrimage. He was greeting all the pilgrims and I saw the Hand of the Cause doing what he seemed to enjoy, mingling with Bahá'ís from all over the world.

Despite his advanced age, his loving and all-embracing smile could be seen on his illumined face at all times— the same smile that attracted me to this distinguished personage the first time I met him when I was a youth. Dr Varqá always manifested a natural dignity and nobility while radiating great humility and self-effacement, which is even more praiseworthy given that he came from a distinguished Bahá'í family. Such a pattern of family consecration had its roots during the time of the Báb, continued throughout the ministries of Bahá'u'lláh, 'Abdu'l-Bahá and Shoghi Effendi, shone during the custodianship of the Hands of the Cause, and ended in a blaze of glory in the service of the Universal House of Justice. Dr Varqá's grandfather, 'Alí Muḥammad Varqá, was posthumously elevated to the rank of Hand of the Cause. While he was alive, Dr Varqá's father, Valíyu'lláh Varqá, was also appointed a Hand of the Cause. Thus, within a space of sixty years this family raised two glorious martyrs and three Hands of the Cause. Certainly, this was a blessed family whose members were characterised by dedication, courage and sacrifice, and whose services spanned over 170 years.

The narrative of their services was miraculously preserved primarily through story-telling and oral accounts more than by any other means hence the continuous referencing to primary and secondary sources. This book contains 101 vignettes documenting this spiritual legacy to the world. To transport our modern minds to a different time and space, care has been taken to interpolate glimpses of Iranian culture, history, geography and even the language. As the title of the book implies, a story-telling approach has been adopted on the basis of true historical events which have been properly referenced through numerous footnotes and the bibliographical list at the end of the book. At times when the available sources were silent, the author has offered his own interpretation which is indicated in the text.

Should we attempt to understand the humanness of Varqá and his son Rúḥu'lláh as well as their grandiosity, it is necessary to refer to the context in which they lived. To encounter those personal traces, those that make us similar to them, we need to consider the external forces to which Varqá and his son Rúḥu'lláh were subjected to, and how they reacted to the crises and victories they faced. The author has attempted his best to represent the contrast between what they actually managed to change and what they could not, despite their efforts. The result of these two contrasts was certainly the result of divine intervention because they passed into history with unsurpassed heroism and brilliance.

With the same satisfaction that the author shared, thirty five years ago, with Dr Varqá the modest thirty-page article on Rúḥu'lláh and his father, he now submits this expanded work in the hope that the light of their blessings, traversing epochs and eras, as 'Abdu'l-Bahá promised, illumines and confirms the reader, whatever time he or she lives in.

Boris Handal
Sydney, Australia
February 2025

Acknowledgements

This book would not have been possible without the exceptional support of Bahá'í institutions, colleagues, friends and family members. I would like to thank the Research Department and the Audio-Visual Department of the Bahá'í World Centre, as well as the Archive Department of the US Bahá'í National Centre and George Ronald Publisher for providing several of the photos included in the book. Old photos are mostly public domain unless indicated. I want to show my appreciation as well to the National Spiritual Assembly of the Bahá'ís of Australia for their logistic support, nurturing and encouragement. I also would like to express my gratitude to Dr Melanie Lotfali and Dr Felicity Rawlings-Sanaei for their careful editorial work including proofreading. I must also acknowledge Dr Iraj Ayman, Dr Moojan Momen, Dr Wendi Momen, Dr Stephen Lambden, Nur Mihrshahi, Dr Soroush Sedaghat, the Vargha family, Camelia Handal, and Greg Dahl for their assistance with translations, historical research and general commentary. Marta and Vicente Lopez also contributed with important historical and photographic information. Also thanks to Farzad Naziri and Habib Hosseiny for translating Rúhu'lláh's letter to his aunt and the personal supplication, respectively.

Many friends such as Enrique Sanchez Jr, Gary Khamsi, Martha and Vicente Lopez, Shahnaz Talebzadeh, Farhad Radmehr, Mirna Leon, Dr Farid Tebyani, Dr Ron Tingook, Dr Omar Brdarevic, Gloria Sadeghi Mogharabi, Michael Day, Dr Janet Khan, among other believers, wrote their touching impressions about the Hand of the Cause of God Dr Varqá. Many thanks also to Allan Waters for letting me quote from his article about Dr Varqá's contribution to the Institution of Ḥuqúqu'lláh and to Vafa Lalehzari for his most valued technical support with the photographs and particularly with the narrative literacy. Hoda Seioshansian and Mary Victoria were very helpful by assisting in the translation of some of Varqá's poems. Without my wife Parvin's encouragement and trust, this book would never have been produced.

To the Kazemzadeh family in the persons of Monireh Kazemzadeh and Marina Banuazizi for providing so generously historical information to enrich the narrative, I should express my deepest gratitude. To Ian Andrew from Leschenault Press for going the extra mile to meet my publishing requirements. My thanks also go to Juxta Publishing for giving permission to use the beautiful portrait of Rúḥu'lláh drawn by Jill Hatcher. Similarly, I would like to acknowledge the English translations of Rúḥu'lláh and Varqá's poetry published by Julio Savi, Faeze Mardani, John Hatcher and Amrollah Hemmat. Likewise, I am grateful to Pedro Donaires for drawing the plane of the Anbár prison and the maps of Iran. The facsimile of Rúḥu'lláh's calligraphy is reproduced with permission from the Bahá'í World Centre.

A Short Note on Bahá'í Orthography

Readers are advised that to a feasible extent the author has used the transliteration standard adopted by Shoghi Effendi in 1923 for Bahá'í literature in the Persian and Arabic language. The system was adapted from the standards set by the Tenth International Congress of Orientalists held in Geneva in 1894.

Due to the lack of a uniform system before Shoghi Effendi's ministry, the writing of Bahá'í terms was inconsistent. For early texts, this book has kept as much as possible the integrity of the original source although at times the correct transliteration has been used to assist with the flow of the narrative. Hence, the spelling of some terms in this book remains as in the original sources. For instance, the word Bahá'í sometimes is spelt as Bahai or Baha'i in some early publications.

In order to facilitate the understanding of some oriental words the table below outlines the variations of some Bahá'í terms that the reader may come across. In some cases, for practicality reasons, the most popular form of the name has been kept such as *Varqá* instead of *Varqa*, *Vargha* and *Wargha*, or Tehran instead of *Ṭihrán*.

Bahá'í transliteration	**Variations**
'Á<u>dh</u>irbayján	Azerbayjan, Azerbaijan,
'Ishqábád	Ashkhabad
Áqá	Aqa, Agha
Asadu'lláh	Asadollah
Bahá'u'lláh	Baha'o'llah
Jináb	Jinab, Jenab, Jenabe
Khán	Sir designation
Khánum	Lady designation
Mahmúd	Mahmoud
Mihdí	Mehdi, Mahdi
Riḍá	Reza, Riḍa
Rúḥu'lláh	Ruhu'lláh, Ruhollah
Siyyid	Sayyed, Sayyid
Tiḥrán	Tihrán, Tehran, Tehrán, Teheran
Varqá	Vargha, Wargha, Varga

Table of Contents

Foreword..*i*

Preface..*v*

Acknowledgements.. *ix*

A Short Note on Bahá'í Orthography.. *xi*

Table of Contents..*xiii*

Table of Illustrations..*xv*

Glossary.. *xix*

Introduction..*21*

I - In Yazd...*27*

II - In Tabríz..*35*

III - Varqá's First Pilgrimage...*41*

IV - Back in Tabríz..*47*

V - Prison in Yazd and Iṣfahán..*63*

VI - Rúḥu'lláh...*71*

VII - The Second Pilgrimage...*84*

VIII - The Furious Mother-in-law.. *102*

IX - In Zanján.. *107*

X - Arrested in Zanján... *117*

XI – The Mystery of Martyrdom.. *133*

XII – The Poetry in the Dove.. *151*

XIII - The Long Horseback March to Tehran.. *160*

XIV - The Anbár Prison... *171*

XV - The Martyrdom of Varqá and Rúḥu'lláh *205*

XVI - After the Martyrdom *213*

XVII – In the Aftermath *218*

XVIII - Valíyu'lláh Varqá *232*

XIX - Dr 'Alí-Muḥammad Varqá *244*

XX - Final Reflections *286*

Appendix I: A Tribute to Dr 'Alí-Muḥammad Varqá by Shahbaz Fatheazam *299*

Appendix II: Ḥuqúqu'lláh (The Right of God) – A Talk by the Hand of the Cause Dr 'Alí-Muḥammad Varqá *303*

Bibliography *313*

Index of Names *329*

Table of Illustrations

Figure 1: Panorama of Yazd in the 19th century. Source: Nabíl's Narrative. 91

Figure 2: A Nineteenth Century Persian Caravanserai in Sabzevar, Iran, by Alireza Javaheri (CC BY-SA 4.0). 91

Figure 4: An old view of the city of Tabríz. 92

Figure 3: Map of Iran. Courtesy: Pedro Donaires. 92

Figure 5: Bíbí Yazdí who married Ḥájí Mírzá Ḥusayn Yazdí (Varqá's brother). Source: MyHeritage.com 93

Figure 7: Prince Malek-Qasim Mírzá's palace in Urúmíyyih were the Báb's portrait was drawn. Source: Nabíl's Narrative. 94

Figure 6: Muẓaffari'd-Dín Mírzá's Court as the Heir Prince in Tabríz. 94

Figure 8: A group of Bahá'ís in Tabríz in 1891. Seated third from right is 'Alí Muḥammad Varqá. Front row, second from left is Rúḥu'lláh Varqá and the other boys seated with him are probably his brothers. Courtesy: George Ronald Oxford. 95

Figure 9: A group of Bahá'ís in Tabríz in 1882. Left to right, front row: Siyyid Mihdí Yazdí, unknown, Mír Sulaymán Yazdí (brother of Siyyid Yazdí). Left to right, middle row, seated: Ḥájí Amín, unknown, 'Alí Muḥammad Varqá, Ḥájí Mírzá Ḥusayn Yazdí (Varqá's brother). Back row: unknown, unknown. Courtesy: George Ronald Oxford. 96

Figure 11: Cities associated with Bahá'í history. Courtesy: Pedro Donaires. 97

Figure 10: The city of 'Akká at the beginning of the 19th Century. 97

Figure 12: Mansion of Mazra'ih, c. 1900. Courtesy: Bahá'í World Centre 98

Figure 13: The House of ‘Abbúd in ‘Akká. 98

Figure 14: Headstone of Ḥájí Mullá Mihdí in the cemetery of Mazra’ih © Bahá’í World Centre. 99

Figure 15: The Mansion of Bahjí at the beginning of the 19th Century. 99

Figure 16: A street of ‘Akká at the beginning of the 19th Century. Courtesy: Bahá’í World Centre. 100

Figure 17: The Soltanieh in Zanján (Public domain) 101

Figure 18: View of Zanján in the 19th century. 101

Figure 19: Laqá’íyyih Khánum. Courtesy: Monireh Kazemzadeh. 192

Figure 20: ‘Alá’u’d-Dawlih, the Governor of Zanján. 193

Figure 21: Kámrán Mírzá, Governor of Tehran. 194

Figure 22: Mas’úd Mírzá, Governor of Isfahan, the Sháh’s oldest son. 195

Figure 23: Naṣiri’d-Dín Sháh (reigned 1848 – 1896). 196

Figure 24: Photograph of the scene depicting the assassination of Naṣiri’d-Dín Sháh in the film Soltan-e Sahebgharan. 197

Figure 25: Map of the Royal Complex of Tehran in the 19th Century. 197

Figure 26: The first Ḥájíbu’d-Dawlih Ḥájí ‘Alí Khán Mughaddam Maraghí (1807–1867), responsible for the assassination of Ṭáhirih in 1852 and the death of many believers 198

Figure 28: Plane of the Anbár prison. Adapted from: Yaghoub Khazaei (2018). 199

Figure 30: A criminal being punished with the bastinado in Iran.. 200

Figure 29: Political prisoners in the Anbár prison. 200

Figure 31: Rúḥu’lláh Varqá in 1891. 201

Figure 32: View of Ferdowsi avenue (formerly, Alaé-Doulah) Tehran (1915) where Rúḥu’lláh, Varqá, Mírzá Ḥusayn Zanjání and Ḥájí Ímám Zanjání were paraded in 1896 before being sent to prison.. 201

Figure 33: Facsimile of Rúḥu'llah's Calligraphy. Source: Bahá'í World Centre.. 202

Figure 34: Rúḥu'lláh portrait by Jill Hatcher. Courtesy: Juxta Media. 203

Figure 36: Rúḥu'lláh and Varqá in chains. 204

Figure 35: The Hand of the Cause 'Alí Muḥammad Varqá. Courtesy: George Ronald. 204

Figure 38: The mausoleum of Varqá and Rúḥu'lláh in Tehran. 273

Figure 37: Varqá, Rúḥu'lláh, Mírzá Ḥusayn Zanjání and Ḥájí Ímám Zanjání chained to each other in the Anbár prison from left to right. 273

Figure 39: Muẓaffari'd-Dín Sháh (reigned 1896–1907)............... 274

Figure 40: Rúḥu'lláh's surviving brothers: Mírzá Valíyu'lláh Varqá (left) and Mírzá 'Azízu'lláh Varqá (right), in Tehran in 1908. 274

Figure 41:'Abdu'l-Bahá in Dublin, New Hampshire, in 1912. Valíyu'lláh Varqá is second from the right. Source: National Bahá'í Archives, United States... 275

Figure 42: Valíyu'lláh Varqá as a young man. 275

Figure 44: Bahá'is of Lima welcoming Hand of the Cause Valíyu'lláh Varqá in Lima, Peru, August 1953. 276

Figure 43: First National Spiritual Assembly of Iran formed in 1934. The future Hands of the Cause Shu'á'u'lláh 'Alá'í and Valíyu'lláh Varqá are seated first and second from the left, respectively. 276

Figure 45: Hand of the Cause and Trustee of the Ḥuqúqu'lláh Valíyu'lláh Varqá. 277

Figure 46: Members of the first Spiritual Assembly of Tehran (1897). Mírzá 'Azízu'lláh Varqá is seated in the middle of the front row holding the Greatest Name. On the middle row three of the four Hands of the Cause are seated: (from left to right) Mírzá Ḥasan-i-Adíb, Ibn-i- Aṣdaq, Ḥájí Mullá Akbar (Ḥájí Akhund). The covered faces are those of Covenant-breakers. Courtesy: George Ronald Oxford. ... 278

Figure 47. Childhood photograph of Dr Varqá on which ‘Abdu’l-Bahá wrote “Hand”, “Confirmed” and “Yá Bahá u’l-Abhá” (O Thou Glory of the Most Glorious). 279

Figure 48: Members of Iran’s National Youth Committee in 98 BE. Seated from right to left: Mr ‘Alí-Muḥammad Varqá (later Hand of the Cause), Mr ‘Alí Nakhjavání, Mrs Rúḥangiz Mutivayyih, Dr Míhdí Samandarí and Mr Muḥammad Yazdání. Standing from right to left: Mr ‘Abdu’lláh Misbáh, unknown, Mr Salim Nunu, Mr Zikru’lláh Khádem (later Hand of the Cause) and Mr Abu’l-Qásim Faizi (later Hand of the Cause) 280

Figure 49: Hand of the Cause Dr ‘Alí-Muḥammad Varqá (front row, second right) and members of the first National Spiritual Assembly of Congo and Gabon (1971). Courtesy: Bahá’í World Centre. 281

Figure 50: Dr Varqá attending the 1985 International Bahá’í Youth Conference in Lima. The author is on the left. 281

Figure 51: Hand of the Cause of God and Trustee of the Ḥuqúqu’lláh Dr ‘Alí-Muḥammad Varqá. Courtesy: Bahá’í World Centre. 282

Figure 52: 1985 International Bahá’í Youth Conference, Lima, Peru. 283

Figure 53: Gathered on the steps of the Seat of the Universal House of Justice on Mount Carmel, Haifa, Israel are members of the Continental Boards of Counsellors together with members of the Universal House of Justice, the International Teaching Centre, and, at front, centre, the Hand of the Cause of God Dr ‘Alí-Muḥammad Varqá, December 2005. Courtesy: Bahá’í World Centre. 284

Figure 54: Hand of the Cause Dr Varqá with members of the Universal House of Justice, 2007. Courtesy: Bahá’í World Centre. 285

Glossary

Abu'l:	Father of …
A.D.	(In Latin, *Anno Domini* – "In the year of the Lord") or Christian Era.
A.H.	"After Hijrah". Date of Muḥammad's migration from Mecca to Medina setting the beginning of the Islamic calendar.
Áqá:	Master, Sire.
Bábí:	A follower of the Faith of the Báb.
Caravanserai:	An inn or accommodation for caravans.
Farrásh:	Footman, guard, lictor. A Farrásh Báshí is the head of the farráshs, the equivalent to head of the royal house and master of ceremonies.
Ḥájí:	A person who has successfully completed the pilgrimage to Mecca.
Hand of the Cause:	An appointed position for the propagation and protection of the Bahá'í Faith. They were designated by Bahá'u'lláh, 'Abdu'l-Bahá and Shoghi Effendi.
Howdah	Litter carried by a mule, horse or camel to transport people in caravans.
Ḥuqúqu'lláh:	(In Arabic, "Right of God"). It is an ordinance enunciated by Bahá'u'lláh in the Kitáb-i-Aqdas. It is a voluntary payment offered to the Center of the Cause. The funds are used to advance the Cause of God, for socio-economic projects or for philanthropic purposes.
Khán:	Courtesy for males, e.g., Muḥammad Khán.
Khánum:	Courtesy for females, e.g., Maryam Khánum.
Jináb:	His/Her Excellency.

Mírzá:	If the term precedes the name it refers to an educated person, e.g., Mírzá Muḥammad. After the name it stands for Prince, e.g. Muḥammad Mírzá.
Muhtajid	A high Islamic level cleric.
Mullá:	An Islamic clergyman.
Shaykh:	A religious leader.
Siyyid:	A descendant from Prophet Muḥammad.

Titles can be combined in a single name such as in *Ḥájí Mírzá Siyyid ‘Alí Shírází,* meaning a person whose name is *‘Alí*, from an educated background, a descendant from Prophet Muḥammad and having been born in the city of *Shíráz.*

Introduction

Who was Varqá? Varqá was a man of many talents. He was a physician, a religious scholar and a poet, as well as a devout servant of the Cause of Bahá'u'lláh endowed with great eloquence. He was an avid Bahá'í travel teacher, a gifted speaker and a prominent public figure in the early Bahá'í community of Persia, now called Iran.

Bahá'u'lláh and 'Abdu'l-Bahá spoke highly of him. Born Mírzá 'Alí-Muḥammad, he was given the designation *Varqá* (Dove) by Bahá'u'lláh because of his eloquence as a poet and a Bahá'í speaker and travel teacher.

Our poet was referred to as the "revered martyr",[4] "the illustrious Varqá, may my soul be sacrificed for his sake",[5] by 'Abdu'l-Bahá, Who posthumously designated him as a Hand of the Cause of God.[6] In 1930, Shoghi Effendi listed Varqá as one of the Nineteen Apostles of Bahá'u'lláh.[7]

As a travel teacher, Varqá travelled constantly, visiting Bahá'ís in innumerable villages and towns. Martha Root wrote that the "family moved about from place to place because he was a Bahá'í teacher and travelled throughout Persia"[8] For his teaching activities he was imprisoned in various cities such as Yazd, Iṣfahán, Zanján and Tehran. Describing the way in which Varqá addressed ecclesiastical and civil authorities, 'Abdu'l-Bahá said he was "perfect in eloquence,

---

4 'Abdu'l-Bahá, Memorials of the Faithful (Wilmette, IL: Bahá'í Publishing Trust, 1971), 5.

5 Youness Afroukhteh, Memories of Nine Years in 'Akká (Translated by R. Masrour. Oxford: George Ronald, 2003), 173-74.

6 'Abdu'l-Bahá, Memorials of the Faithful, 5.

7 Shoghi Effendi, "The Apostles of Bahá'u'lláh", The Bahá'í World, vol. 3 (1928-1930), 80.

8 Martha Root, "White Roses of Persia (Part 2)," Star of the West, vol. 23, issue 6, (September 1932), 180.

his speech was convincing, his arguments were evident. Highly knowledgeable of religious matters, no one could withstand him …”[9]

Varqá was a Renaissance man, with “a good hand at calligraphy and other arts … [as well as] knowledge of medicine, scriptures, and the history and literature of his country….”[10] At that time in Iran, poetry and artistic calligraphy were among the finest arts through which a cultivated Persian man could demonstrate the skills and capacities he acquired through education. According to Mírzá Abu’l-Faḍl, Varqá “wrote poetry in Persian with the utmost elegance and beauty.”[11]

Varqá was also well-versed in medicine and chemistry as practised in 19th century Persia.[12] Mírzá Abu’l-Faḍl referred to Varqá as an “expert in medical science”.[13] He even had the opportunity to use his medical knowledge to treat Bahá’u’lláh Himself.[14]

For his era, Varqá was certainly a polymath. Shoghi Effendi refers to him as the “renowned teacher and poet”.[15] Furthermore, ‘Abdu-l-Baha has remarked that, “Even Zillu’s-Sultan (the Sháh’s eldest son) who murdered Bahá’ís, in My presence confirmed that Mírzá Varqá is the only fully accomplished Iranian”[16].

He was also exceptional in the realm of the spirit. ‘Abdu’l-Bahá mentioned that Varqá “from his youth time, rather, from his childhood, became a Bahá’í”[17] and that he “was accepted at the Holy

[9] Bahá’í News Service, "Abdul-Baha Introduces Mirza Wargha to the New York Friends," Star of the West, vol. 12, no. 4, Persian section (February 1913), 91-93.
[10] Hasan Balyuzi, Eminent Bahá'ís in the Time of Bahá'u'lláh (Oxford: George Ronald, 1986), 77.
[11] Mírzá Abu'l-Faḍl-i-Gulpáygání, Bahá'í Proofs, 99. (New York: J.W. Pratt & Co, 1902), https://bahai-library.com/gulpaygani_bahai_proofs.
[12] Encyclopædia Iranica, s.v. "Ali-Moḥammad Varqā," http://www.iranicaonline.org/articles/varqa-ali-mohammad.
[13] Mírzá Abu'l-Faḍl-i-Gulpáygání, 2.
[14] Balyuzi, Eminent Bahá'ís in the Time of Bahá'u'lláh, 1986, 82.
[15] Shoghi Effendi, God Passes By (Wilmette, IL: Bahá’í Publishing Trust, ed. 1979), 296.
[16] Star of the West, vol. 3, No. 18 (February 1913), 362-364.
[17] Star of the West, vol. 3, No. 18 (February 1913), 362-364.

Threshold ... He was the essence of the love of God".[18] His unlimited love for 'Abdu'l-Bahá and Bahá'u'lláh was the source of his tireless service and dedication.

No mention of Varqá can be made without talking about his son Rúḥu'lláh. A talented junior youth who had inherited his father's literary and spiritual keenness as shown by verses like these:

> O the joy of that day, when eyes at me stare
> As on gallows-tree, I the praise of the King of Glory declare.[19]

Both attained the presence of Bahá'u'lláh and 'Abdu'l-Bahá. Much loved, the stories narrated in this book reveal the strong bonds between Bahá'u'lláh and 'Abdu'l-Bahá, and Varqá and Rúḥu'lláh. Following their last pilgrimage both encountered a tragic death in 1896 at Tehran's main prison when Varqá was forty years old and his son Rúḥu'lláh just twelve.

Due to his spiritual insight, Bahá'u'lláh once called Rúḥu'lláh "Jináb-i-Mubaligh" (honourable religious teacher)[20] and 'Abdu'l-Bahá stated that the Cause of Bahá'u'lláh would be proclaimed to the world through him.[21] Mírzá Abu-Faḍl affirmed: "The child, although only eleven or twelve years old, had been educated and trained by his father and was very intelligent".[22]

On one occasion, after recounting the assassination of these two souls to American believers in New York in 1913, 'Abdu'l-Bahá said:

> Therefore you shall remember their level of attachment and their attraction to the Beloved, especially the attachment of that child, who was full of the love of God, and with what such

---

[18] Star of the West, vol. 3, No. 18 (February 1913), 362-364.
[19] Balyuzi, Eminent Bahá'ís in the Time of Bahá'u'lláh, 81.
[20] Darius Shahrokh, Varqá and Son: The Heavenly Doves (1992), Varqá and Son: The Heavenly Doves (1992), 2, https://bahai-library.com/shahrokh_varqa_son, https://bahai-library.com/shahrokh_varqa_son.
[21] Faizi, Fire on the Mountain Top, 91.
[22] Mírzá Abu'l-Faḍl-i-Gulpáygání, Bahá'í Proofs, 99, 1902.

> spiritual gladness and happiness, he sacrificed his life in the path of the Beloved and attained the rank of martyrdom.[23]

Upon delivering the address, it is written that 'Abdu'l-Bahá went up to His room and cried so much that the guests downstairs sitting in silence could hear Him.[24]

To an American couple to whom 'Abdu'l-Bahá advised to call their son Rúḥu'lláh after the young martyr Varqá,[25] He wrote:

> O thou who art attracted by the Fragrances of God!
>
> Thank God for giving and granting thee "sight of eyes" (i.e., a son) whereby thy bosom becomes dilated and thy heart rejoiced.
>
> Then make his name "Ruhullah" (i.e., the Spirit of God), so that the Spirit of thy Lord, the Merciful of the Merciful, will confirm him.
>
> O maid-servant of God! Know, verily, that the one who bore similar name (i.e., Ruhullah), son of Varga, was martyred in the path of God in the twelfth year of his life. While he was beneath the unsheathed sword he called out "Ya Baha-el-ABHA!" until he was killed in the path of God.
>
> We called thy son by this noble name so that he may have a great station in the Kingdom of God.[26]

In relation to the martyrdom of father and son, Shoghi Effendi wrote:

> Even the Sháh's assassination had at first been laid at the door of that community, as evidenced by the cruel death suffered, immediately after the murder of the sovereign, by the renowned teacher and poet, Mírzá 'Alí-Muḥammad, surnamed "Varqá" (Dove) by Bahá'u'lláh, who, together with his

---

[23] Star of the West, vol. 3, No. 18 (February 1913), 362-364.

[24] Mable R Garis, Martha Root: Lioness at the Threshold (Wilmette: Ill: Bahá'í Publishing Trust, 1983), 54.

[25] Thornton Chase, In Galilee (Kalimat Press, 1985), viii.

[26] 'Abdu'l-Bahá, Tablets of Abdul-Baha Abbas (Chicago: Baha'i Publishing Society, 1909-19), 19.

> twelve-year-old son, Rúḥu'lláh, was inhumanly put to death in the prison of Tihrán, by the brutal Hajíbu'd-Dawlih, who, after thrusting his dagger into the belly of the father and cutting him into pieces, before the eyes of his son, adjured the boy to recant, and, meeting with a blunt refusal, strangled him with a rope.[27]

The legend of the Varqá family began when the patriarch of the family, the respected Mullá Mihdí, a perfume-maker, accepted the Faith of the Báb in 1846.

[27] Shoghi Effendi, God Passes By, 296.

I - In Yazd

Yazd is known for the strong religiosity of its population most of whom follow one of three main religions: the Bahá'í Faith, Islam and Zoroastrianism. In the ancient Persian language the word Yazd meant holy. Many consecrated Bahá'ís and martyrs of the Cause have originated from Yazd. Among them was the Varqá family.

1.1 Mullá Mihdí, 'Aṭrí, the Perfume-Maker

Whether located on the cooler mountain areas or in the sub-tropical regions, Persian towns of 200 years ago followed a similar design which included the maydan (main square), bazaar, main mosque, governorate and the *madreseh* (religious school). Other amenities surrounding the main square included the public bath and the caravanserai. The social and economic life of the town revolved around those places.

A number of these cities were located on the Silk Road —the highway of ancient times. The tableland of Iran was geographically the bridge between China and Europe, many commodities were carried by traders along this road including rugs, textiles and carpets, saffron, dates, pistachios, spices, perfume, sugar, handicrafts and plants. Through widespread trade routes Iran was connected to Turkey, Ádhirbáyján, Syria, Lebanon, Georgia, Armenia, Iraq, India, Afghanistan, Pakistan, and Central Asia.

To the West, however, most of the interior of Iran remained largely unknown due to the geography of Iran. The country was flanked by the Caspian Sea and the Persian Gulf. To its west and east Iran was guarded by rugged mountains and arid deserts respectively, which prevented ready access to the people of that region. Thus, with the exception of centres located on the Silk Road, little was known of Iran by the Europeans.

Yazd was one of the fortunate cities accessible by the Silk Road. Marco Polo visited it in 1272 and observed: "Yasdi also is properly in Persia; it is a good and noble city, and has a great amount of trade. They weave there quantities of a certain silk tissue known as Yasdi, which merchants carry into many quarters to dispose of." [28]

Though similar in layout, each Iranian town manifested its own character. Due to the impact of the desert, Yazd was renowned to be the driest Iranian city. Its temperatures routinely reached more than forty degress Celcius and it experienced low average rainfall. To compensate for this, the inhabitants of Yazd created the world-famous wind towers resembling modern air conditioners called *badgirs* (wind-catchers). In order to catch fresh wind, towers were built on top of houses. These ingenious feats of engineering directed fresh wind into the building, producing a cooling effect in the interior.

The people of Yazd also developed *qanats* in response to the arid environment. By means of this simple hydraulic mechanism water for irrigation was extracted from surrounding hills using vertical shafts and distributed by aqueducts constructed for this purpose. Thus this ancient Persian technology of *qanats* made it possible for agriculture to flourish in the midst of a hot and inhospitable terrain.

Geographically the centre of Iran, and at the intersection of important trade routes including those linking India and Central Asia, Yazd benefited from continuous and intense trading. One of the successful citizens of the city was Ḥájí Mullá Mihdíy-i-Yazdí. His name reveals his background: Ḥájí is a title that designated a person who had observed the Hájj, that is, the pilgrimage to Mecca as prescribed in the Qur'án. The term Mullá denotes a student of religion or a Muslim priest. The word Yazdí indicates a native from Yazd. His given name was simply Mullá Mihdí and he had no surname, as these were

[28] Henry Yule, The Travels of Marco Polo (Cambridge University Press, 2010), 84.

adopted only one hundred years ago in Iran. He was born in approximately 1830.[29] [30]

1.2 The Conversion of Mullá Mihdí

In the year of 1846, a champion of the Faith in those times passed through the city of Yazd. His name was Siyyid Yahyáy-i-Dárábí but was better known as Vahíd —Peerless— and he was coming from the capital to the city of Shíráz on a very significant state mission. Being one of the most learned theologians of the kingdom, Muḥammad Sháh, the King of Iran, personally had commissioned him to independently investigate the teachings of the Báb and produce a report. As Vahíd passed through Yazd en route to Shiraz he announced the nature of his royal assignment in a public square.[31]

As a result of three interviews with the Báb, astonishingly Vahíd recognized the truth of His mission, communicating later his findings to the sovereign. On his way back home, already a believer, he passed again through Yazd and, imperturbably, proclaimed the Manifestation of the Báb and invited those who listened to him to join him in the recognition of the Lord of the Age.

Vaḥíd was highly renowned for his impressive theological knowledge. During his public speech in the same square he used on his way to Shíraz, a crowd eager to hear him gathered to learn of his findings. As a result, a group of prominent citizens and religious people were enrolled into the new Faith. These souls immediately rose up with enthusiasm to spread the teachings recently embraced. Among these early converts was our Mullá Mihdí. Mullá Mihdí must have been about sixteen years of age when he accepted the Faith.

[29] Bahá'í Chronicles, "Ḥájí Mullá Mihdí-i-Yazdí Aka Ḥájí Mullá Mihdí-i-'Atrí." 31 October 2015, accessed 20 May 2020, https://bahaichronicles.org/ḥaji-mulla-mihdiy-i-yazdi/.
[30] Source: MyHeritage.com
[31] Boris Handal, El Concurso En Lo Alto (Lima: PROPACEB, 1985).

Mullá Mihdí, like his companions, began practicing the precepts of the rising Faith in his personal life and wholeheartedly dedicated himself to promoting and disseminating the new Teachings. 'Abdu'l-Bahá said: "As a teacher of the Faith he was never at a loss for words, forgetting, as he taught, all restraint, pouring forth one upon another sacred traditions and texts … When news of him spread around the town and he was everywhere charged, by prince and pauper alike, with bearing this new name, he freely declared his adherence and on this account was publicly disgraced".[32]

Having heard of Bahá'u'lláh's sojourn in Baghdad, Mullá Mihdí set out to meet Him sometime before 1860 with his eldest son Mírzá Ḥusayn Yazdí. Mullá Mihdí was graced with several Tablets revealed by the Blessed Beauty. His son had the privilege of attaining His presence in Baghdad on a second occasion, and on his return brought the first copy of the Hidden Words to Yazd. Mírzá Ḥusayn Yazdí also intimated to the friends that Bahá'u'lláh was the Promised One foretold by the Báb as "Him Whom God shall make manifest".[33]

The Báb had proclaimed Himself to be a Manifestation of God, an assertion that the religious leaders rejected. They strongly believed that Muḥammad was the last Messenger of God. From the perspective of the ecclesiastical leaders no one could claim access to divine revelation after Muḥammad without committing heresy. Further, any Muslim who joined the Faith of the Báb was considered an apostate and was punishable by death.

When the city clerics learned of the followers and their activities they became alarmed at the threat to their power. Hence a decision was made by the council to declare any new follower as an infidel who is to be sentenced to death.

1.3 The Family of Mullá Mihdí

Ḥájí Mullá Mihdíy-i-Yazdí was also known as 'Aṭrí. This designation derives from the Persian word *'Aṭr* for rose-water, products of which

[32] 'Abdu'l-Bahá, Memorials of the Faithful, 84-85.
[33] Taherzadeh, The Revelation of Bahá'u'lláh, vol. 4, 147.

he was a producer.[34] The term literally means (distiller of attar) or, more generally, perfume-maker. In Iran people called 'Aṭrí are normally the local apotecaries selling perfumes and medicinal plants as well as spices. If so, it is likely that Varqá acquired his medical knowledge working at his father's business.

Yazd had an extensive agricultural sector despite its arid soil. Up to 5,000 kg of rose petals are needed to obtain only 1 kg of rose essential oil.[35] Also, the generic attar of rose is produced not only from roses but also from a variety of other flowers and herbs through a range of chemical procedures, mainly distillation.

From Mullá Mihdí's marriage four children came to the world: one girl named Bíbí Túbá and three boys, namely, Mírzá Ḥusayn Yazdí, Mírzá Ḥasan Yazdí and Mírzá 'Alí Muḥammad, better known as Varqá. Varqá was born in approximately 1855.[36] Mullá Mihdí himself had become a Bábí, that is, a follower of the Báb, in 1846. Members of his whole family also declared their belief in the Báb.

Mullá Mihdí's wife was a wise and pious women and one of the believers in Islam who was aware of the prophecies concerning the Manifestation of the Báb. When Mullá Mihdí became a Bábí, he began talking to his wife about the Faith and taking home any other believer visiting Yazd to initiate conversations about the Faith of the Báb. At one point, Mullá Mihdí brought a Bahá'í teacher to especially talk to his wife about the Faith of the Báb. As per the custom of the time which dictated that women must separate themselves from men, she had to sit behind a curtain for the conversations. According to Martha Root, based on interviews with 'Azízu'lláh and Valíyu'lláh Varqá[37] in Tehran,

---

[34] Adib Taherzadeh, The Revelation of Bahá'u'lláh. Vol 4: Mazra'ih & Bahji 1877-92, vol. 4, 50 (Oxford: George Ronald, 1988).

[35] Danièle Ryman, "Aromatherapy Bible," 2016, accessed 30 August 2020, http://aromatherapybible.com/rose/.

[36] Source: MyHeritage.com

[37] 'Azízu'lláh and Valíyu'lláh Varqá were the surviving children of Mírzá 'Alí-Muḥammad, the Martyr.

> Her husband had had a Bahá'í teacher come to speak with her (which he did without seeing her, for she sat behind a curtain to receive her lessons). When she heard about the Bahá'í Cause and that a Prophet had appeared she said, "We are not waiting for a Prophet; I have studied all the Books, and we are waiting for a Manifestation of God." The teacher had used the word "Prophet" so as not to startle her, but to try to tell her gradually that the great World Teacher was here, but she was an apt pupil and more ready than he thought to receive the Truth. She at once became a believer.[38]

A similar version reveals that Mullá Mihdí's wife was related to Fátimih Zahrá, the daughter of Prophet Muḥammad. A second version of her conversion relates that when one of the teachers of the Faith entered Yazd, at the request of Mullá Mihdí, he engaged in conversation with her to address her concerns about the Faith of the Báb. At that time Bahá'u'lláh had not declared His mission. By the end of their talk, she told the teacher that his statements to prove the revelation of the Báb as the Qá'im[39] were sufficient and acceptable; however, she said that we were waiting for the appearance of two prophets, the first of whom was the Qá'im whereas the second one would be greater than the first. Mullá Mihdí's wife finally became a believer.[40]

'Abdu'l-Bahá spoke highly of Mullá Mihdí:

> Although to all appearances this excellent man was not of the learned class, he was an expert in the field of Muslim sacred traditions and an eloquent interpreter of orally transmitted texts. Persevering in his devotions, known for holy practices and nightly communings and vigils, his heart was illumined, and he was spiritual of mind and soul. He spent most of his

---

[38] Root, White Roses of Persia (Part 2), 180.

[39] The Qá'im (In Arabic, the Ariser) and the Qayyúm (In Arabic, the Self-Subsisting) were the two consecutive Messengers promised in Islam, represented by the Báb and Bahá'u'lláh, respectively.

[40] 'Azízu'lláh Sulaymání, Masábíh-i-Hidáyat, vol. 1 (Tehran 1964). Available also at: http://aeenebahai.org/en/node/3444.

> time repeating communes, performing the obligatory prayers, confessing his failings and supplicating the Lord. He was one of those who penetrate mysteries, and was a confidant of the righteous … He was an eminent soul, with his heart fixed on the beauty of God. From the day he was first created and came into this world, he single-mindedly devoted all his efforts to acquiring grace for the day he should be born into the next. His heart was illumined, his mind spiritual, his soul aspiring, his destination Heaven.[41]

1.4 Mullá Mihdí is Expelled from Yazd

One day Mullá Mihdí organized a large Bábí gathering at his home. Prior to this, most of the meetings were held discretely in order to avoid harassment. The boldness and public presence of the community attracted the fury of one of the top religious leaders of Yazd. His name was Shaykh Muḥammad-Ḥasan-i-Sabzivárí. An account of those times relates:

> One day he held a large meeting in his house in Yazd and invited the Bahá'ís, including the members of the Afnán family,[42] to attend. About two hundred believers attended this meeting. Among them was a certain Dervish Mihdí, who was a Bahá'í and had a melodious voice. He chanted Bahá'í songs in a very loud voice and a few others chanted Tablets. No such meeting had ever been held in Yazd since the Cause began in that city.[43]

The aforementioned cleric was so upset that Mullá Mihdí was summoned the next day to his office. To avoid the danger, Mírzá Ḥusayn Yazdí and Varqá went into hiding while Mírzá Ḥasan left the city to a neighbouring town.[44] Mullá Mihdí was violently flogged in front of the cleric. A death sentence was issued, but another cleric

41 'Abdu'l-Bahá, Memorials of the Faithful, 84-85.
42 The term Afnán denotes a member of the Báb's family.
43 Taherzadeh, The Revelation of Bahá'u'lláh, vol. 4, 50-51.
44 Taherzadeh, The Revelation of Bahá'u'lláh, vol. 4, 51.

named Mullá Báqir of Ardakán refused to confirm the order. Saved from imminent execution Mullá Mihdí was forced to leave the city, which he did in the company of his two sons, Mírzá Ḥusayn Yazdí and Varqá, who had stayed in the neighbouring town. At that time, Varqá was about 22 years old.

Their final destination was Bahá'u'lláh's abode, in 'Akká, Palestine. En route they passed through Tabríz, located more than one thousand kilometers from Yazd where they were welcomed by the Ahmadofs, another strong Bahá'í family. Paying tribute to the qualities shown by Mullá Mihdí in those days, 'Abdu'l-Bahá said:

> In every town and village along the way, he ably spread the Faith, adducing clear arguments and proofs, quoting from and interpreting the sacred traditions and evident signs. He did not rest for a moment; everywhere he shed abroad the attar of the love of God, and diffused the sweet breathings of holiness. And he inspired the friends, making them eager to teach others in their turn, and to excel in knowledge. [45]

[45] 'Abdu'l-Bahá, Memorials of the Faithful, 85.

II - In Tabríz

It was 1873 [46] when Varqá along with his brother, Mírzá Ḥusayn Yazdí and father, Mullá Mihdí, reached Tabríz from Yazd after a journey of 1,250 km. To traverse that distance on horseback may have taken more than a month.

Varqá eventually mastered the Azari language. He settled in Tabríz and in the years that followed travelled extensively through the province of Ádhirbáyján teaching the Baha'i Faith and visiting believers in rural villages and small towns. Tabríz was also the place where Varqá married and started a family of his own.

2.1 The Qájár Crown Prince and the Bahá'ís

If Yazd was the hottest place in Iran, Tabríz was the coldest. Yazd is known for being the last bastion of the Zoroastrian culture, language and religion, the base itself of the Iranian civilization that was violently subdued by the Arab invaders between 632 to 654 CE. Tabríz, by contrast, had fully adopted Islam through the traditional Azarí language that is still spoken. People from Yazd were proud to call themselves Persians while the people of Tabríz strongly identified as Iranian Turks. The Azarí language derives from the same Turkic language family as the Turkish language. Tabríz is also the northwest gateway to Turkey and a traditional producer of beautiful rugs and carpets.

The Azarís descended originally from tribes of Central Asia whereas the Persians had Indo-European roots. Because of these ethnic differences Azarí and Persian languages are completely separate.

Interestingly, Persian and English come from the same Indo-European family of languages sharing linguistic features. Tribal migrations from the old Persian geography to Europe horizons took place 3,000-4,000

[46] 1290 AH

years ago in search of better agricultural land and climates, over hundreds of years. Moving slowy and intermittently on their way, from west to east following the earth rotation direction, these proto Indo-Iranian groups mythified as the Aryans, merged with other etnias mutating into new languages and dialects although preserving a number of linguistic features.[47] For example, most of the nouns in the following English words in the following sentences have the same origin with proto-Persian languages including Sanscrit: "In his *van*, my *young brother* had a *magic guitar* and a *bronze tambour* from *China. Margaret* in her *Paradise kiosk* sold *lemon, sugar, saffron, pistachio, spinach* and *candies. Father, mother* and *daughter* bought a *rustic tapestry* with *jasmines, a scarlet shawl* and a *khaki pajama* from the *bazar.*"

Returning to the subject of the Azarís, they flourished as a culture on their own with a distinct literature, poetry and folklore developed in their own language. Nowadays, Azarí people comprise up to twenty percent of the Iranian population, many of whom reside in the province of Ádhirbáyján which has Tabríz as its capital.

During Mullá Mihdí's life, Qájár was the ruling dynasty. The Qajars were initially a Turkic-speaking tribe based in the Azerbaijan region, especially near Astarabad (modern-day Gorgan) in northeastern Iran. However, as their empire grew, they developed close connections with the northwestern part of the country, particularly with Tabriz, which emerged as the region's most significant city. This diminished their popularity, as did their reputation for corruption, abuse of power and public mismanagement. "The Qájárs, members of the alien Turkoman tribe, had, indeed, usurped the Persian throne", wrote Shoghi Effendi.[48]

---

[47] Birgit Anette Olsen, Thomas Olander, and Kristian Kristiansen, Tracing the Indo-Europeans: New Evidence from Archaeology and Historical Linguistics, 126 (Oxbow Books, 2019).
[48] Shoghi Effendi, The Promised Day Has Come (Wimette, Illinois: Bahá'í Publishing Trust, 1980), 66.

Ádhirbáyján, literally the "Land of Fire" in old Persian, was famous for three things. Firstly, it is mentioned in the Qur'án[49] and in Islamic traditions as a place of an Islamic prophecy which was corroborated by the Báb:

> What must needs befall us in Ádhirbayján is inevitable and without parallel. When this happeneth, rest ye in your homes and remain patient as we have remained patient. As soon as the Mover moveth make ye haste to attain unto Him, even though ye have to crawl over the snow.[50]

Secondly, the "Land of Fire" is also the place where the Báb was martyred. Five of the seven Qajar monarchs were born in Ádhirbáyján and it became a tradition that the Crown Prince had to be the governor of that province.

Naṣiri'd-Dín Sháh (r. 1848-1896) was the fourth Qáján monarch during Varqá's life. He was notorious for his corruption, cruelty, nepotism and ineptitude throughout the 50 years of his reign. He was also notorious for having 27 wives, 14 sons and 14 daughters though this paled compared to his great grandfather Fatḥ ʿAlī Sháh who had 160 wives. Násiri'd-Dín Sháh was responsible for the killing of the Báb and for the banishment of Bahá'u'lláh to a forty-year exile. Of his three oldest surviving sons, Muẓaffari'd-Dín Mírzá the Crown Prince, was the governor of the province of Ádhirbáyján.

The other two influential sons of Naṣiri'd-Dín Sháh were Mas'úd Mírzá and Kámrán Mírzá. Mas'úd Mírzá was firstborn but his mother was not of royal blood and therefore he could not inherit the throne. Mas'úd Mírzá was the governor of Iṣfahán while his son, Jalál'ud-Dawlih, as cruel as his father, was the governor of Yazd. Kámrán Mírzá was the third surviving son and governor of Tehran from the age of six years!

---

[49] Marzieh Gail, Six Lessons on Islam, 14 (Wilmette, Ill.: Bahá'í Pub. Trust, 1973).

[50] Cited in Selections from the Writings of the Báb (Haifa: Bahá'í World Centre, 1976), 16-17.

These two last sons, like their father the Sháh, manifested hatred towards the Bahá'ís and engaged in their persecution and murder. Both gloried in their pompous titles Zillu's-Sultán (the King's Shadow) and Náyibu's-Saltanih (the Viceregent). Although they competed which each other for power, they were united in their jealousy of their brother the Crown Prince. Due to the complexities of the Qájár politics, the Sháh was not in good terms with the Crown Prince and so favoured Mas'úd Mírzá and Kámrán Mírzá. As a result of constant intrigues, the three brothers grew up distrusting one another and regarding each other as rivals.

Muẓaffari'd-Dín Mírzá, the Crown Prince, loved poetry and engaged in literary and religious discussions at his palace. Varqá was a perfect candidate for these popular evening gatherings. It was from Varqá that the prince learned a lot about the Bahá'í Faith which led to a more positive attitude towards the believers. The Crown Prince was happy to protect the Bahá'ís in Ádhirbáyján from violence. As a result, many Bahá'í families moved to the province of Ádhirbáyján. Many settled in Tabríz and practiced their faith with relative freedom and safety.

However, the Crown Prince was also a product of his environment, and Shoghi Effendi referred him as "the weak and timid Muẓaffari'd-Dín Mírzá, the heir to his throne, who had fallen under the influence of the Shaykhí sect, and was showing a marked respect to the mullás."[51]

2.2 Varqá's Wedding

The Qájár was once a powerful Iranian tribe that took power and established a dynasty in the transition between the 18th and 19th centuries. Iran was composed of many other large tribes with various degrees of influence in society and the government. One of them was the Shahsavan tribe. The Shahsavan tribe comprises 32 nomadic sub-tribes [52] with a common leadership and total population of 100,000-

[51] Shoghi Effendi, God Passes By, 198.
[52] Richard Tapper, "Black Sheep, White Sheep and Red-Heads: A Historical Sketch of the Shāhsavan of Āzarbāijān," Iran 4, no. 1, 61-62 (1966).

120,000 in the last century.[53] In a previous dynasty they were one of the Sháh's preferred tribes because they fought wars supporting the monarchy.

A prominent woman from the Shahsavan tribe lived in Tabríz became related to the Varqá family. Coming from the upper echelons of the Tabríz society she was well connected with the government as well as with the clerical establishment. She was a strong Muslim.[54] Her husband, 'Abdu'lláh Núrí had been a Muslim, but about two years before Varqá's arrival to Tabríz he had converted to the Bahá'í Faith thanks to the effort of Nabíl, the great historian of the Faith. 'Abdu'lláh Núrí, as his name implies, was from Núr, Bahá'u'lláh's ancestral town. As the court chamberlain and head of the royal house,[55] 'Abdu'lláh Núrí was a person of great influence on the Crown Prince.

The aforementioned lady never accepted her husband's faith. Rather, she had a profound resentment of anything associated with the Bahá'í Faith. As a prominent governmental figure, 'Abdu'lláh Núrí's declaration of faith became a sensitive issue in the court, one that could be used against him by enemies of the Faith. There was also risk for the Crown Prince to be endangered, should he be accused of changing his religion due to the influence of one of his officers. Converting to the Bahá'í Faith would have seemed unforgivable in the eyes of his father Naṣiri'd-Dín Sháh.

'Abdu'lláh Núrí welcomed any Bahá'í that travelled through the city. It is not surprising then that one day he invited Varqá, his brother and father to his house for dinner. Particularly, as 'Abdu'lláh Núrí had an interest in poetry and medicine, Varqá was seen as a distinguished guest due to his renown in these areas of learning. On that occasion something happened that changed Varqá's life forever. Marriage

[53] Fereydoun Safizadeh, "Shahsavan in the Grip of Development," Cultural Survival Quarterly Magazine, March, 1984, https://www.culturalsurvival.org/publications/cultural-survival-quarterly/shahsavan-grip-development.
[54] Darius Shahrokh, Varqá and Son: The Heavenly Doves, 4.
[55] 'Abdu'lláh Núrí's official position was farrash-bashi.

knocked at his door in a very unusual way. ‘Abdu’lláh Núrí and his wife had only one daughter, Núríyyih,[56] and desperately wanted more descendants. As Varqá was a doctor, ‘Abdu’lláh Núrí encouraged his wife to approach Varqá for a cure, which led to the extension of a dinner invitation to Mullá Mihdí’s family. Darius Shahrokh recounts the story in this way:

> Desperately wanting another child, she agreed. After supper, Varqá prescribed a pearly pill; however, before the evening was over, Mírzá told his wife privately that maybe they should ask Varqá and the family to stay as their guests to see if the medicine would become effective or not. Well, she consented to that also. Before long it was discovered that she was pregnant. Mírzá told her that he had pledged to God that whoever gives them the bounty of another child, he would give his daughter to marry him. The wife felt very reluctant. Her family background and the wealth and position of Mírzá made her very conceited. The thought of giving her precious daughter to a stranger who not only was a Bahá’í but also was considered by her to be below their class, was very hard to swallow. Mírzá showed his concern that if he does not keep his pledge, they might lose the unborn baby. She found herself at an impasse and consented. The next event was a big wedding for Mírzá [‘Abdu’lláh Núrí]’s daughter.[57]

---

[56] Moojan Momen, The Bahá’í Communities of Iran 1851-1921: The North of Iran, vol. I (Oxford: George Ronald, 2015), 417.

[57] Darius Shahrokh, Varqá and Son: The Heavenly Doves, 4.

III - Varqá's First Pilgrimage

In 1878, about six years after arriving in Tabríz,[58] Mullá Mihdí with his two sons, Varqá and Mírzá Ḥusayn Yazdí set out for the longed for destination: The Most Great Prison in 'Akká, Palestine. This was going to be the greatest experience of Varqá's life— attaining the presence of Bahá'u'lláh. His father and brother had already met Bahá'u'lláh in Baghdad and, after listening to all their wonderful stories, Varqá knew this was going to be the pinnacle moment of his life.

3.1 The Passing of Mullá Mihdí

The 2000 km overland trip was exhausting for Mullá Mihdí because of his advanced age. Despite this, as he travelled he was invariably engaged in the teaching work. 'Abdu'l-Bahá said in this regard:

> He travelled some distances by walking on foot and some distances by riding. He endured much hardship and disasters in his travel. While walking on foot he was always reciting prayers, while weeping, and lamenting about the sufferings of the Wronged One [Bahá'u'lláh] ...[59]

> He was imprisoned along his way; and as he crossed the deserts and climbed and descended the mountain slopes he endured terrible, uncounted hardships. But the light of faith shone from his brow and in his breast the longing was aflame, and thus he joyously, gladly passed over the frontiers until at last he came to Beirut. In that city, ill, restive, his patience gone, he spent some days. His yearning grew, and his agitation was such that weak and sick as he was, he could wait no more.

---

[58] 1296 AH

[59] Star of the West, vol. 3, No. 18 (February 1913), 362-364.

> He set out on foot for the house of Bahá'u'lláh. Because he lacked proper shoes for the journey, his feet were bruised and torn; his sickness worsened; he could hardly move, but still he went on; somehow he reached the village of Mazra'ih and here, close by the Mansion, he died. His heart found his Well-Beloved One, when he could bear the separation no more. Let lovers be warned by his story; let them know how he gambled away his life in his yearning after the Light of the World.[60] May God give him to drink of a brimming cup in the everlasting gardens; in the Supreme Assemblage, may God shed upon his face rays of light. Upon him be the glory of the Lord. His sanctified tomb is in Mazra'ih, beside 'Akká.[61]

This was not what Varqá expected for this trip. Losing his father was a major blow for him and his brother. They had to reconcile the idea of visiting the Manifestation of God and not sharing that joy with the presence of their beloved father whom Bahá'u'lláh loved so much from the previous encounter in Baghdad. Varqá was about 23 years old at this time. Both brothers stayed in the Holy Land for several months grieving the loss of their father under Bahá'u'lláh's loving care Who was at that time residing between Mazra'ih and 'Akká.

3.2 Mullá Mihdí's grave

'Abdu'l-Bahá said that He built Mullá Mihdí's "sanctified grave" [62] in Mazra'ih. Bahá'u'lláh revealed a beautiful Tablet of Visitation to be recited at his graveside. The historian Adib Taherzadeh wrote:

> Whenever the Blessed Beauty passed by his grave on His way to 'Akká or Mazra'ih, He would pause there, put His blessed foot on the grave and stop beside it for a few moments. Although Ḥájí did not attain the presence of Bahá'u'lláh this time, he had, on a previous occasion, visited Baghdad with his eldest son Mírzá Ḥusayn where he met his Lord face to face.

---

[60] According to Adib Taherzadeh, Mullá Mihdí died sometime between 15 and 26 April 1878.
[61] 'Abdu'l-Bahá, Memorials of the Faithful, 86.
[62] 'Abdu'l-Bahá, Memorials of the Faithful, 86.

> Bahá'u'lláh had revealed Tablets for him for many years, all indicative of his deep love and devotion to the Cause. The outpouring of Bahá'u'lláh's blessings upon him were indeed boundless. In a Tablet addressed to Varqá, Bahá'u'lláh, in the words of His amanuensis describes the way in which He and some of His companions once on their way to Mazra'ih stopped at the grave of his father and revealed such exalted verses in his honour that no pen could describe the glory with which his soul was invested. Bahá'u'lláh has revealed for him a Tablet of Visitation which clearly indicates how exalted was his rank among the Concourse on High" [63]

The epitaph on his gravestone summarises in few words his life:

> He is the Everlasting
> Verily, Hájí Mihdí [Mullá Mihdí] was enlightened by the burning bush of [Mount] Sinai and answered the call that attracted him to the Concourse on High. Al-Fátiḥa.[64]
> Deceased in the year 1296 AH (1878 AD)

3.3 "Asnam-i-uham ra bisuzan"

Two stories have remained of Varqá's sojourn in the Holy Land: Varqá testing Bahá'u'lláh's spiritual powers, and Bahá'u'lláh commanding him to burn away all veils. The expression "Asnam-i-uham ra bisuzan" reads in Persian "Burn away the idols of vain imaginings".

Throughout the lengthy trip Varqá was curious about how his first encounter with Bahá'u'lláh would be. He had heard wonderful stories from his father and brother Ḥusayn about the magnetic presence of Bahá'u'lláh, experienced during their visit to the House of Bahá'u'lláh in Baghdad in the previous decade. The Báb Himself has

[63] Taherzadeh, The Revelation of Bahá'u'lláh, vol. 4, 51.

[64] Al-Fátiḥah is the very first short devotional prayer in Qur'án, like an "opening", which is also recited for the dead for blessings. It is symbolic of commencing a new life in the next world. This was a gravestone formality in those countries.

spoken about the bounty of visiting Him Whom God shall make manifest:

> There is no paradise more wondrous for any soul than to be exposed to God's Manifestation in His Day, to hear His verses and believe in them, to attain His presence, which is naught but the presence of God, to sail upon the sea of the heavenly kingdom of His good-pleasure, and to partake of the choice fruits of the paradise of His divine Oneness.[65]

Arriving in the Holy Land, Varqá had to confront his own emotions as he contemplated the figure of Bahá'u'lláh for the first time. When he was a child he had had a dream of playing in the garden with dolls when suddenly God Himself turned up, collected all the dolls and threw them into fire. The next day Varqá told his parents about the dream. They reprimanded him for his vain imaginings, as God cannot be seen. He was told not to share his strange dream with anyone else.

On pilgrimage he unexpectedly had the sense that he had seen Bahá'u'lláh's face somewhere sometime. Then, in the course of one meeting, Bahá'u'lláh commanded him to "burn away the idols of vain imaginings".[66] Suddenly he realized that the face of God in his childhood dream was the same as Bahá'u'lláh's face. The meaning of his dream about burning the dolls thus became apparent.

3.4 "Inham kafi bud?"

"You of little faith. Why did you doubt?"[67] were Jesus's words to Peter when his faith was tested on the rough waters in the Sea of Galilee. According to the the Bible, after asking this question, Jesus extended His hand to Peter and almost immediately the strong wind calmed down. The Bible says that once in the boat safe, everyone prostrated unto Jesus and said: "Verily, Thou art the Son of God".[68]

---

[65] The Báb, Selections from the Writings of the Báb, 77.
[66] Taherzadeh, The Revelation of Bahá'u'lláh, vol. 4, 55.
[67] Matthew 14:31
[68] Matthew 14:22-34

Varqá had an experience similar to Peter when, in a moment of doubt he tried to test the spiritual powers of the Manifestation of God. Listening quietly to what Bahá'u'lláh was elaborating on in a meeting, Varqá entertained the thought of asking, without words, for a special sign. He thought: "I know that Bahá'u'lláh is the supreme Manifestation of God, but I wish He would give me a sign to this effect". Suddenly a verse of the Qur'án came to his mind with which to test the Manifestation of God. It was the verse "Thou seest the earth barren and lifeless, but when We pour down rain on it, it is stirred to life, it swells, and it puts forth every kind of luxuriant growth in pairs" (22:5).

No sooner had Varqá thought this than Bahá'u'lláh wove the aforementioned verse into His speech. But Varqá thought: "Could this have been a mere coincidence?" [69] Suddenly Bahá'u'lláh turned towards Varqá and exclaimed "Inham kafi bud?" ("Wasn't this sufficient proof for you?")

In this connection the Báb said: "It is for God to test His servants, and not for His servants to judge Him in accordance with their deficient standards".[70] Varqá, like Peter, was tested by doubting the powers of the Manifestation of God. However, similar to Peter's incident, Varqá emerged from this test with more certitude and complete faith.

3.5 Mírzá Abu'l-Faḍl, the Father of Wisdom

Mírzá Abu'l-Faḍl (1844–1914) meaning the "Father of Virtues" is a title given by Bahá'u'lláh to a very knowledgeable and devoted believer. The following incident took place during Varqá's first pilgrimage. Mírzá Abu'l-Faḍl writes:

> In the early years of my conversion, I refused to write books, supporting that in the days in which the Supreme Pen was moving, its sound would be heard in all regions. Therefore, I

[69] Taherzadeh, The Revelation of Bahá'u'lláh, vol. 4, 54.

[70] Nabíl-i-A'zam, The Dawn-Breakers: Nabíl's Narrative of the Early Days of the Bahá'í Revelation (Wilmette, IL: Bahá'í Publishing Trust, 1970), 61.

reasoned, it would be a great presumption for a man to attempt writing and composition. Finally in 1887, when in Ádhirbáyján, I was favored with the privilege of meeting Varqá the Martyr, and he encouraged me to write and compose. He said: "During the days when I was at the brilliant city of 'Akká, and attained the honor of meeting the Blessed Perfection, the Blessed Tongue repeated the Command of the 'First Point,' [The Báb] which was that the believers should each one write books demonstrating the truth of 'He whom God shall manifest.' I inquired if He deemed it advisable to employ Mírzá Abu'l-Faḍl in this service. Then He said, "As the "First Point" has commanded it, such persons should employ themselves in writing and propounding arguments."[71]

[71] Mírzá Abu'l-Faḍl-i-Gulpáygání, Bahá'í Proofs, 1902.

IV - Back in Tabríz

After that pilgrimage, Bahá'u'lláh arranged for Varqá and Mírzá Ḥusayn Yazdí to return to Iran to teach the Bahá'í Faith. They did so and with renewed spirit, they dedicated themselves to that service. On the way back both brothers, now in their twenties, stopped at their father's fresh grave and said some prayers for him.

A new life laid ahead of them in Tabríz. Varqá was going to raise a family and live a life full of blessings as well as tests. He was himself a new creation willing to offer what he had to serve his beloved Bahá'u'lláh. It is noteworthy that in all his endeavours while in Tabríz, Varqá always had the protection of his father-in-law 'Abdu'lláh Núrí, the influential court chamberlain.

4.1 The Birth of Rúḥu'lláh

From Varqá and Núríyyih's marriage four children were born after the first pilgrimage: 'Azízu'lláh (about 1881), Rúḥu'lláh (about 1883), Valíyu'lláh (1884) and Badí'u'lláh who died in childhood.[72] [73] The first three of them shone with glory in the Cause of Bahá'u'lláh. Rúḥu'lláh, the most brilliant of all of them was born on an April day two years after 'Azízu'lláh the eldest brother. Since we know that Rúḥu'lláh was 12 years old when he passed away in May 1896 the boy must have been born around 1883.[74]

Rúḥu'lláh means the "Spirit of God", a title composed of the terms "Rúh" and "Alláh", meaning "Spirit" and "God", respectively. The

---

[72] The family registrar book containing the birth dates of family members was confiscated by the police when Varqá was arrested in 1895 in Zanján as he was being transferred to the prison in Tehran. Hence there is no accurate knowledge of their birthday (Martha Root).

[73] Martha Root, "White Roses of Persia (Part 4)," Star of the West, vol. 23, issue 8, (November 1932), 255-259.

[74] Martha Root, "White Roses of Persia (Part 1)," Star of the West, vol. 23, issue 6, (June 1932), 179-181.

title is commonly used in the Islamic world to refer to Jesus Christ. The Qur'án says: "The Messiah, Jesus, the son of Mary, was but an Apostle of God, and His Word, which He conveyed into Mary and a *Spirit* proceeding from Himself" (4: 169). In the same way in the Islamic tradition, the names 'Azízu'lláh ("Dear to God"), Valíyu'lláh ("Friend of God"), and Badí'u'lláh (Creation of God) seek to bestow favour on the child by associating him with God.

Adib Taherzadeh[75] states that all four sons of Varqá received tablets from Bahá'u'lláh when they were children, showing the special connection between the Manifestation of God and this dear family.

According to Martha Root:

> There was glad rejoicing when Bahá'u'lláh from 'Akká sent these parents a Tablet (a letter) about this new babe and in it the reader with insight will discern the introduction to this thrilling story which follows. Bahá'u'lláh wrote:
>
> "O Varqá! It is for thee to chant in both ears of this little one three times:
>
> "Verily, thou hast come by the Command of God! Thou hast appeared to speak of Him, and thou hast been created to serve Him Who is the Dear, the Beloved!"
>
> "We mentioned this before when his mother implored us, and now We are mentioning it again. We are the Generous and the Giver!" (His mother sent no petition by letter, but it was perhaps when this little one was coming into this world that she cried out to Bahá'u'lláh.)[76]
>
> While Rúḥu'lláh was still a little child, Bahá'u'lláh sent a second Tablet. It read:

[75] Taherzadeh, The Revelation of Bahá'u'lláh, vol. 4, 59.
[76] Root, "White Roses of Persia (Part 1)," 71.

"He is the Hearer and the Seer! "Blessed art thou, for thou hast witnessed the grandeur and greatness of God while still a child. Blessed is the mother who nursed thee and has arisen to do what is becoming of her! We beg God to write for thee from His Supreme Pen that which is fitting to His Generosity, Bounty and Favour. Verily, He is the Generous and the Bountiful! Praise be to God, the Lord of the Worlds!"[77]

Another Tablet to Rúḥu'lláh from Bahá'u'lláh reads:

"O thou Rúḥu'lláh! Verily, the Greatest Spirit has inclined towards thee from the Prison and is mentioning thee with such a station that its fragrance will continue as long as My Kingdom and My Grandeur endure!

"Thou, when thou bindeth and knoweth (the mention) say: 'Praise be to Thee, O Ocean of Bounty! Thanks be to Thee that Thou hast made me to appear and in my first days speak Thy mention and Thy praise. Verily, Thou art the Forgiving and the Compassionate!'" [78]

4.2 Travel Teaching

During the next four years after his first encounter with Bahá'u'lláh, Varqá was transformed into a person entirely consecrated to teaching the Faith either in Tabríz at the prince's court or in private homes, or travelling throughout the province of Ádhirbáyján visiting villages and small Bahá'í communities.

It is noteworthy that after his first pilgrimage, Varqá visited Baha'u'llah one more time. Subsequent to Baha'u'llah's passing Varqá went to the Holy Land again this time to visit 'Abdul-Bahá. From those pilgrimages, as well as from the many Tablets he received through continuous correspondence, Varqá gained guidance and strength.

---

[77] Root, "White Roses of Persia (Part 1)," 71-72.
[78] Root, "White Roses of Persia (Part 1)," 72.

At that time there were few Bahá'ís who were mostly isolated from each other and spread across various cities and rural villages. There was also a small and informal network of known travel teachers travelling throughout Iran called "Mubalighs" meaning "religious instructor". Their teaching work was conducted either overtly or covertly depending on the circumstances and dangers. According to the Shariah law an individual who left Islam for another religion was regarded as an apostate and this choice was punishable by death.

Very often, the believers had to visit each other and have their devotional and deepening meetings in secrecy at night. There were no Bahá'í institutions at that time so believers had to rely on a small number of these travel teachers who moved continuously place to place to teach, and to deepen those nascent Bahá'í communities. With no printed literature, the believers had to copy Tablets by hand or pass them from one to another. These Tablets came through pilgrims returning to Iran or from regular travelers to the Holy Land such as Shaykh Salman, the courier of the Merciful,[79] or the trustees of the Ḥuqúqu'lláh, namely, Ḥájí Sháh-Muḥammad Manshádi and Abu'l-Ḥasan Ardikání known as Ḥájí Amín.

For his extraordinary services in the field of teaching, Varqá was posthumously appointed a Hand of the Cause of God by 'Abdu'l-Bahá. Bahá'u'lláh commanded Varqá to travel extensively to teach the Faith and managed to convert many people to the Faith. Happily coming back from pilgrimage he had to confront a sad reality. His mother-in-law's animosity at home had intensified and thus to avoid confrontation he spent more time travel teaching in country villages. It was in one of those villages that Varqá came across an extraordinary discovery.

4.3 The Báb's Portrait

The largest lake in Iran is called Urúmíyyih. It stands as a barrier between the town of the same name and Tabríz, the province capital.

[79] Boris Handal, A Trilogy of Consecration: The Courier, the Historian and the Missionary, 3-35 (IngramSparks, 2020).

The Urúmíyyih lake is so extensive that it has 102 islands with 13 tributaries becoming the second largest saltwater lake on Earth. It is so salty that, like in the Dead Sea, people easily float on the surface and it never freezes. Due to the salinity there are no fish although it is home to 226 native species of birds. The lake has an area of 5,200 km^2 about the size of the island of Puerto Rico. The beautiful city of Urúmíyyih is located on the shores of this lake.

In the summer of June-July 1848, the Báb passed through Urúmíyyih. He was being taken from the castle of Chihriq to the capital, Tabríz, for cross-examination when He passed through the city of Urúmíyyih. He stayed there a number of days as a guest of the Prince Malek-Qasim Mírzá. Two important events happened during His time in Urúmíyyih. The first involved the testing of the Báb's supernatural powers by Prince Malek-Qasim Mírzá and the second one was the paiting made of the Báb. According to Nabíl:

> On a certain Friday when the Báb was going to the public bath, the prince, who was curious to test the courage and power of his Guest, ordered his groom to offer Him one of his wildest horses to ride. Apprehensive lest the Báb might suffer any harm, the attendant secretly approached Him and tried to induce Him to refuse to mount a horse that had already overthrown the bravest and most skilful of horsemen. "Fear not," was His reply. "Do as you have been bidden, and commit Us to the care of the Almighty." The inhabitants of Urúmíyyih, who had been informed of the intention of the prince, had filled the public square, eager to witness what might befall the Báb. As soon as the horse was brought to Him, He quietly approached it and, taking hold of the bridle which the groom had offered Him, gently caressed it and placed His foot in the stirrup. The horse stood still and motionless beside Him as if conscious of the power which was dominating it. The multitude that watched this most unusual spectacle marvelled at the behaviour of the animal. To their simple minds this extraordinary incident appeared little short of a miracle. They hastened in their enthusiasm to kiss the stirrups of the Báb, but were prevented by the attendants of the prince, who feared lest

> so great an onrush of people might harm Him. The prince himself, who had accompanied his Guest on foot as far as the vicinity of the bath, was bidden by Him, ere they reached its entrance, to return to his residence. All the way, the prince's footmen were endeavouring to restrain the people who, from every side, were pressing forward to catch a glimpse of the Báb. Upon His arrival, He dismissed all those who had accompanied Him except the prince's private attendant and Siyyid Ḥasan, who waited in the antechamber and aided Him in undressing. On His return from the bath, He again mounted the same horse and was acclaimed by the same multitude. The prince came on foot to meet Him, and escorted Him back to his residence.[80]

The prince, a son of the second Sháh of the Qájár dynasty, was a well-educated royal who was raised and tutored by a French lady. He was a lover of Western traditions very much admired by foreign people and diplomats.

It is in the prince's environment that the only painting of the Báb was ever produced. The chief painter of the court named Áqá Bashí was the artist that produced such a historical portrait. More than two decades later, during a teaching trip, Varqá managed to teach the Faith to this painter who happily embraced it.[81]

It is thanks to Varqá that there exists a single painting of the blessed Báb, a painting that might otherwise have been lost to posterity. When the Báb was painted it was the first time in human history that a Manifestation of God had been authentically portrayed. This unique painting of the Báb is now in the International Archives of the Bahá'í Faith on Mount Carmel, Israel. One version of the story about the painting of the Báb in Urúmíyyih is given by Muḥammad 'Alí-Faizí:

---

[80] Nabíl-i-A'zam, The Dawn-Breakers: Nabíl's Narrative of the Early Days of the Bahá'í Revelation, 309-11.

[81] Bijan Masumian, and Adib Masumian, "The Báb in the World of Images," Bahá'í Studies Review 19, no. 1, 171-190 (2013).

> In three sessions, he would gaze intently upon the Báb's face in the latter's room. Áqá Balá Bayg [82] [the painter] would then leave the room and gradually complete the sketch. Each time the artist entered the room, the Báb would put on his cloak, sit down, pull up his sleeves, and place his hands upon his knees. [83]

According to Darius Shahrokh:

> After his conversion, he [Áqá Bashí] told Varqá how in Urúmíyyih the Báb rode the unruly horse which the mayor had given Him to test Him. He said, "I was among the anxious crowd who flooded the house of the mayor to have a glance at the miracle maker, the Báb. After seeing Him, I decided to draw His picture, so I focused intently upon His face. When the Báb noticed me, He fixed His cloak on His knee, and posed with His hand on the cloak." Obviously, the Báb understood the intention of the artist who was among the crowd. They had not been introduced. To continue the narrative, "I left the room, and made a rough sketch on a paper, and went back a couple more times. Every time I went in, the Báb resumed the same position and would look at me." Oh! What a majestic scene! He later composed a full-scale portrait in black and white. Varqá wrote to Bahá'u'lláh about this tremendous discovery. Bahá'u'lláh instructed Varqá to have the artist make two water color copies, one to be sent to Himself, and the other to be kept by Varqá. When Bahá'u'lláh received this copy, the brother of the wife of the Báb, Afnan-i-Kabir, was in Akká. Bahá'u'lláh asked him how much the drawing resembled the Báb, and he confirmed that it was an accurate likeness. Then Bahá'u'lláh sent his own fur overcoat as a gift to the artist.[84]

Valíyu'lláh Varqá adds in this regard:

---

[82] Same person as Áqá Bashí but with a different spelling.
[83] Masumian, and Masumian The Báb in the World of Images, 5.
[84] Darius Shahrokh, Varqá and Son: The Heavenly Doves, 11.

Bahá'u'lláh called one of the uncles of the Báb, showed him the painting and asked, 'Do you know this face?' Instantly the uncle replied, 'Yes, it is the Báb!' "Bahá'u'lláh at once sent one of His 'abas to my father asking him to give it to the painter. My father, at the time he had sent the painting, had asked permission from Bahá'u'lláh to have nine paintings made and sent to nine important cities in Persia to be kept by believers in special places. In answer Bahá'u'lláh had given permission for the painter to make only one more and that was to be given to my father. No more were to be made. This painting of the Báb which my father had was confiscated by the Government with other papers, but when I was in the presence of 'Abdu'l-Baha He promised me that sometime this will be given back to our family. Seyid Assadullah found the sketch made by this painter in the home of a Bahá'í family in Persia and he sent it to 'Abdu'l-Bahá in 'Akká. Thus the painting of His Holiness the Báb and the one sketch are now preserved in Haifa, the other painting is lost for the present, and aside from these there is no other authentic painting or photograph of the Báb.[85]

4.4 At the Court meetings

At this time in the Tabríz court, Varqá attended meetings, usually accompanied by his father-in-law 'Abdu'lláh Núrí, who by that time was publicly known as a Bahá'í. Actually, it was the Crown Prince Muzaffari'd-Din Mírzá who used to remind 'Abdu'lláh Núrí to bring his son-in-law to the palace.

The prince himself liked reading Varqá's poems to the audience showering praise upon him. At those meetings philosophical, religious and literary matters were discussed to the delight of the prince who seemed to enjoy these elevated conversations. Varqá was able to demonstrate the supremacy of his intelligence and the weight of the

[85] Martha Root, "The Only Pictures of the Báb," The Star of the West, vol. 21, No. 2, (May, 1930), 54-55.

Bahá'í teachings, though this sometimes incurred the displeasure of the clergy.

At the prince's request Varqá recited his poems with pleasure but he tried to be quiet in the religious discussions where he was an expert. Those were very dangerous times for the Bahá'ís due to the power the clerics had on the population, authorities and the court. Wisdom was needed to present the Bahá'í teachings without arousing animosity.

An interesting incident occurred when a high ranking Mullá described his view on how Bahá'ís converted people to their faith. He stated that:

> The Bahá'í teachers used to, at one time, feed their unsuspecting guests with a certain kind of date which made them into Bahá'ís. Now that people have found out about this trick, the Bahá'ís extract the essence of dates which their teachers then make into pills to be used on those whom they want to make Bahá'ís. They have a cunning way of doing this. First the teacher seats himself in such a position as to face all those who are gathered in a room, then he charms his hearers with a most fascinating speech so that everybody's mouth is opened with admiration. When this stage is reached, the Bahá'í teacher cleverly shoots out a pill from between his fingers into the mouth of each of his audience who, having swallowed it, cannot help becoming a Bahá'í.[86]

Though others present considered this explanation unlikely, most would not dare to publicly challenge the pronouncements of such a senior cleric. Varqá asked for permission to respond to the mullá's arguments. After all, he was a physician and an expert in chemistry. With authority he stood up and said:

> I have knowledge of medicine and am aware of many extracts, but never heard about the date extract. Such pill-throwing

---

[86] Gloria Faizi, Fire on the Mountain Top (New Delhi, India: Bahá'í Publishing Trust, 1973), 76.

> requires years of practice and marksmanship so they don't miss the mouth, and thirdly, regardless of how eloquent a speaker, seldom does one see every jaw drop in awe, and finally, if the pill gets into the mouth, people still have to swallow it, which no one has reported. [87]

The priest was left speechless and unable to reply.

4.5 Tablets to Varqá

Varqá was the recipient of many Tablets of Bahá'u'lláh and this had a powerful effect on his teaching endeavours and on the special missions with which he was engaged. The Tablets were usually revealed in response to Varqá's requests and reports. Varqá treasured those Tablets very much.

It has been said that the numbers of Tablets received by Varqá from Bahá'u'lláh could amount to a large volume.[88] The length of those Tablets varied. For example, the Lawḥ-i-Varqá (Tablet to Varqá) comprises about forty pages and was revealed in 'Akká in 1885 over a period of more than one month.[89] These epistles address a broad variety of mystic, theological and social issues.[90] [91] "The Tablets of Bahá'u'lláh to Varqá", wrote Adib Taherzadeh, "are replete with passages in which He extols with great eloquence the loftiness and grandeur of the Cause He has revealed, glorifies the Person of its Author, unravels some of the mysterious and superhuman forces which have been released by Him in this age and lays bare some of the truths which are enshrined in His Writings."[92]

---

[87] Darius Shahrokh, Varqá and Son: The Heavenly Doves, 6-7.
[88] Taherzadeh, The Revelation of Bahá'u'lláh, 74.
[89] Sen McGlinn, "The Leiden List of the Writings of Bahá'u'lláh," 1997, https://www.h-net.org/~bahai/notes/bhtabs.htm.
[90] Moojan Momen, "Relativism: A Basis for Bahá'í Metaphysics," Studies in Honor of the Late Hasan M. Balyuzi, 185-217 (1988).
[91] Taherzadeh, The Revelation of Bahá'u'lláh, vol. 4, 64-72.
[92] Taherzadeh, The Revelation of Bahá'u'lláh, vol. 4, 66.

In one of those Tablets, Varqá and the believers are encouraged by the Blessed Beauty in these beautiful terms:

> O Varqá! … We found thy letter a mirror reflecting thy love for the Beloved of the world and thy turning towards Him. Great is thy blessedness for having drawn nigh, for having drunk thy fill, and for having been caused to attain. Verily, thy Lord is the Resplendent Expounder. Verily, We witness the fire that hath encompassed thee in thy love for thy Lord. We see its flaring up and hear the crackling of its flames. Exalted be He Who hath ignited it, He Who hath made its flames leap high, He Who hath revealed it to all men. He is that Almighty Lord before the evidence of Whose might the essence of power acknowledgeth its helplessness. Verily, thy Lord is He who heareth and seeth, and is the All-Knowing. Rejoice, for this Wronged One maketh mention of thee as He hath in the past, and even in this instant, as He paceth, He giveth utterance to these words: 'Verily, We have sensed the sweet scent of thy love, and have witnessed thy sincerity and thy humility, as thy heart was occupied with the mention of Me and thy tongue with My wondrous praise.' Thus hath the Sea of life sprinkled its waters upon thee, that thou mayest rejoice in the days of thy glorious, incomparable Lord …
>
> Say: O friends! Ye have endured much in the path of thy love for the Beloved of the worlds; ye have witnessed that which it was not seemly to behold, and have heard that which ill became thine ears, and have endured such burdens in the path of the Friend as were truly heavier than mountains. Great is the blessedness of your backs, your eyes and your ears, for that which they bore and they saw and they heard. Now ye should value this highly exalted station, and not allow it to be squandered. In all cases, this ephemeral world and all who are therein will suffer death, and all things therein will be caught in the claws of change. At all times ask ye God —exalted be He— to keep thee in His safekeeping, and to cause thee to be constant in the path of His Cause. Know ye well that whatever ye have endured or seen or heard for His sake hath been as a

> token of His special bounty unto you. And among His eternal bestowals is the mention of thee in His Tablets. Verily, ye have tasted the cup of calamity in His path; now drink your fill of the purest elixir from the goblets of His remembrance of you and of His tender mercy unto you. . . . Be not saddened by what appeareth to be thy weakness, thine abasement and thy distress. I swear by the Sun of the Heaven of Independence that honour, wealth and affluence are revolving around thee, and making mention of thee and are turning unto thee. We beseech God that men will partake of the sweetness of His divine Utterance.[93]

In the Lawḥ-i-Varqá (Tablet of Varqá) the Manifestation of God also explains to him complex theological themes such as the concept of *Malakút*, literally the *Angelical Kingdom*, meaning the *Concourse on High* or *Abhá Kingdom*. The term *Malakút* is from the same root as the biblical name Malachias meaning "angel" in Semitic languages such as Hebrew, Arabic and Aramaic (Jesus' spoken language). By *Concourse on High* the Bahá'í Scriptures refer to the congregation of holy souls in the life to come. In different passages of the Writings we can find that this glorious company acts as the ferment and yeast that make the world of humanity develop:

> The meaning of the Kingdom [*Malakút*] in its primary sense and degree is the scene of His transcendent glory. In another sense it is the world of similitudes which existeth between the Dominion on high and this mortal realm; whatever is in the heavens or on the earth hath its counterpart in that world. Whilst a thing remaineth hidden and concealed within the power of utterance it is said to be of the Dominion and this is the first stage of its substantiation. Whenever it becometh manifest it is said to be of the Kingdom. The power and potency it deriveth from the first stage, it bestoweth upon whatever lieth below. [94]

[93] Balyuzi, Eminent Bahá'ís in the Time of Bahá'u'lláh, 49-51.
[94] Momen, "Relativism: A Basis for Bahá'í Metaphysics," 185-217.

Varqá and Rúhu'lláh

The historian Adib Taherzadeh in his book "The Revelation of Bahá'u'lláh" wrote about the Tablets that the Blessed Beauty revealed in honour of Varqá:

> There are numerous Tablets revealed by Bahá'u'lláh for Varqá which, if compiled, would make up a large volume. A common feature of them all is the outpouring of grace and manifold favours upon him. Bahá'u'lláh refers to Varqá as one who has truly recognized the exalted station of His Lord, and has had the honour of attaining His presence. He testifies that Varqá has immersed himself in the ocean of His words, soared in the heaven of His love, drunk deep of the living waters of His remembrance, turned himself wholly towards Him, and served His Cause with utter dedication. He showers praises upon him for his devotion and love, his steadfastness, his sincerity, his faithfulness and his meritorious teaching activities.
>
> In one of His Tablets revealed about 1888-9 Bahá'u'lláh highly commends Varqá for having adorned his being with the mantle of servitude and assures him that it is God who has desired that same mantle for him...
>
> The Tablets of Bahá'u'lláh to Varqá are replete with passages in which He extols with great eloquence the loftiness and grandeur of the Cause He has revealed, glorifies the Person of its Author, unravels some of the mysterious and superhuman forces which have been released by Him in this age and lays bare some of the truths which are enshrined in His Writings.
>
> In a lengthy Tablet revealed for Varqá in about 1887-8, several years before His ascension, Bahá'u'lláh lauds in glowing terms the greatness of His Revelation, affirms that the verses of God have been sent down in great profusion, that proofs and testimonies of His Cause have encompassed the world, that the pearls of wisdom and utterance have been brought forth for all to see, and that the Tongue of Grandeur has uttered His call to the nations, and yet in spite of this outpouring of God's grace

and bounty the people of the world have remained for the most part uninformed. Some have heard the Call of God but remained heedless. Only a few have witnessed the glory of His Revelation and embraced His Cause…

In this Tablet Bahá'u'lláh calls upon the believers to render Him victorious by the hosts of goodly deeds and praiseworthy character. He states that day and night His tongue is engaged in exhorting His loved ones to a virtuous life and saintly conduct, through which His Cause will be glorified and His Word exalted. He urges the believers to teach His Cause, but counsels them to carry out this injunction with great wisdom, reminds them that speech in moderation acts as the water of life for the soul, whereas if it is carried beyond the bounds of moderation it will give birth to fanaticism and malice.

In an earlier Tablet to Varqá revealed about 1880-81 Bahá'u'lláh describes the condition of humanity as grievous. Man can clearly see the instability of this mortal life and the continued disturbances and changes which overtake the world. He can witness at all times in every created thing the signs and tokens of ultimate extinction. And yet he is utterly heedless of his own extinction. Wayward and negligent he roams over the earth, occupies himself with that which perishes, and commits such deeds as will bring upon him everlasting loss and deprivation…

In another Tablet to Varqá and expounding the same theme, Bahá'u'lláh states that even the German Templers,[95] who had discovered through the Gospels that the coming of the Lord was nigh, and had gone to the Holy Land with the express purpose of coming face to face with Him, had utterly failed to recognize their Lord when He manifested Himself to them.[96]

[95] A group pf German Protestants who left their homes and took up residence mainly on the slopes of Mt. Carmel, Haifa, in anticipation of the return of Christ. (A.T).
[96] Taherzadeh, The Revelation of Bahá'u'lláh, vol 4, 64-72.

4.6 'Abdu'l-Bahá as the Centre of the Covenant of Bahá'u'lláh

Varqá also wrote to 'Abdu'l-Bahá asking for guidance and blessings. However, 'Abdu'l-Bahá never responded to him. One day Varqá, in a state of frustration, wrote to Bahá'u'lláh's secretary. The Blessed Beauty heard of it and instructed 'Abdu'l-Bahá to write back to Varqá. In a short reply, 'Abdu'l-Bahá informed him that He felt unable to write when the Supreme Pen is writing.[97]

Such was 'Abdu'l-Bahá's sense of humility and reverence. As Adib Taherzadeh remarked, "Indeed, whatever 'Abdu'l-Bahá wrote during the lifetime of Bahá'u'lláh was directed by Him and received His sanction".[98] Many decades later while in New York in 1912 'Abdu'l-Bahá said:

> In the days of the Blessed Beauty, I never had a desire to write: The friends even complained about it. In reply I finally wrote to Varqá saying, 'When the shrill of the Supreme Pen can be heard, what is the need of my writing?' However, in the days of the Most Great Luminary others wrote, referring to themselves as the great sun of God.[99]

Varqá loved 'Abdu'l-Bahá very much. Once a discussion arose among believers from Tabríz about whether 'Abdu'l-Bahá or His brother Muḥammad 'Alí should be Bahá'u'lláh's successor. Varqá asked Bahá'u'lláh to explain the meaning of the following verse of the "Kitáb-i-Aqdas" (The Most Holy Book):

> When the ocean of My presence hath ebbed and the Book of My Revelation is ended, turn your faces toward Him Whom

---

[97] Adib Taherzadeh, The Covenant of Bahá'u'lláh, 128 (Oxford: George Ronald, 1992).

[98] Taherzadeh, The Covenant of Bahá'u'lláh, 128.

[99] Mahmúd Zarqání, Mahmúd's Diary the Diary of Mírzá Mahmúd-i-Zarqání Chronicling `Abdu'l-Bahá's Journey to America, trans. Mohi Sobhani with the assistance of Shirley Macias (Oxford: George Ronald, 1998), 135. Sunday, June 16, 1912

> God hath purposed, Who hath branched from this Ancient Root.[100]

Varqá said that 'Abdu'l-Bahá would be the chosen one, while another believer thought of Bahá'u'lláh's secretary and a third one believed that the successor would be Muḥammad 'Alí. Varqá said: "Bahá'u'lláh has stated that if there is anything which we do not understand we should write to Him."[101] Hence Varqá wrote a request to the Holy Land to which Bahá'u'lláh responded on 29 June 1881 indicating that the verse of the Kitáb-i-Aqdas refers to 'Abdu'l-Bahá.[102]

In 1892 Bahá'u'lláh ascended in the Mansion of Bahjí. This news filled the Bahá'ís with great dismay. In His Testament, called the "Kitáb-i-'Ahd" (The Book of Covenant), Bahá'u'lláh again designated 'Abdu'l-Bahá as the Head of Faith and Interpreter of His teachings. This sacred document, which establishes the Covenant of Bahá'u'lláh with 'Abdu'l-Bahá as its Center, was opened nine days after His passing in front of the members of the Holy Family and the resident Bahá'ís and pilgrims in the Holy Land.

The great majority of the believers obeyed without reserve the last words of the Blessed Beauty, but there were those who rebelled and pursued the path of error leading ultimately to complete spiritual loss. Varqá remained firm and a few years after his second pilgrimage, he again visited 'Abdu'l-Bahá in the Holy Land. Varqá was blessed with numerous Tablets from 'Abdu'l-Bahá after Bahá'u'lláh's ascension.

---

[100] Bahá'u'lláh, The Kitáb-i-Aqdas: The Most Holy Book (Wilmette, Illinois: Bahá'í Publishing Trust, 1993), 63.
[101] Root, "White Roses of Persia (Part 2)," 180.
[102] Christopher Buck, and Youli A Ioannesyan, "The 1893 Russian Publication of Bahá'u'lláh's Last Will and Testament: An Academic Attestation of 'Abdu'l-Bahá's Successorship," Bahá'í Studies Review 19, no. 1, 4 (2013).

V - Prison in Yazd and Iṣfahán

Varqá stayed in Tabríz until he went to Yazd, his homeland, to both visit his sister and also engage in travel teaching. This journey took place in approximately 1300 AH[103] (1882-1883)[104].

5.1 Mas'úd Mírzá, The Infernal Tree

Mas'úd Mírzá (1850-1918), the eldest son of the Sháh, was the Governor of Iṣfahán from 1874. He was known as Yamín-al-Dowleh (Right Hand of the Government) [105] and as Zillu's-Sultán, (the Shadow of the King), but Bahá'u'lláh referred to him as the "Infernal Tree".[106] An overly ambitious man, he was at the centre of Iran's political life, engaged in intrigue, extortion and bribery, with a single central objective: becoming the next Sháh of Iran.

Mas'úd Mírzá would have been in direct line to the throne but for the fact that he was the son of a concubine. However, the Qájár dynasty did not have clear succession rules. For example, his father Naṣiri'd-Dín Sháh was the youngest of his siblings when he became sovereign in 1848 but he was appointed king as a result of the machinations of his mother who was able to manipulate the various heads of the Qájár tribe to achieve her purpose.

Mas'úd Mírzá became blinded by the pursuit of power. At certain times he was one of the Sháh's favourite princes and accrued much power and wealth. In addition to serving as the Governor of the important provinces of Fars and Mázindarán, he was in charge of

---

[103] "After Hijrah". Date of Muḥammad's migration from Mecca to Medina setting the beginning of the Islamic calendar.
[104] Balyuzi, Eminent Bahá'ís in the Time of Bahá'u'lláh, 78, 1986.
[105] Abbas Amanat, Pivot of the Universe: Nasir Al-Din Shah Qajar and the Iranian Monarchy, 1831-1896, 403 (Univ of California Press, 1997).
[106] Shoghi Effendi, God Passes By, 232.

Iṣfahán for a total of 40 years[107]. At one point this prince ruled two-fifths of the country.[108] His father may have come to suspect his engagement in conspiracy because in 1888 Mas'úd Mírzá's domain was reduced to Iṣfahán only.

In his greed he was unscrupulous. At times he befriended the Muslim ecclesiastical hierarchy but this relationship was characterized by corruption of both parties. In 1888 he dispatched a secret emissary[109] to meet Bahá'u'lláh in 'Akká looking for political support to overthrow the Sháh, a request that Baha'u'llah blatantly rejected. A few years later, this emissary was arrested in the capital and Mas'úd Mírzá, fearful of his treason being revealed, ordered a systematic campaign of persecution against the Bahá'ís in Iṣfahán and Yazd. This served the double purpose of distracting attention away from his treachery and 'providing evidence' of his loyalty to the crown.[110]

Yazd was another of Mas'úd Mírzá's domains administered by his eldest son, Jalál'ud-Dawlih. Jalál'ud-Dawlih was referred to by Baha'u'llah as the tyrant of the land of Ya (Yazd) who "committed that which hath caused the Concourse on High to shed tears of blood".[111] Like his father, the "Infernal Tree", Jalál'ud-Dawlih manifested cruelty in his dealings with the Bahá'í communities under his jurisdiction. Jalál'ud-Dawlih was responsible for the martyrdom of the Seven Martyrs of Yazd in 1891, like his father before him who had responsibility for the execution of two brothers entitled the King and Beloved of the Martyrs in 1879, as well as many other barbarities.[112]

---

[107] Amanat, Pivot of the universe: Nasir al-Din Shah Qajar and the Iranian monarchy, 1831-96, 997.
[108] Shoghi Effendi, God Passes By, 232.
[109] His name was Ḥájí Muhammad-'Alí-i-Maḥallátí better known as Sayyáḥ (traveller).
[110] Balyuzi, Eminent Bahá'ís in the Time of Bahá'u'lláh, 79, 1986.
[111] Bahá'u'lláh, Tablets of Bahá'u'lláh: Revealed after the Kitáb-i-Aqdas, 85 (Wilmette, Illinois: Bahá'i Publishing Trust, 1988)..
[112] Shoghi Effendi, God Passes By, 201.

5.2 Rúḥu'lláh's Aunt

Through letters Varqá's only sister Bíbí Túbá had been lamenting separation from him and was begging Varqá to visit her. After her father's and brother's exile she had been feeling lonely for a long time.

Bíbí Túbá was married to Áqá Mírzá Ḥusayn 'Alí Tabib and the couple had two daughters, Farahangiz Bahjí and Riḍváníyyih, and two sons, Áqá Mírzá Habib'u'lláh, Mírzá Vajíh'u'lláh. These children were Rúḥu'lláh's cousins.[113]

Rúḥu'lláh was very fond of his aunt Bíbí Túbá. A letter exists in Rúḥu'lláh's handwriting to a member of his family refering to her in very affectionate terms and showing that, despite living in different cities and going through various vicissitudes, the family was still connected.[114] The letter is accompanied by a supplication[115] in his beautiful calligraphy both of which are shown on the book illustrations. This is Rúḥu'lláh's letter:

> He is the All-Glorious.
> God is the Most Magnificent.
> God willing, may my spirit and my whole being be sacrificed for you.
> I hope that your glorious and blessed existence had been and is without any unhappiness and worries.
> As my brother, may the God's Glory of the Most Glorious be upon him, used to write to you, this humbled one also would like, in a couple of words (i.e. briefly), remind your exalted self of me so that I won't be among the forgotten ones. This is the purpose of me sending you this brief letter, and bothering you.
> If you ask about my health, thanks God, the gift of health which is the greatest of God's gifts, is bestowed upon me.

---

113 Source: MyHeritage.com

114 'Andalíb Magazine, vol. 10, no. 39 (Summer 1991) 16.

115 Momen, The Bahá'í Communities of Iran 1851-1921: The North of Iran, 68.

I spending all my days and nights in the hope of attaining your presence and the presence of my exalted aunt and my cousins. "Perhaps, we may be able to see the sight of friends again, and pick the garden flowers by our hands"
I extend my greetings and Alláh-u-Abhá to the esteemed and respected aunt, and also to my cousins.
With the utmost desire looking forward to it.
Upon you be Al-Bahá
Rúḥu'lláh

Rúḥu'lláh's accompanying supplication reads as follows:

He is the Most Glorious

All praise and worship are to the Creator Who hath illuminated this darkened world with a ray of the Sun of His Beauty and, with a drop of the Ocean of His Blessings and Magnanimity, He hath quenched the whole world. O my God, my Master, and my Desire, Thou seest this lowly, sinful, poor, and needy servant of Thine in the claws of Thine enemies and knowest, O my God, my burning heart and trembling limbs in Thine remoteness and separation. Verily, Thou art the Most Rich, the Most Able, the Most Powerful, the Incomparable, and the Most Mighty. O my Creator, my Master and my Beloved, I thank Thee for freeing Thy servants from the shackles of idle fancies and vain imaginings and illuminated them with the Light of Thy Guidance and Faith. And Thou hast enlightened these weak ones bewildered in the wilderness of ignorance and waywardness with the brilliance of the Rays of Thy Light. Thou art the One Whom the earthly circumstances do not stop from vouchsafing Thy Blessings and Benevolence. O my Beloved, Thou seest this sinful servant of Thine who is standing before the Gate of Thy Mercy and Thy Compassion begging Thine Forgiveness and asking for Thy Munificence and Generosity. He supplicates: O Compassionate Lord, quench these lowly servants from Thine Life-Giving Chalice and grant these wanderers with the Hand of Thy Grace and Bestowal a share. Thou art the King Whom the armies of the world and the peoples therein are incapable to stop Thy Sovereignty. O Beneficent One, Thy Beneficence hath encompassed all, and O Merciful One, Thy Mercy hath surrounded all the inhabitants of the earth. We beseech Thee not to deprive us from Thy Blessings. Thou art the Gracious, Thou art the Generous.

5.3 The Jalál'ud-Dawlih

Around that time a wave of persecution against the Bahá'ís erupted throughout Iran where state, religious and local authorities joined hands.[116] As a result, soon after his arrival to Yazd, Varqá was chained and put in jail along with criminals. The order came from the governor, Jalál'ud-Dawlih but the divines of Yazd who, ten years previously, had expelled Varqá's father from the city, had a great deal of responsibility. Varqá was imprisoned for one year. Although Jalál'ud-Dawlih was the governor, Yazd was under the authority of his father Mas'úd Mírzá, the Governor of Iṣfahán.

Iranian prisons of that period were the antithesis of modern Western penitentiaries. There was no judiciary system. Instead, the fate of the accused was determined by the arbitrary judgement of despotic regional governors and the central power, all susceptible to corruption in the form of bribery and to other influences. Innocent people were routinely jailed to advance the vested interests of those in power.

Connection to someone in Iranian high society was important in order to attain protection against abuses. In the absence of connections, the accused would be obliged to pay vast sums in bribes to a chain of corrupt prison officers. The concept of rehabilitation was non-existent. Prisoners languished for years in dungeons with no windows or ventilation and only brief occasional access to sunlight and amenities. As the official rations were literally dry bread and water, food had to be provided by family and friends.

---

[116] Ahang Rabbani, Witnesses to Bábí and Bahá'í History, vol. 5, Ponder Thou Upon the Martyrdom of Hájí Muhammad-Ridá: Nineteen Historical Accounts, ed. Ahang Rabbani, 22 (2007). https://bahai-library.com/pdf/r/rabbani_martyrdom_haji_muhammad-rida.pdf.

5.4 In the Prison of Iṣfahán

Mas'úd Mírzá desperately wanted the Iranian throne and was willing to go to unimaginable extremes to achieve his goal. As seen earlier, Mas'úd Mírzá went so far as to approach Bahá'u'lláh in 'Akká through his emissary Sayyáḥ seeking support from the Bahá'ís of Iran to dethrone his father. This request was of course totally rejected.

In pursuit of the same goal, Mas'úd Mírzá sent one of his confidants called Sayyáḥ to murder the Crown Prince in Ádhirbáyján. As soon this plot was exposed, Sayyáḥ was condemned to the gallows. It was actually 'Abdu'lláh Núrí , Varqá's father-in-law and the court chamberlain, who pleaded with the prince to spare Sayyáḥ's life and instead expel him from the city. 'Abdu'lláh Núrí was successful and the wisdom of it would become apparent later. Sayyáḥ went back to Iṣfahán happy to have avoided death thanks to the intervention of this Bahá'í.

After one year in the prison in Yazd, Varqá was transferred to a prison in Iṣfahán two to three hundred kilometres away. This is one of the most beautiful Iranian cities due to the splendor of its architecture. The locals proudly call their city "Esfahan nesf-e jahan" (In Persian, "Iṣfahán is half the world"). In 1598, the Safavid dynasty made this city the capital of its empire until the Qájárs transferred it to Tehran eventually. Iṣfahán was also the seat of Mas'úd Mírzá's power.

The trip between prisons entailed a ten-day journey by mule in chains and fetters. By that time, Varqá was about 26 or 28 years old and a robust man. According to Balyuzi: "The guards escorting him from Yazd to Iṣfahán had been so insolently abusive that to spare himself the taunts of those brutish men Varqá had pretended to be deaf and dumb"[117].

[117] Balyuzi, Eminent Bahá'ís in the Time of Bahá'u'lláh, 1986, 97.

Sometime prior to Varqá's arrival at the prison in Iṣfahán, a Bahá'í poet by the name of Síná had been released from the same prison. When Síná heard that Varqá had been sent to the prison in Iṣfahán he began mobilizing the local Bahá'ís to either facilitate his release or ameliorate his severe imprisonment restrictions, particularly when Varqá was being forced to associate with hardened criminals. The local Bahá'ís approached Sayyáḥ who had much influence on Mas'úd Mírzá and who in return for having his life spared through the intervention of a Bahá'í, arranged for Varqá to be transferred to a better prison where only political prisoners were kept. [118]

At this prison an imprisoned nobleman befriended Varqá. Isfandíyár was the son of Ḥusayn-Qulí, a chieftain of the powerful Bakhtíyarí tribe. Ḥusayn-Qulí had been assassinated at Mas'úd Mírzá's orders. Varqá shared poems that he and others had written with Isfandíyár. This poetry had a profound effect on Isfandíyár who became enchanted by Varqá's talent.

Probably because Mas'úd Mírzá was hoping to be given a ransom to release Isfandíyár he came often to the prison and engaged in conversation. One day, the prince noticed the distinguished presence of Varqá and asked about his identity. The prince was told that he was a believer from Yazd. The prince replied with sarcasm, saying that if he was a prophet he should perform the miracle of relieving himself from the fetters. Varqá replied he never claimed to be a prophet nor the power to create miracles.[119]

At the same time an attendant informed the prince that Varqá was a poet and an educated person. Persians have a great respect for poets. A famous Islamic tradition, repeated by the Báb, states, "Treasures lie hidden beneath the throne of God; the key to those treasures is the tongue of poets."[120]

---

[118] Darius Shahrokh, Varqá and Son: The Heavenly Doves, 7, 1992.
[119] Handal, El Concurso En Lo Alto, 371.
[120] Nabíl-i-A'zam, The Dawn-Breakers: Nabíl's Narrative of the Early Days of the Bahá'í Revelation, 258-59.

Impressed by a piece of Varqá's poetry which was followed by a lively conversation with the poet, the prince ordered that his fetters be removed.[121] Isfandíyár found this amusing and exclaimed: "Behold! Varqá's prophet has performed a miracle!"[122]

Isfandíyár asked Varqá about his religious beliefs. A series of conversations ensued leading Isfandíyár to become a Bahá'í in the prison.[123] [124] Varqá was finally released by Mas'úd Mírzá and, penniless, he made the 900 km journey from Iṣfahán to his home in Tabríz and much missed children.

---

[121] Kazem Kazemzadeh, "Varqá and Rúhu'llah: Deathless in Martyrdom," World Order, Winter 1974-1975, 33.

[122] Kazemzadeh, "Varqá and Rúhu'llah: Deathless in Martyrdom," World Order, Winter 1974-75, 33.

[123] Balyuzi, Eminent Bahá'ís in the Time of Bahá'u'lláh, 80, 1986.

[124] Moojan Momen, "Persecution and Resilience: A History of the Baha'i Religion in Qajar Isfahan," Journal of Religious History 36, no. 4, 471-485 (2012).

VI - Rúḥu'lláh

Rúḥu'lláh was such a delightful child that his graceful nature attracted the special attention of Bahá'u'lláh, 'Abdu'l-Bahá and Bahíyyih Khánum in the Holy Land. He was a child endowed with profound spiritual insights, displaying advanced literary abilities, focused on deep mystical themes, and confronting with maturity adults on religious themes.

Bahá'u'lláh and 'Abdu'l-Bahá were very fond of Rúḥu'lláh and praised his determination to teach in various circumstances. He was known for his capacity to introduce the Faith into any conversation under any circumstance. Thus, he earned from Bahá'u'lláh and 'Abdu'l-Bahá the designation of "mubaligh" مبلغ (religious teacher).

Rúḥu'lláh was "a boy so timid that he would never even go alone into the garden in the evening" and yet "always remarkably courageous when it came to doing anything for the Bahá'í Cause".[125] He became an adolescent who embraced death to avoid recanting his Faith, the personification of Bahá'u'lláh's statement "The source of courage and power is the promotion of the Word of God, and steadfastness in His Love".[126]

6.1 A Prodigy Child

Rúḥu'lláh was mostly educated at home. Credit for his education is due to his father, Varqá. Martha Root wrote:

> All fathers who read this tale will see in the life of this Persian the highest ideal of fatherhood, a height not reached in every home, and too high to be understood by many fathers.[127]

[125] Martha Root, "White Roses of Persia (Part 3)," Star of the West, vol. 23, issue 7, (October, 1932), 226-27.
[126] Bahá'u'lláh, Tablets of Bahá'u'lláh: Revealed after the Kitáb-i-Aqdas, 156.
[127] Root, "White Roses of Persia (Part 1)," 72.

Rúḥu'lláh grew up surrounded by spirituality, wisdom and literary abilities. When he was eleven years old, his father sent 'Abdu'l-Bahá a letter attaching samples of Rúḥu'lláh's calligraphy. In response to Varqá, 'Abdu'l-Bahá wrote in His own handwriting a letter for Rúḥu'lláh.

> He is the Most Glorious!
>
> O thou who art nearer to the sucking age! The impression of the musk like writing of that sign of the Love of God (Rúḥu'lláh) was seen. Verily, in a short time thou hast improved greatly, and seeing this great progress is the cause of my joy and happiness. Certainly, thou must try thy utmost that thy writing may become better day by day and in the world of writing it may become the glory and the bounty of the Supreme Pen!
>
> Always I must hear from thee, and thou must describe and explain about those whom thou dost teach (spiritually). Upon thee be Bahá![128]

"When 'Alí Muḥammad Varqá read this Tablet", Martha Root wrote, "with great reverence and solemnity he knelt with forehead to the floor and said: "This is the son who will give his life as promised by Bahá'u'lláh, because a pen of wood could not have such an effect, the effect of the Supreme Pen would be the mighty pen of martyrdom."[129]

The following episode during Rúḥu'lláh's second pilgrimage reveals how careful Varqá was with regard to the education of his children. In Martha Root's words,

> The little group stayed for several months in 'Akká and in Bahjí. Rúḥu'lláh studied Persian writing every day and every

[128] Root, "White Roses of Persia (Part 2)," 181.
[129] Root, "White Roses of Persia (Part 2)," 181.

> Friday he used to show a copy of his writing to 'Abdu'l-Bahá Who often praised it. Rúḥu'lláh's father was very insistent about their lessons and very severe when they did not study, for he knew the importance of education."[130]

Rúḥu'lláh's paternal grandmother, paternal and maternal grandfathers and father were all believers. This ensured that Rúḥu'lláh's innate spiritual capacity was nurtured and enabled to blossom. Only his maternal grandmother, in her blind fanaticism, tried to undermine the faith of her grandchildren. However, she was unsuccessful because their faith was strong.

Although his father was a Bahá'í, Rúḥu'lláh did not accept the Faith passively. He had a direct personal relationship with and belief in Bahá'u'lláh. One day he was asked why he was a Bahá'í, to which he replied: "Because I have investigated it for myself. I am not a Bahá'í because my father is one, but because I have thoroughly investigated it."[131]

At about nine years of age Rúḥu'lláh had to be separated from his mother —a painful blow for a child of that age. The death threats against Varqá led by his mother-in-law were intensifying forcing him to flee the city with his two oldest children. Rúḥu'lláh's grandmother's home was no longer safe. Varqá left the two younger sons behind, one of whom was Valíyu'lláh. Many years later Valíyu'lláh said:

> She [Rúḥu'lláh's grandmother] had such a deep hatred of the Cause that she began to make evil suggestions to me against my father and to sow the seeds of hatred and enmity in my soul against him. She was able to impress my tender soul to such an extent that in my Islamic prayers, which I was obliged to

[130] Root, "White Roses of Persia (Part 1)," 73.

[131] Jan Teofil Jasion, 'Abdu'l-Bahá in France 1911-1913 (Paris: Editions Bahá'íes France, 2017), 572.

> say, I wept in bitter grief for my father's deviation which had earned him so much hatred from the public.[132]

Psychologists argue about whether a child can be gifted without being talented, or the other way around. Regardless of whether or not this is possible, Rúḥu'lláh was both gifted and talented. That is, he was a prodigy. Although he liked to play with his young friends and was full of joy and vivacity, he had great mastery of spiritual subjects. Rúḥu'lláh easily answered the questions asked of him and with a lot of wisdom. He spoke with much courage and enthusiastically taught the Bahá'í Faith to young people and adults.

6.2 A Spirited child

Despite his maturity, Rúḥu'lláh enjoyed playing with other children of his age. The following story, narrated by Martha Root, happened during the last pilgrimage he made with his father to the Holy Land.

> There were many happy incidents during the days spent with 'Abdu'l-Bahá, but I wish to relate one which though not quite so pleasant at the moment, reveals 'Abdu'l-Bahá's great character, the quickness of a father to obey and the wisdom of little Rúḥu'lláh.
>
> A large group of Bahá'í children were playing together when one little boy uttered a naughty word; Rúḥu'lláh quickly slapped him on the mouth saying he deserved punishment. This child who had said the word was the son of a great martyr and since he had come to 'Akká he had been very favoured by the Holy Family and all the believers. The other children marched in a body with this little boy to tell Rúḥu'lláh's father and to complain about this matter. Rúḥu'lláh, when he saw them going, ran into the court and up the prison stairs, through the open door into 'Abdu'l-Bahá's room and sat down close beside Him. 'Abdu'l-Bahá was by the window writing Tablets.

[132] Bahá'í World Centre, "Váliyu'lláh Varqá 1884—1955," in The Bahá'í World, vol. XIII (Haifa, Israel: Bahá'í World Centre, 1970), 831-34.

> As soon as 'Alí Muḥammad Varqá heard the children's story he started out to find his son. Going into the court, he saw Rúḥu'lláh sitting beside 'Abdu'l-Bahá upstairs near the window. He motioned him to come down. Rúḥu'lláh was vigorously nodding "no", and 'Abdu'l-Bahá attracted by this motion said, "Why are you nodding out the window?" Then Rúḥu'lláh related the whole story of how he had slapped the little boy on the mouth and said he knew if he went down to the court his father was going to punish him. 'Abdu'l-Bahá called the father to come upstairs and said very sternly: "No one must say anything to Rúḥu'lláh about this matter!" Usually 'Abdu'l-Bahá was very careful that children must obey their parents, but He repeated it a second time: "No one must say anything to Rúḥu'lláh about this matter!" From that time on 'Alí Muḥammad was very respectful to his little son Rúḥu'lláh and he never again reproved him for anything. He was a good father and Rúḥu'lláh was a good son; he never consciously did wrong.[133]

6.3 Talking to the Divines

Throughout his life Varqá engaged in discussions with high level theologians. "At times, Varqá would turn to his son Rúḥu'lláh and ask him to answer on his behalf. Rúḥu'lláh charmed his hearers.[134] Hatcher adds that "Normally, after Varqá used to end his speech, he would then ask his young son to deliver a speech"[135]. The Governor of Zanján once said: "This child's strange power of argument is a miracle in itself".[136] Ḥájí Mírzá Ḥaydar-'Alí adds:

> Since the defeat of the divines in their argument became evident to the Governor, who was a powerful and courageous personality, the divines did not dare to label Varqá as an infidel and issue his death warrant. In these meetings 'Alá'u'd-

[133] Root, "White Roses of Persia (Part 2)," 180-81.
[134] Faizi, Fire on the Mountain Top, 80.
[135] John S. Hatcher, and Amrollah Hemmat, Reunion with the Beloved: Poetry and Martyrdom (Hong Kong: Juxta Publishing Limited, 2004), 168.
[136] Faizi, Fire on the Mountain Top, 80.

> Dawlih often permitted the twelve-year-old Rúḥu'lláh to speak with the divines. He used to prove the subject with amazing courage, eloquence and profundity. His talks were so sweet that the Governor admitted that the proofs which that child had adduced were a great miracle in his sight . . .[137]

6.4 The Donkey

There is another moment in the life of Rúḥu'lláh, related by Mr 'Azízu'lláh Sulaymání, which shows his cheerful character:

> Rúḥu'lláh and his brother were walking in the streets of Zanján one day when a be-turbanned, awe-inspiring muhtajid [138] came riding along on his donkey. The muhtajid could tell by the clothes the boys were wearing that they were not natives of Zanján.
>
> > "Whose children are you?" he asked them.
> >
> > Rúḥu'lláh answered: "We are the sons of Varqá of Yazd."
> >
> > "What is your name?" the mujtahid enquired of the boy.
> >
> > "My name is Rúḥu'lláh," the child replied.
> >
> > "Oho! What a great name!" said the Muhtajid. "This is the title of His Holiness Christ who raised the dead."
> >
> > "If you will ride a little more slowly, sir," was Rúḥu'lláh's prompt reply, "I, too, will also raise you from the dead."

---

[137] Taherzadeh, The Revelation of Bahá'u'lláh. Vol 4: Mazra'ih & Bahji 1877-92, 63.
[138] High-ranking Muslim cleric.

> "You must be Bábís!"[139] growled the priest as he hastened along.[140]

6.5 Meaning of the "Return"

As a young child, Rúḥu'lláh enthusiastically taught the Bahá'í Faith to all around him with intrepidity and depth. Kazem Kazemzadeh relates the following story:

> One day Bahá'u'lláh asked Rúḥu'lláh what he had been doing. "Studying", the boy replied. Bahá'u'lláh asked what the subject was. When Rúḥu'lláh said that the subject he had been discussing with his teacher was the return of God's Messengers, Bahá'u'lláh asked him to interpret the term "return." Rúḥu'lláh explained that by "the return" was meant the reappearance in a human being of divine qualities and attributes. "This", Bahá'u'lláh commented, "is a literal, parrotlike repetition of the explanation given by your teacher. How do you understand the term?" "This year", Rúḥu'lláh proceeded, "a rose bush produced a rose. We have cut the flower and placed it in a vase on the shelf. The same bush will produce another rose next year, but that rose will not be identical with this year's flower, though it will be similar in qualities: shape, color, aroma." Bahá'u'lláh praised Rúḥu'lláh for his understanding and from then on referred to him as his excellency the teacher (Jináb-i-Mubaligh).[141]

6.6 Teaching by the Eyes

Martha Root tells a story about Rúḥu'lláh and 'Azízu'lláh visiting Bahíyyih Khánum, 'Abdu'l-Bahá's sister known as the Greatest Holy Leaf. The future enemies of the Faith (Covenant breakers), her half-brothers, Mírzá Ḍiá'u'lláh and Mírzá Badí'u'lláh, were also in the room.

---

[139] The term Bábí continued to be used for many years to refer to the Bahá'ís.
[140] Faizi, Fire on the Mountain Top, 95.
[141] Kazemzadeh, Varqá and Rúhu'llah: Deathless in Martyrdom, 33.

The next day they were all invited, the grandfather, father, and two small sons to visit Bahá'u'lláh in His own room. Then when the visit was over, the two boys were invited to the room of Bahá'u'lláh's daughter, Báhíyyih, known throughout the world as the Greatest Holy Leaf. She was then perhaps about forty-five years old. She said to her little guests: "What are you doing in Persia?" and Rúḥu'lláh replied: "We are teaching the Bahá'í Cause in Persia".

"What do you say in speaking to people", she queried, and Rúḥu'lláh answered: "I tell them God has appeared again on this earth." The Greatest Holy Leaf smiled but said: "When you are speaking you must not say this openly." The child replied: "I do not say it to everybody, I know to whom I must say it." "How do you know the people to whom to speak?" she continued, and he said: "I know people from their eyes; when I see their eyes I know."

In fun, Bahá'u'lláh's great daughter said: "Rúḥu'lláh look into my eyes and see if you could speak to me?" Naively he searched her eyes and told her: "No, I cannot speak to you, because you know everything."

Two young men sitting and doing their writing lessons in the other part of the room began to laugh over the conversation and the Greatest Holy Leaf said: "Look into their eyes and see whether you could speak with them and convince them." The child looked at them long and carefully, and then answered:

"It is very difficult and it is of no use to try to convince them." (These two young men were Ḍíyá'u'lláh and Badí'u'lláh who afterwards turned against the Cause.) When this conversation was told to Bahá'u'lláh He said: "Rúḥu'lláh is a Bahá'í teacher."[142]

---

[142] Root, "White Roses of Persia (Part 1)," 73.

6.7 What if the Qá'im…?

At some point, the Master wanted to prove the firmness of Rúḥu'lláh's faith and asked him, what would he do if after the coming of the Báb someone appeared proclaiming to be the Qá'im [143] and performed miracles and literally produced all the symbolic and material signs of the prophecies? Rúḥú'lláh's response was: "We would have to teach him the Faith". [144]

'Abdu'l-Bahá said that Rúḥu'lláh was now ready to face a high-ranking cleric ('ulamá). When saying goodbye to the prison-city of 'Akká for the last time, the Master had said while congratulating him with an affectionate patting on the shoulder, that, "If God so ordains …He will proclaim His Cause through Rúḥu'lláh".[145] And Rúḥu'lláh always mentioned that happy moment with pride. Indeed, the child had a brilliant future.

6.8 The Poems of Rúḥu'lláh

Rúḥu'lláh inherited the literary genius of his father. The form and the content of these poems reveal knowledge of a broad vocabulary, rich use of figures of speech as well as mastery of rhythm, meter and other technicalities characterising classic Persian poetry. Rúḥu'lláh's poetry also portrays a passion for teaching the Faith and for a broad range of mystical matters such as communion with God, love for Bahá'u'lláh and for 'Abdu'l-Bahá as well the spiritual notion of martyrdom. For instance, probably alluding to Bahá'u'lláh's ascension in 1892, Rúḥu'lláh wrote "Help O King of the Kingdom of the Souls / my heart in its remoteness from you… rescue this bird from the snare of despondency."[146]

The mastery of these concepts at that early age reveals a prodigious spiritual reasoning and complex higher order thinking. On communing with God, the young Rúḥu'lláh wrote:

---

[143] The Messenger promised in Islám.

[144] Kazemzadeh, Varqá and Rúhu'llah: Deathless in Martyrdom, 34.

[145] Faizi, Fire on the Mountain Top, 91.

[146] Hatcher, and Hemmat, Reunion with the Beloved: Poetry and Martyrdom, 32.

O Cupbearer, fill my cup to the brim!
Fill my heart's túr[147] with the fire of Your wine!

Bestow a goblet of the wine of "Am I not. . .?"
that I may awaken from intoxicated sleep,

that I may rend the veils of fancies and vain imaginings,
that I may ascend to the zenith of the seventh heaven,

that I may escape the dark snare of water and clay,
that I may take my flight to the sanctified kingdom,

that I may free myself from this realm of toil and tests,
that I may turn my face towards the native land of my soul

and inhale from that garden of the spirit the fragrance of the Friend
then return like breezes blowing from the abode of the Friend …[148]

6.9 Rúḥu'lláh's Poetry of Martyrdom

'Abdu'l-Bahá relates that once "When he [Rúḥu'lláh] was in Acca ['Akká], with his father I asked him one day, 'Tell me Rúḥu'lláh, what is the greatest desire of thy life?' immediately he answered. 'I long martyrdom in the path of God'".[149] Years later when the child was killed, the Master said that "no one has yet shown the joy, the passion and the ecstasy shown by Rúḥu'lláh in the arena of martyrdom".[150]

Martyrdom in the path of God is one of the main themes in Rúḥu'lláh's poetry. One wonders how a person of that age can arrive at such mystical understanding and deep insight. In other verses

---

[147] Túr is a Koranic term کوه طور referring to Mount Sinai (the place where Moses is said to have received the Ten Commandments).
[148] Hatcher, and Hemmat, Reunion with the Beloved: Poetry and Martyrdom, 69.
[149] Jasion, 'Abdu'l-Bahá in France 1911-13, 2017, 572.
[150] Kazemzadeh, Varqá and Rúhu'llah: Deathless in Martyrdom, 44.

Rúḥu'lláh senses the nearness of his own sacrifice in the Cause of Bahá'u'lláh:

> Cupbearer! Kindly proffer the cup of Thy gifts,
> That I may be cleansed from crimes and faults.
>
> Even with my countless transgressions,
> I hopefully expect the favor of my God.
>
> Hail, O Cupbearer at the eternal banquet,
> Graciously pour a wine drop on this dust,
>
> That these patterns may be brightened by Thy bounty,
> That we may be sacrificed for the One Beloved.
>
> When shall I offer this life, O my Lord,
> In Thy pathway in my love for Thy Face?
>
> Happy the day, when in the field of love I shall tender
> My life on the way of the Sovereign of love!
>
> Blessed the hour, when on the gallows
> The King of Glory I shall exalt!
>
> O God! May soon come the day
> When of this withered body I shall get rid;
>
> When, blooming and happy for His Presence grace,
> Towards the everlasting Heaven I shall direct my steps![151]

A second theme of Rúḥu'lláh's poems is a call to service, a plea for the Bahá'ís to be engaged in service to the Faith of Bahá'u'lláh. The following verses are indicative of Rúḥu'lláh's passion for teaching:

---

[151] Julio Savi, and Faezeh Mardani, "The Mathnaví by Rúhu'lláh Varqá, the Martyr: A Few Notes on Its Historical Context and Poetical Content," Lights of Irfan 9 (2018): 270, http://irfancolloquia.org/pdf/lights19_savi_mardani_ruhullah.pdf.

O companions! Seize the moment!
Assist and help the Cause of God!

Strive, O friends, that this brilliant sun
may shine above all the regions of the earth!

Struggle, that the signs of the almighty Lord
May be spread throughout this globe.

Make an effort, O my friends! The time to serve hath come!
It is now the day to earn bestowals! It is the hour of success!

Hoisting the flags of guidance, march
Towards the world, O lovers of Bahá,

That these intoxicated creatures may awaken
And move away from fancies and doubts,

And the light of God may enlighten their eyes,
And the thorns of their hearts may become roses.

The ancient Ruler hath thus decreed
For all the peoples, in His Kitáb-i-Aqdas.

Whosoever will arise for the Cause of God,
The Lord of Creation will come to his rescue.

Whosoever will lay down his life in this age of God,
To him the Lord will turn His Face.[152]

6.10 Rúḥu'lláh's Love for Abdu'l-Bahá

As we have seen before 'Abdu'l-Bahá loved Rúḥu'lláh much and vice versa. In expressing His love for 'Abdu'l-Bahá and praising Him as the Centre of Bahá'u'lláh's Covenant,

[152] Savi, and Mardani The Mathnaví by Rúhu'lláh Varqá, the Martyr: A Few Notes on its Historical Context and Poetical Content, 270.

Rúḥu'lláh composed the following:

O Lord of the Testament! O King of the Covenant!
O Thou by Whose fire the Sinai of the Pledge hath been lit!

O Thou Whose name is 'Abdu'l-Bahá! For Thee
The flags of Guidance have been unfurled:

Thou art the Dayspring of the Divine mysteries;
Thou art the Wellspring of the Divine signs.

O mighty King of Kings, as an Alif,
Thou risest above the Cause of God,

In Thy servitude, submissive as a Bih,[153]
At the gate of the garden of the Lord of Bahá.

O Most Great Branch of the Tree of the Cause!
O Twig sprouted from the Ancient Essence!

Thou art the spring of God's inspiration! Thou
Illuminest the eyes of the people of Bahá!

Bestow a drop of kindness on this puny bird,
Restless and impatient in his remoteness from Thee!

In this Day, O King of the Kingdom of the heart,
My breast burneth in its separation from Thee.[154]

"He wrote poems that when you read them you think a very skilled poet has composed them," the Hand of the Cause 'Alí Akbar Furútan commented. "His calligraphy is so beautiful that it rivals the best. His writings are so beautiful that they are the envy of scholars".[155]

---

[153] The letter alif (ا) and bih (ب) stands for a and b in the Arabic alphabet. For its upright and laying position alif and bá represent honour and humility, respectively.
[154] Savi, and Mardani The Mathnaví by Rúhu'lláh Varqá, the Martyr: A Few Notes on its Historical Context and Poetical Content, 271.
[155] Í.F. Muhájir, Hand of the Cause of God Furútan (Bahá'í Publishing Trust, 2017), 211.

VII - The Second Pilgrimage

Varqá returned to Tabríz to teach in about 1885. The distance to Tabríz from Iṣfahán is 900 km and the trip might have taken one month. Upon his return he recommenced actively teaching the Faith, and travelling extensively despite increased opposition from his mother-in-law.

About five years later, sometime between 1890 or 1891, he undertook his second pilgrimage to the Holy Land.[156] He travelled with his father-in-law 'Abdu'lláh Núrí and children Rúḥu'lláh and 'Azízu'lláh, who were eleven and thirteen, respectively.[157] Some of the incidents have been related in the previous chapter. This time they stayed for seven months.

7.1 Visiting Bahjí

At the time of the second pilgrimage, Bahá'u'lláh was residing in the Mansion of Bahjí and in the House of Abbúd in 'Akká. Bahjí, meaning delight in Arabic, was Bahá'u'lláh's dwelling from 1880, where He spent the last 12 twelve years of his life. Situated in the countryside of Akká, surrounded by trees and the Akká plains, this beautiful residence belonged to a rich Christian merchant who fled the city because of a cholera outbreak in 1879. 'Abdu'l-Bahá had managed to rent it for a cheap price. There is a plaque on the main door of the mansion, placed there by the original builder, with the inscription:

> Greetings and salutation rest upon this Mansion which increaseth in splendour through the passage of time. Manifold

[156] 1308 AH began in August 1890 and ended in July 1891.
[157] Root, "White Roses of Persia (Part 2)", 180.

> wonders and marvels are found therein, and pens are baffled in attempting to describe them.[158]

Endowed with plenty of fresh water and air, Bahjí was a place to escape from 'Akká's pestilence. With its peaceful and tranquil atmosphere surrounded by birds, trees, flowers and swept by breezes, Bahjí was true to its name a source of delight. Bahá'u'lláh characterized the Mansion of Bahjí as the "lofty mansion".[159]

Bahá'u'lláh resided mostly in Bahjí throughout the year, with occasional trips to 'Akká, where most pilgrims stayed. Most of the time Bahá'u'lláh remained in His room where He revealed Tablets, responded to His correspondence, conducted interviews and carried out the work of the Faith of God. In the evenings, accompanied by an attendant, Bahá'u'lláh walked among the tall cypress trees.

In order to meet the Manifestation of God, the pilgrims walked about four kilometres through the orchards situated from 'Akká to Bahjí. On foot it took about one hour though it is now a ten-minute drive. The simple but majestic two-storey structures of the Mansion of Bahjí were visible to the approaching pilgrim from a distance.

For pilgrims like Varqá, 'Abdu'lláh Núrí and the two boys, it was the first time they went to this wonderful mansion, the spot which "God hath ordained as the most sublime vision of mankind[160] as Bahá'u'lláh characterised it. The long march to the mansion of Bahjí from 'Akká must have been a delightful experience as it provided an opportunity for each to prepare spiritually as they walked towards their personal encounter with the Manifestation of God.

7.2 Meeting Bahá'u'lláh

According to Martha Root:

---

[158] David S Ruhe, Door of Hope: A Century of the Bahá'í Faith in the Holy Land (George Ronald, 1983), 103.
[159] Shoghi Effendi, God Passes By, 193.
[160] Shoghi Effendi, God Passes By, 193.

> Many were the incidents of that historic visit to Bahá'u'lláh but I [will] only tell you a few of them. 'Azízu'lláh Varqá told me that when the maternal grandfather, the father and Rúḥu'lláh arrived in 'Akká, they went to the room of the secretary of Bahá'u'lláh. It was furnished with a mat and they sat down on this, for they had been told that Bahá'u'lláh would come to this room to meet them. In the distance there were steps leading to an upper room and the father told 'Azízu'lláh to go and stay near those steps to watch the approach of the Blessed Beauty and then to inform them. The child went but when he looked and saw Bahá'u'lláh at the head of the stairs he mounted several steps and knelt at the feet of His Lord. He was crying so hard his very bones were shaking. Bahá'u'lláh stopped and made him [be] happy and they came down the stairway together, the little boy just behind Bahá'u'lláh. It was a great meeting, but when the visitation was over, the father said to his little son: "Why did you not do what I asked you to do? Why did you not run and tell us?" 'Azízu'lláh replied: "I do not know. I do not know how I mounted those steps, I was not conscious that I went up the stairs." We know how moved Professor Edward G. Browne of Cambridge University, England, was, when he first met Bahá'u'lláh but here is an account of what it meant to a very young Persian boy.[161]

7.3 How Tablets were Revealed

This is a beautiful story portraying the power of the Word of God when Bahá'u'lláh revealed Tablets and how His room was filled with atmosphere charged with a marvellous power:

> 'Azízu'lláh recounted another incident of the visit saying that when Bahá'u'lláh wished to reveal a Tablet, he used to dismiss everybody with great haste. 'Azízu'lláh, said:
>
> "One day I was in Bahá'u'lláh's Presence with the whole family and He called for the secretary to bring ink and paper

[161] Root, "White Roses of Persia (Part 1)," 72-73.

quickly and in the same moment He requested us all to go. I was just a child, but seeing this haste to send every one away, I had a great longing to be present sometime when a Tablet is revealed. I had asked from one of the members of His family to ask Bahá'u'lláh if I could come, please, to see a Tablet revealed. A few weeks later in the Garden at Bahjí, when I was playing with some children, the door of the home was opened and one member of the family called me and said that Bahá'u'lláh wished to see me. I ran to His room and entering I saw that He was chanting revealed Tablets and poems. So entering His room that day, I thought everything was the same as on other days, that Bahá'u'lláh was only chanting. I stood near the door which I had entered, and was only a few moments in the room when I began trembling in my whole body. I felt I could not stand any more on my feet. His Holiness Bahá'u'lláh turning to me said 'Good bye'. As I lifted the curtain to go out, I fell on the threshold and was unconscious. They took me to the room of the wife of His Holiness Bahá'u'lláh where they poured rose water and cold water on my face until I revived. The members of the Family asked me what had happened and I told them about going to Bahá'u'lláh to hear the chanting. When I was relating this, the lady who had called me first, came in, and she said to me: 'You, yourself, had asked me to permit you to be present, now that was the time when a Tablet was being revealed."

"Then I understood why Bahá'u'lláh in haste dismissed everybody. It is because the people cannot endure it, there is such a Power in the room." [162]

'Azízu'lláh Varqá said that his father had a similar experience during his first visit to 'Akká:

"Father had been asked by someone to implore Bahá'u'lláh's help concerning a certain matter and to beg that a Tablet be sent. When my father presented this petition, Bahá'u'lláh

[162] Root, "White Roses of Persia (Part 2)," 73-74.

> called a secretary to bring ink and paper, and He also sent for His brother Músá Kalím and another one of the relatives. He put a hand on each one's shoulder and began to walk up and down revealing the Tablet. Father began to tremble and he said he couldn't say what was happening. He heard Bahá'u'lláh's voice but He could not understand His Words. Some minutes passed and He dismissed them all. Then outside they began to discuss and none of the three had understood Him, they had only felt the Power. It is certainly interesting to hear about Bahá'u'lláh from those who saw and spoke with Him. They said they could not look upon His Face, it was so glorious, the eyes so shining. There was such a vibration that everyone began to tremble and they could not understand His Words; there was such a Power there."[163]

7.4 How Would the Cause Spread?

Varqá had a question for Bahá'u'lláh: If the Bahá'í Faith was going to be universally recognized, how would this process take place? The Blessed Beauty responded:

> … that the nations will fully arm themselves and like blood-thirsty beasts attack each other resulting in tremendous bloodshed. Then the wise from all nations would investigate the cause of this, and conclude that prejudice is the cause, the worst being religious prejudice. Then they would try to eliminate religion as the culprit, but soon they would realize that man cannot exist without religion. Then they would study the teachings of all religions to see which one addresses the requirements of the age. That is the time that the Faith would become universal.[164]

---

[163] Root, "White Roses of Persia (Part 2)," 73-74.
[164] Darius Shahrokh, Varqá and Son: The Heavenly Doves, 1992, 9

7.5 Varqá Cured Bahá'u'lláh

Persian doctors like Varqá were given the title tabib طبیب which carried the prestige equivalent to that enjoyed by the modern physician.[165] In the absence of medical schools or hospitals, tabibs gained knowledge of the profession by apprenticeship and by studying textbooks mostly based on Avicenna and Galenic medicine.[166] Unlike traditional quacks or medicasters, tabbibs were educated individuals who usually came from middle and upper classes although reliying on other economic activity for their financial subsistence. Healing was undertaken mainly by prescribing diet and medication. In the course of his life, Varqá applied his medical knowledge to the treatment of Bahá'ís and non-Bahá'ís alike.

During Varqá's second visit to the Holy Land, Bahá'u'lláh fell ill and Varqá was asked to prescribe medicine for Him. The Blessed Beauty took the medicine and Varqá was called again the same evening.[167] According to Shahrokh:

> That evening, again He summoned Varqá, and told him He had taken the medicine, and as a patient, He liked His physician. Oh! What a compliment![168]

Certainly, Varqá was the embodiment of the Bahá'í doctor as revealed by Bahá'u'lláh: "Well is it with the physician who cureth ailments in My hallowed and dearly-cherished Name."[169]

---

165 Misagh Ziaei, "The Lawh-i-Tibb (Tablet to the Physician)–Beyond Health Maxims," The Journal of Bahá'í Studies 29, no. 3, 67-82 (2019).

166 At that time there were not professional faculties of medicine in Iran. The first one of these universities, Dár ul-Funun, was established in Tehran in 1851 which delivered a curriculum in both traditional Persian and Western medicine with a very small number of candidates.

167 Balyuzi, Eminent Bahá'ís in the Time of Bahá'u'lláh, 1986, 82.

168 Darius Shahrokh, Varqá and Son: The Heavenly Doves, 9, 1992.

169 Bahá'í World Centre, The Compilation of Compilations, vol. I (Maryborough, Victoria: Bahá'í Publications Australia, 2000), 459.

The pilgrimage came to its end and a few months later Bahá'u'lláh passed away on 29 May 1892 in the Mansion of Bahjí. As we are going to read further, Varqá, Rúḥu'lláh and 'Azízu'lláh returned again to the Holy Land a few years after the ascension to meet 'Abdu'l-Bahá.

Figure 1: Panorama of Yazd in the 19th century. Source: Nabíl's Narrative.

Figure 2: A Nineteenth Century Persian Caravanserai in Sabzevar, Iran, by Alireza Javaheri (CC BY-SA 4.0).

Figure 3: Map of Iran. Courtesy: Pedro Donaires.

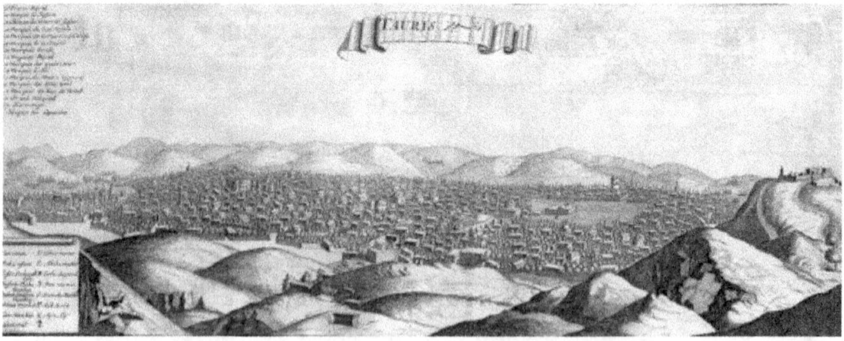

Figure 4: An old view of the city of Tabríz.

Figure 5: Bíbí Yazdí who married Ḥájí Mírzá Ḥusayn Yazdí (Varqá's brother). Source: MyHeritage.com

Figure 6: Muẓaffari'd-Dín Mírzá's Court as the Heir Prince in Tabríz.

THE HOUSE OCCUPIED BY THE BÁB IN URÚMÍYYIH. THE BÁLÁ-KHÁNIH (UPPER ROOM) MARKED X IS THE ROOM IN WHICH HE STAYED

Figure 7: Prince Malek-Qasim Mírzá's palace in Urúmíyyih were the Báb's portrait was drawn. Source: Nabíl's Narrative.

Figure 8: A group of Bahá'ís in Tabríz in 1891. Seated third from right is 'Alí Muḥammad Varqá. Front row, second from left is Rúḥu'lláh Varqá and the other boys seated with him are probably his brothers. Courtesy: George Ronald Oxford.

Figure 9: A group of Bahá'ís in Tabríz in 1882. Left to right, front row: Siyyid Mihdí Yazdí, unknown, Mír Sulaymán Yazdí (brother of Siyyid Yazdí). Left to right, middle row, seated: Ḥájí Amín, unknown, 'Alí Muḥammad Varqá, Ḥájí Mírzá Ḥusayn Yazdí (Varqá's brother). Back row: unknown, unknown. Courtesy: George Ronald Oxford.

Figure 10: The city of 'Akká at the beginning of the 19th Century.

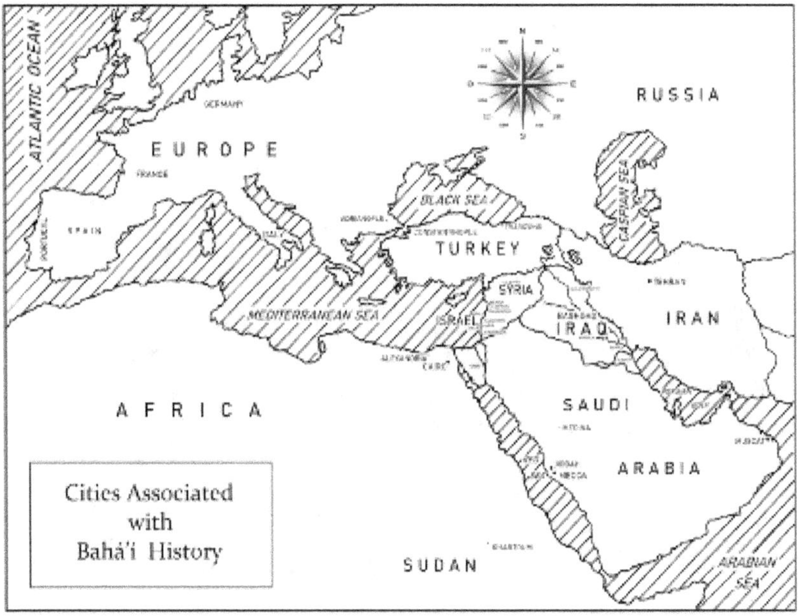

Figure 11: Cities associated with Bahá'í history. Courtesy: Pedro Donaires.

Figure 12: Mansion of Mazra'ih, c. 1900. Courtesy: Bahá'í World Centre.

Figure 13: The House of 'Abbúd in 'Akká.

Figure 14: Headstone of Ḥájí Mullá Mihdí in the cemetery of Mazra'ih © Bahá'í World Centre.

Figure 15: The Mansion of Bahjí at the beginning of the 19th Century.

Figure 16: A street of ‘Akká at the beginning of the 19th Century. Courtesy: Bahá’í World Centre.

Figure 17: The Soltanieh in Zanján (Public domain).

Figure 18: View of Zanján in the 19th century.

VIII - The Furious Mother-in-law

The seven-month family pilgrimage bore many sweet fruits. Varqá attained the Holy Presence for the second time and the two children were greatly touched by the experience. Varqá's father-in-law also felt confirmed and similarly planned to return to Tabríz to give everything he had to the Faith. His wife (Varqá's mother-in-law), had become more aggressive in her opposition to the Bahá'ís.

8.1 Rúḥu'lláh and the Muhtajid

> "O Thou Who art the Lord of all names and the Maker of the heavens! I beseech Thee by them Who are the Day-Springs of Thine invisible Essence, the Most Exalted, the All-Glorious, to make of my prayer a fire that will burn away the veils which have shut me out from Thy beauty, and a light that will lead me unto the ocean of Thy Presence" —Bahá'u'lláh—

These are the initial words of the long obligatory prayer which Rúḥu'lláh began to recite to the high-level priest (known as mujtahid) and to his grandmother when she took him to the *muhtajid* telling him: "A friend of your father wishes to meet you."[170] The *muhtajid* asked Rúḥu'lláh to recite a Bahá'í obligatory prayer.

Rúḥu'lláh then asked for two things: the location of the Qiblih[171] and to be allowed to do his ablutions. Imperturbable despite his audience, with absolute devotion and with beautiful intonations the child began reciting by heart the 1,500 words of the long obligatory prayer. As he recited the prayer Rúḥu'lláh performed all the required genuflexions.

---

[170] Darius Shahrokh, Varqá and Son: The Heavenly Doves, 14.

[171] The Qiblih (or direction, in Arabic) is the point to which Bahá'ís turn to say their obligatory prayers. The Qiblih is fixed at the Shrine of Bahá'u'lláh in 'Akká. In the Islamic dispensation the Qiblih is in Mecca.

The priest was shaken by such spirituality. Unexpectedly, he had witnessed a manifestation of pure religiosity and love of God from a young soul.

"Shame on you," the *muhtajid* said to the lady, "for seeking the execution of a man who raised his little son in such a spirit of faith, piety, and devotion".[172] The grandmother felt defeated and frustrated as she had failed to secure ecclesiastical permission to kill Varqá, her son-in-law. In her quest for that permission, the lady had brought Rúḥu'lláh as evidence that his father Varqá was a heretic and an apostate from Islam deserving death as prescribed by the Shariah law.

Previously, the lady had individually met the *muhtajid* who had challenged her to bring a fair proof of any falsehood in the Bahá'í beliefs. "How can I issue such a verdict," he said, "not knowing the accused?" to which the lady responded, "I can give you ample proof. I shall bring you one of his own children who has been taught by Varqá himself, and after you have seen this child you will have no more doubts."[173]

Despite the fact that the *muhtajid* was a relative of the furious grandmother, he approved the spiritual disposition of Rúḥu'lláh and rebuked her. That was one of the last attempts to get rid of her son-in-law. Previously, she had sought to uproot the influence that her Bahá'í husband had on the Crown Prince. With the alliance of fanatical enemies of the Bahá'í Faith, the lady plotted against her own husband 'Abdu'lláh Núrí raising suspicions in the court that he was conspiring against the government. For her, the proof was that her husband was holding Bahá'í meetings at home having put his house at the disposal of the believers to plot against the government. The Prince, once an admirer of 'Abdu'lláh Núrí, his court chamberlain and chief of the royal house, unfortunately paid attention to those rumours and eventually changed his attitude toward 'Abdu'lláh Núrí. So tense and uncertain were the circumstances that 'Abdu'lláh Núrí could have been arrested at any time. He therefore fled Tabríz for Tehran.

---

[172] Kazemzadeh, Varqá and Rúhu'llah: Deathless in Martyrdom, 35.
[173] Faizi, Fire on the Mountain Top, 95.

When 'Abdu'lláh Núrí left Tabríz, Varqá lost the support he needed at the court level. His mother-in-law made his life impossible in the home she owned and where the family lived. He considered divorcing his wife and joining his father-in-law in the capital, however, his father-in-law recommended that he travel teaches throughout the province. At that point 'Abdu'lláh Núrí himself was not considering divorcing his wife either and he encouraged Varqá to tread the same path and be patience.

When her husband ran away to the capital, the lady recovered her hope in destroying her son-in-law. Allied with a leading local priest named Shaykh Músá Thiqat ul-Islam, known as Moses, she began plotting to assassinate Varqá. 'Abdu'l-Bahá advised Varqá to move to Tehran or Zanján.[174] Zanján is a city between Tehran and Tabríz.

8.3 Plot to Assassinate Varqá

The situation rapidly deteriorated such that the only solution was to leave Tabríz. It was a disappointment considering that the last pilgrimage (1890-1891)[175] had left Varqá, 'Azízu'lláh and Rúḥu'lláh spiritually empowered, enamoured of the Manifestation of God and committed to widely propagating the Faith. However, at the return, they were facing many obstacles from inside the court and from their own family. They wanted to live as a loving Bahá'í family, particularly after seeing the way in which Bahá'u'lláh and 'Abdu'l-Bahá interacted.

As the tension escalated including physical threats, after two years there was no other possibility but to split the family. It was evident that the family atmosphere had become very toxic for Varqá and the children. This may have been a difficult decision for Varqá as well as a painful experience for the children being separated from their mother. Varqá's wife, at her mother's insistence, had sought divorce

[174] Momen, The Bahá'í Communities of Iran 1851-1921: The North of Iran, 372.
[175] 1308 AH beginning in August 1890.

on the basis that the father was an infidel.[176] [177] In the Islamic culture, only men could divorce with the children remaining with the father. It is not clear the details as to when the final divorce happened but it seems that Varqá did not apply for the divorce until later when he moved to Zanján and the whole marriage had collapsed.

The situation in Tabríz became unbearable for Varqá when he learned that his mother-in-law was trying to kill him. Frustrated by not getting a death sentence for her son-in-law, she decided to eliminate Varqá by her own means. To do that, she bribed one of his servants named Khalíl with 250 tumans and a horse as reward to assassinate Varqá. However, he was already a Bahá'í thanks to Varqá's efforts. Khalíl went to see him at night on the pretext of seeking medical advice for a stomach illness and informed him of his mother-in-law's intentions.

8.4 Fleeing to Zanján

That same night the poet decided to flee to Zanján taking his two older children, 'Azízu'lláh and Rúḥu'lláh. He threw his Bahá'í books out the window to pick them up once outside the house and went to stay in another believer's house. According to Darius Shahrokh:

> The next morning when his wife and mother-in-law had taken the youngest son to the public bath, he returned home, and took his two older sons, 'Azízu'lláh and Rúḥu'lláh, with him.[178]

When the mother-in-law noticed Varqá's escape, he was already out of reach en route to Zanján. It was 1892. He and the two oldest boys headed to the city of Zanján, 300 km south-east. He thought of going to Tehran but eventually he settled in Zanján, a town in between Tabríz and Tehran.

---

[176] Kazemzadeh, Varqá and Rúhu'llah: Deathless in Martyrdom, 34.
[177] Darius Shahrokh, Varqá and Son: The Heavenly Doves, 13.
[178] Darius Shahrokh, Varqá and Son: The Heavenly Doves, 15.

The two younger children, Valíyu'lláh and Badí'u'lláh, remained in Tabríz with their antagonistic grandmother. She set herself the mission of converting these two children to the Islamic faith. She had a prayer after which the little ones had to say 'amen'. She used to pray: "Oh God, if these two children grow up as good Muslims, make them happy and rich, give them the joy of a pilgrimage to Mecca. But if they become like their father, destroy them right now".[179] In response, the children had to say amen.

According to Valíyu'lláh Varqá: "She was able to impress my tender soul to such an extent that in my Islamic prayers, which I was obliged to say, I wept in bitter grief for my father's deviation which had earned him so much hatred from the public".[180]

---

[179] Kazemzadeh, Varqá and Rúhu'llah: DeathlesMartyrdom, 35.
[180] The Universal House of Justice, "In Memoriam: Valíyu'lláh Varqá," The Bahá'í World (1954-1963), 1970.

IX - In Zanján

Zanján gave Varqá an oasis of peace, away from his difficult mother-in-law whose machinations nearly led to the collapse of his marriage. The Zanján Bahá'í community which had suffered a massacre four decades previously was resurging and Varqá made a valuable contribution to its progress. The Varqás were received with open arms by the local believers and settled into their new Bahá'í community well. From Zanján he undertook his third pilgrimage to the Holy Land to see 'Abdu'l-Bahá accompanied by his sons, 'Azízu'lláh and Rúḥu'lláh, for whom it was their second pilgrimage.

9.1. Travelling in Iran

During the time Varqá was alive, individuals and families did not travel alone but in large groups called caravans to mitigate the danger posed by highwaymen. Caravans were escorted by riflemen circling around the moving group. Some travelled on foot and others by horse or mules. Children, the elderly, women and the sick usually travelled in wagons pulled by these animals. Typical of Persian caravans was the *howdah* which consisted of a litter carried by an animal to transport people. Caravans were also used to transport food and agricultural products from town to town.

Camels, mules and donkeys were used to transport heavier loads including merchandise. Camels were adorned with small ringing bells whose jingling produced a beautiful and sweet sound breaking the monotony of those long journeys. The caravans advanced in single file, beginning the journey early in the morning after prayers supplicating the protection of, and dedicating themselves to God. They would thus travel all day long until a caravanserai was reached. Caravans were not only used to traverse deserts but also mountains, valleys and plains.

Caravanserais were places of accommodation located at the roadside for rest after a long day trip. These establishments were situated at intervals of 20 or 30 km. In order to facilitate trade on the various routes of the Silk Road, 999 caravanserais were built by Sháh Abbas during his reign between the 16th and the 17th centuries.

Caravanserais provided not only accommodation but also bathing facilities and food to travellers. Animals were similarly supplied with fodder and water. These commercial-oriented establishments were like oases in the middle of nowhere and provided opportunity for travellers to restore spent energy and prepare for the subsequent legs of their journeys. As they travelled it was common for the travellers to sing and chant poems. The leaders of the caravans were called *sárabáns*.

The distance from Tabríz to Zanján was 300 km. This would usually take at least 10 days to traverse on horseback. At that time Varqá, 'Azízu'lláh and Rúḥu'lláh, were aged 37, 11 and 9 years old respectively. Their destination was the capital, however, they stayed about three years in Zanján before their martyrdom in 1896 in Tehran.

Zanján is a very special city in terms of the history of the Faith. The Báb called it Arḍ-i-A'lá —The Exalted Place. The Tree of the Faith in Zanján was watered with the blood of more than 1,500 believers who were killed by Persian government forces during the years 1850-1851 at the fort of 'Alí-Mardán Khán. The memory of the massacre was still fresh. According to the historian Moojan Momen "In Zanján, Varqá revived the Bahá'í community and converted many".[181]

9.2 Umm-i-Ashraf, a Marvellous Mother

In Zanján, Varqá lived for a time in the house of a well-known Bahá'í lady named Anbár Khánum. In Bahá'í history she is better known as Umm-i-A<u>sh</u>raf meaning the mother of Ashraf. [182] Umm-i-Ashraf's husband was a martyr in the aforementioned massacre.

---

[181] Momen, The Bahá'í Communities of Iran 1851-1921: The North of Iran, 462.
[182] Adib Taherzadeh, The Revelation of Bahá'u'lláh. Vol. 2: Adrianople 1863-68, vol. 2, 223. (Oxford: George Ronald, 1987).

Their son Ashraf was born during the siege of the fort of 'Alí-Mardán Khán. He was a young Bahá'í who met Bahá'u'lláh in Adrianople. There is a beautiful story involving Bahá'u'lláh, Ashraf and his mother:

> Many non-Bahá'í members of the family, particularly three paternal uncles, of Ashraf gave his mother a rough time. They constantly harassed her as the force behind the enthusiasm of her husband and now the children. While Ashraf and company were in Adrianople the three uncles came and tongue-lashed Umm-i-Ashraf [in Zanján]. When they began to suggest immoral intention on the part of her daughter who had accompanied Ashraf, Umm-i-Ashraf could no longer take it. She left the room, crying bitterly, raised her hands supplicating Bahá'u'lláh to send her children home. The next morning Baha'u'llah summoned Ashraf and companions and told them that the night before He heard the supplication of Umm-i-Ashraf asking for their return. Therefore, they were to leave at once. Then He showered His praise and bounties upon Umm-i-Ashraf.[183]

When he returned from his pilgrimage, Ashraf was ordered by the priests to deny his faith in Bahá'u'lláh. Ashraf refused to do it and then they sent for his mother, hoping she would induce her son to recant. His mother, the great Umm-i-A<u>sh</u>raf urged him to remain firm until the end. Consequently, Ashraf was martyred in 1870 in front of the populace, twenty years after the martyrdom of his father. A<u>sh</u>raf was beaten and beheaded publicly, but before he was killed, he was hit so hard that blood ran under his fingernails. Nabíl wrote:[184]

> Faithful to his mother's admonitions, Ashraf met his death with intrepid calm. Though herself a witness to the cruelties inflicted on her son, she made no lamentation, neither did she shed a tear. This marvellous mother [Umm-i-A<u>sh</u>raf] showed

---

[183] Darius Shahrokh, ed., The Mystery of Sacrifice (1992), 7, https://bahai-library.com/wttp/PDF/The%20Mystery%20of%20Martyrdom.pdf.
[184] Nabíl-i-A'zam, The Dawn-Breakers: Nabíl's Narrative of the Early Days of the Bahá'í Revelation, 562.

> a courage and fortitude that amazed the perpetrators of that shameless deed. “I have now in mind”, she exclaimed, as she cast a parting glance at the corpse of her son, “the vow I made on the day of your birth, while besieged in the fort of ‘Alí-Mardán Khán. I rejoice that you, the only son whom God gave me, have enabled me to redeem that pledge.”

Bahá’u’lláh has extolled the memory of mother and son in eloquent terms:

> Call thou to mind the behavior of Ashraf’s mother, whose son laid down his life in the Land of Zá (Zanján). He, most certainly, is in the seat of truth, in the presence of One Who is the Most Powerful, the Almighty.
>
> When the infidels, so unjustly, decided to put him to death, they sent and fetched his mother, that perchance she might admonish him, and induce him to recant his faith, and follow in the footsteps of them that have repudiated the truth of God, the Lord of all worlds.
>
> No sooner did she behold the face of her son, than she spoke to him such words as caused the hearts of the lovers of God, and beyond them those of the Concourse on high, to cry out and be sore pained with grief. Truly, thy Lord knoweth what My tongue speaketh. He Himself beareth witness to My words.
>
> And when addressing him she said: “My son, mine own son! Fail not to offer up thyself in the path of thy Lord. Beware that thou betray not thy faith in Him before Whose face have bowed down in adoration all who are in the heavens and all who are on the earth. Go thou straight on, O my son, and persevere in the path of the Lord, thy God. Haste thee to attain the presence of Him Who is the Well-Beloved of all worlds.”

> On her be My blessings, and My mercy, and My praise, and My glory. I Myself shall atone for the loss of her son—a son who now dwelleth within the tabernacle of My majesty and glory, and whose face beameth with a light that envelopeth with its radiance the Maids of Heaven in their celestial chambers, and beyond them the inmates of My Paradise, and the denizens of the Cities of Holiness. Were any eye to gaze on his face, he would exclaim: "Lo, this is no other than a noble angel!"[185]

Soon Rúḥu'lláh conquered Umm-i-Ashraf's affection whom he addressed as mother. The words of the historian Kazem Kazemzadeh illustrate the tenderness and innocence of this wonderful child:

> Rúḥu'lláh frequently questioned Umm-i-Ashraf about the execution of her son, telling her not to grieve. "Think, mother," he would say, "if Siyyid Ashraf had not been executed, he would have died in bed some years later. What would have been the advantage of that? But now he is the pride of his family and friends, and the subject of endless praises and mercies of Bahá'u'lláh. I wish I could attain such joy." Umm-i-Ashraf would reply: "Do not say such things. You must live to teach." "Then let me teach you," the boy would say. "You will be a Muslim and I will be a Bahá'í teacher." But Umm-i-Ashraf would not consent even to pretend to be a Muslim. "After all I have suffered, I cannot be a Muslim and argue with you," she would say. Rúḥu'lláh would give up and instead would make a speech about Bahá'u'lláh's religion. Though his voice was sonorous and clear, he would occasionally stop and cough, explaining that all adult orators coughed when they spoke, to clear the throat.[186]

---

[185] Bahá'u'lláh, Gleanings from the Writings of Bahá'u'lláh, trans. Shoghi Effendi (London: Bahá'í Publishing Trust, 1978), LXIX, 134-35.
[186] Kazemzadeh, Varqá and Rúhu'llah: Deathless in Martyrdom, 36.

9.3 How Varqá Taught the Faith?

Here is a beautiful story as to how Varqá taught the Faith in the context of the Jewish community. The story took place in Hamadán which was a city known for the number of believers from that religion.

> Mírzá Khalíl was one of the respected and confident members of Jewish socicty, and therefore, his conversion to the Cause of the Blessed Beauty created much commotion. One day, Ḥájí Eliahu [a new believer from Jewish background], as I have mentioned, was taking refuge in the home of Núr-Mahmúd out of fear of his enemies, and in the meantime was secretly teaching the Faith to Mírzá Mahmúd's son-in-law, Mírzá Ayyúb. After embracing the Faith, Mírzá Khalíl, who had a very modest home in the [Jewish] Ghetto, put his house in the service of Bahá'í teachers and many would frequent his house. For instance, one day Jináb-i-Ḥájí Mírzá Ḥaydar 'Alí and Jináb-i-Varqá-i-Shahíd [His Excellency Varqá the Martyr] entered that home where I met them as I also visited this place often for deepening.
>
> Jináb-i-Varqá had recently returned from the Holy Land and Mírzá Khalíl had invited a group of Jews and Rabbis [Jewish priests] to benefit from his teaching and to ask whatever questions they had and present any concerns. We ourselves sat quietly in a corner and were witnessing the discussion taking place. Unfortunately, instead of deriving benefit and learning some truths, they were busy arguing and would often change the subject. Out of prejudice and the habit of clinging to their old beliefs, they were not really ready to listen to any truthful fact whatever. Such was the case until Jináb-i-Varqá stated, "There is a verse from His Holiness Joshua, to this effect: 'Eye to eye, see that they will bring the Lord back to Zion" (a verse of Joshua). And then he said, "I saw this with my own eyes."
>
> The Rabbis, who could not bear to hear things like this, began to insult him. Disregarding manners and courtesy, they said, "If you saw God, may both your eyes be blinded if you lie."

> This contemptuous attitude from them, in contrast to the gracious and courteous manner of Jináb-i-Varqá, who so eloquently marshalled proofs and cited verses from the Torah, moved me to the extent that I recognised the truth, and realized that in every age, the chief source of denial has ever been this kind of unjust, stubborn, and proud people. At any rate, this baseless response from Jewish religious leaders to the powerful and persuasive discourses of Jináb-i-Varqá stirred me to such depths that I surrendered my will right then and there. My faith was confirmed, and I took on the path of service to Bahá'u'lláh.[187]

9. 4 The Last Pilgrimage

About some months after Varqás' arrivals in Zanján, Bahá'u'lláh ascended to *The Most High* in November 1892. The news of His ascension filled the Bahá'ís with dismay. Soon after this Varqá, 'Azízu'llah and Rúḥu'lláh had the opportunity to go again to the Holy Land, arriving in 1893. Although the Beloved was not physically present anymore, Varqá visited the newly designated Shrine, and supplicated to be of even greater service.

In His Testament, called the "Kitáb-i-'Ahdí" (The Book of My Covenant), Bahá'u'lláh designated 'Abdu'l-Bahá as the Head of the Faith and Interpreter of His teachings. This sacred document, which establishes the Covenant of Bahá'u'lláh with 'Abdu'l-Bahá as its Center, was opened nine days after His passing in front of the members of the Holy Family and the resident Bahá'ís and pilgrims in the Holy Land.

The great majority of the believers obeyed without reserve the last words of the Blessed Beauty, but there were those who rebelled and pursued the path of error leading ultimately to complete spiritual loss. Varqá was of those who remained firm.

---

[187] 'Azíz'u'lláh Azízí, Crown of Glory: Memoirs of Jináb-i-'Azíz'u'lláh Azízí. (Iran: Bahá'í Publishing Trust, 1976), 44-45. https://bahai-library.com/pdf/a/azizi_crown_glory.pdf.

In this last pilgrimage, a particular instruction from 'Abdu'l-Bahá was for Varqá to move all his Tablets and Bahá'í archives out of Zanján when he returns to Persia.[188] It appears from this that he was in possession of a vast collection of Bahá'í literature. 'Abdu'l-Bahá said in this regards:

> For a number of times they were with me. Afterwards I ordered them to return to Iran and commence teaching the Faith. Therefore they went to Iran where they were engaged in teaching until they arrived in Zanján.[189]

9.5 Returning to Iran

On the farewell, 'Abdu'l-Bahá said as He was patting the back of the young Rúḥu'lláh: "Should God will it, He can make Rúḥu'lláh ride on the neck of an emperor to proclaim the Cause of God."[190]

Here is another beautiful story about Rúḥu'lláh when he was coming back with his father and brother from the Holy Land in 1896:

> Early in my stay in the new residence, the illustrious teacher of the Cause, Varqá, and his esteemed sons, Mírzá 'Azízu'lláh and Rúḥu'lláh – who was in name Rúḥu'lláh and in essence truly Rúḥu'lláh – came to Rasht from the Holy Land and from the presence of our divine Beloved. They enkindled and enthralled everyone with the spirit of faith. They spent their first night of stay in the home of Mírzá Murtidá-Qulí Massáh. The second night was spent at Áqá 'Alí Arbáb's house, and the third night at the residence of this ephemeral servant, where the chant of prayers by Rúhu'lláh enchanted and mesmerized every hearing soul. All the believers were at their

[188] Momen, The Bahá'í Communities of Iran 1851-1921: The North of Iran, 462.
[189] Star of the West, vol. 3, No. 18 (February 1913), 362-364.
[190] Balyuzi, Eminent Bahá'ís in the Time of Bahá'u'lláh, 98.

> presence all three nights and immensely enjoyed their sweet and awakened discourse.[191]

Upon returning to Iran, Varqá passed through Tehran and gave thought to the idea of settling in Tehran and staying with 'Abdu'lláh Núrí, however, Covenant-breakers prevented this from happening.[192] Varqá stayed about two years in Zanján strengthening the local community and as usual making teaching trips to towns and villages.

Eventually Varqá divorced his first wife and married Laqá'íyyih, a Bahá'í, the granddaughter of Umm-i-Ashraf[193] and daughter of Ḥájí Ímám, sometime in 1893 or 1894.[194] Laqá'íyyih Khánum's mother was Ḍiáy'iyyih Khánum and her siblings were Muḥammad Ímám and Qudsíyyih Khánum Fadá'í. Ḥájí Ímám would later share imprisonment with his new son-in-law Varqá, and with Rúḥu'lláh in the prison of Tehran.

Gradually, Varqá became more interested in living in Tehran, which was 330 km away. He planned to travel accompanied by his two sons 'Azízu'llah and Rúḥu'lláh and later his wife would join them. Zanján was becoming unsafe as a place for Bahá'ís to live, and this obliged 'Azízu'llah and Rúḥu'lláh to move out for their own protection. According to Martha Root:

> Once, when the times were very dangerous a lovely Bahá'í woman near Tihrán took 'Azízu'lláh and Rúḥu'lláh into her own home to try to protect them. This was when the Varqá family was living in Tihrán. The husband of the Bahá'í, who was not a believer, though he was a celebrated lawyer and a great statesman, objected to having the children in the house. He said: "You cannot do this, we too, shall be killed."

---

[191] Mīrzá Yahyá 'Amídu'l-Atibbá Hamadání, "Memoirs of a Bahá'í in Rasht: 1889–1903," Bahá'í Studies Review 18, no. 1 (2012): 12.
[192] Momen, The Bahá'í Communities of Iran 1851-1921: The North of Iran, 62.
[193] Momen, The Bahá'í Communities of Iran 1851-1921: The North of Iran, 462.
[194] 1311 AH began in July 1893 and ended in June 1894.

His wife replied: "Let me ask you something. If a man has been a butcher for forty years and in a dark night someone gives him a dog to kill instead of a lamb, do you think he would make a mistake and kill the dog instead of the lamb?" Her husband said, "No." Then she answered: "Be assured you will not be murdered instead of a Bahá'í." She kept the children for several weeks and during that time nothing happened to any of them.[195]

[195] Root, "White Roses of Persia (Part 2)," 180.

X - Arrested in Zanján

One day, Varqá and Rúḥu'lláh were arrested in Zanján along with Mírzá Ḥusayn Zanjání, a local believer. Before issuing a verdict on their lives, the Governor Ahmad Khán had the idea of convening evening meetings where the Bahá'ís and the clergy could debate about the truth of the Faith of Bahá'u'lláh. It is not clear what the reasons were behind the Governor's initiative. He may have wanted to create a spectacle or perhaps he hoped that in the course of the evening the Bahá'ís would make a statement to justify their execution – which was what the clergy were demanding of him. Ahmad Khán, however did not plan on Varqá's eloquence and wisdom, which were overwhelming nor did he appreciate the knowledge and intelligence of the adolescent Rúḥu'lláh. This chapter explore these incidents.

10.1 Cameliers and Shepherds

Ahmad Khán, the Zanján Governor, and his prisoner Varqá were peers in only two respects – they were approximately the same age and they each had a similar number of sons. In all other regards they differed. Ahmad Khán was the cruel and powerful governor of the province of Zanján, while Varqá was a loyal citizen serving humanity. Ahmad Khán's grandiose title was 'Alá'u'd-Dawlih ("Splendor of the State")[196], whereas the latter was designated by Bahá'u'lláh Himself as Dove or Nightingale. Ahmad Khán was rich, vain and aristocratic. Varqá's merits were his spiritual and intellectual qualities and his only possessions were Bahá'í relics consisting of Bahá'u'lláh's Tablets, His white robe, a portrait of the Báb, and his medical books.

Ahmad Khán was described as "imperious, suspicious, unbearably autocratic"[197] and "a grandee demanding obeisance, whose hateur and air of superiority were hard to match and to bear, and who was easily

---

[197] Balyuzi, Eminent Bahá'ís in the Time of Bahá'u'lláh, 85.

swayed by his conflicting and fleeting emotions".[198] In contrast, Varqá was described by 'Abdu'l-Bahá Himself as an "incomparable person, a jewel of kindness".[199]

Further, Ahmad Khán followed in the footsteps of Pontius Pilate from a previous dispensation, when under pressure from the divines, he eventually chose to send Varqá to his death in the gaols of Tehran rather than liberating him. The differences continued to the end: Varqá's death was recorded in history as a glorious martyrdom, while Ahmad Khán was shot dead fifteen years later, a victim of his own political intrigues.

Ahmad Khán was contemporary to the three powerful sons of the Sháh of Iran. They ruled most of the country in the most despotic form under the Sháh's absolutist monarchy. Mas'úd Mírzá governed Iṣfahán and a broad range of provinces, Kamran Mírzá ruled in Tehran and other important provinces while Muẓaffari'd-Dín Mírzá governed only in Ádhirbáyján. The three royal brothers were two years older, five years younger and one year younger than Ahmad Khán, respectively. To reach a governorship Ahmad Khán must have had strong family influences within the Qájár clan. His career flourished within the Qájár bureaucracy and military, and he obtained the title of major general by the time he was appointed Governor of Zanján.

All four of them were from the Qájár dynasty. There was, however, a major difference between Ahmad Khán and the three royal brothers. Ahmad Khán was a second-class Qájár who may have been given the job to keep the alliance between the two more powerful Qájár clans: the Cameliers (Devehlu) and the Shepherds (Quyunlu). In reality, the Qájárs were a confederation of minor tribes united under the Sháh's rule.

In order to keep the Qájár dynasty going the Sháhs of Iran had to keep all the tribes connected through multiple marriages thus paving the way for economic and political favours. In this political geography,

[198] Balyuzi, Eminent Bahá'ís in the Time of Bahá'u'lláh, 88.
[199] Bahá'í News Service, February 1913, 362-364.

the Shepherds comprised the ruling class. For his bad luck, Ahmad Khán was however a Devehlu, a "camelier" not a "shepherd".

10.2 Planning to Settle in Tehran

It was February 1896.[200] About three years previously, after his last pilgrimage to the Holy Land, 'Abdu'l-Bahá had advised him to move his Bahá'í archives and relics to Tehran. Varqá was a prominent believer and the potential target of any attack against the Faith. Varqá did not want his presence to cause harm to the local believers. Varqá was very aware of the latent danger of staying in Zanján and was well aware of the holocaust of 1850 where nearly 1,500 believers were massacred.

According to Kazem Kazemzadeh "They were insulted in the bazaar and threatened in the streets."[201] Shahrokh added:[202]

> A Tablet from 'Abdu'l-Bahá arrived, stressing steadfastness in the face of fierce storms of tests. The dream of Varqá's wife, identical to the dream of a Muslim acquaintance, about a flood the color of blood was foreboding danger.

Animosity against the Bahá'ís had resurged in Zanján and Varqá could be of greater service in Tehran where the Faith was gaining momentum. 'Abdu'lláh Núrí, grandfather of his sons was living in Tehran. As a man of integrity and a dedicated believer he was Varqá's supporter.

Consequently, together with another Bahá'í, his new father-in-law named Ḥájí Ímám, and the children he set out for Tehran. It was a cold Iranian winter and the snow made it difficult to hire horses which could navigate the conditions. Thus there were ongoing delays. Eventually the pressure of the situation affected 'Azízu'lláh to such an extent that though only a teenager, he set off alone and on foot for

[200] Momen, The Bahá'í Communities of Iran 1851-1921: The North of Iran, 462-463.
[201] Kazemzadeh, Varqá and Rúhu'llah: Deathless in Martyrdom, 36.
[202] Darius Shahrokh, Varqá and Son: The Heavenly Doves, 18.

Tehran. As he had not informed anyone of his intention, by the time Varqá learned about it, it was too late to get him back. He was out of reach.

In preparation for the trip Varqá arranged all his Tablets and books in two big cases with locks. Horses also were procured for the trip. On the eve of their departure Varqá, Rúḥu'lláh and his new father-in-law Ḥájí Ímám went to say goodbye to the head of the local telegraph office. On arrival they found some other Bahá'ís of Zanján were visiting 'Alí Akbar Khán, the telegraph operator. He had recently lost his mother and the Bahá'ís were there to offer their condolences and their spiritual support.

A number of public places like telegraph offices and military facilities throughout Iran were under the direct control and protection of the central government. For this reason people used them as a place to seek refuge from the abuses of regional and local authorities. Citizens felt safe because while in those offices, they were in a position to provide immediate report to national authorities. As such, those places were under vigilance by local and regional authorities. Religious shrines were also considered untouchable.

As Varqá and his companions were leaving the telegraph office, they were seen by a Muslim priest named Mullá 'Abdu'l-Vasí who was there to spy for the governor. The priest immediately advised the city master of the curfew. Through the latter the governor was informed that the Bahá'ís had been at the telegraph office and were possibly making a complaint against him.

It is alleged that Ahmad Khán, the governor, became suspicious. He had recently been appointed to his first governorship and any complaints against him to the Sháh would be detrimental to his ambitions. Another version of this story indicates that Ahmad Khán was pursuing Varqá's imprisonment for the purpose of extorting money from him as he had heard that Varqá was rich, which was not the case.[203]

[203] Momen, The Bahá'í Communities of Iran 1851-1921: The North of Iran, 464.

Early the next day, having finalised all the preparations, Rúḥu'lláh, Varqá, and Ḥájí Ímám left town. Mírzá Ḥusayn Zanjání, a Bahá'í of the city, following a farewell custom accompanied them to the first resting place.

10.3 Varqá is Arrested in Zanján

That same morning the governor's guards went to arrest Varqá at the house of Siyyid Faṭṭaḥ where he had been living.[204] As they could not find Varqá there, they invaded the homes of other Bahá'ís. The guards were arresting and torturing the believers. When Mírzá Ḥusayn Zanjání returned to the city he was immediately arrested, imprisoned and subjected to interrogation.

Though Mírzá Ḥusayn Zanjání explained everything that had taken place in the course of the day, the governor's suspicions increased. He ordered a regiment to quickly leave in search of Varqá, Ḥájí Ímám and Rúḥu'lláh. They were found on the road to Tehran. Varqá and Rúḥu'lláh were arrested and brought back to Zanján. Ḥájí Ímám took advantage of the confusion at the time of the arrest and managed to escape with several trunks of Bahá'í books in his possession. He managed to get to Qazvín located 140 km away where he left the sacred possessions in the care of a trustworthy individual. He was then determined to return to Zanján but was arrested en route and imprisoned with Varqá and Rúḥu'lláh. Guards rummaged through the belongings of the prisoners and their surprise, Varqá's only treasure were fifty volumes of the Writings of Bahá'u'lláh[205], on fine quality paper and including drawings and illuminations. According to Martha Root:

> After arresting 'Alí Muḥammad Varqá the policemen had gone to his home and carried off his beautiful painting of the Báb (and there is only one other in the world) taken many of

---

[204] Momen, The Bahá'í Communities of Iran 1851-1921: The North of Iran, 463.
[205] For a discussion on the Tablets to Varqá see The Revelation of Bahá'u'lláh by Adib Taherzadeh, vol. 4, pp. 64-72 and pp. 88-90.

> his precious Tablets, plundered the family books, even the register that gave the dates of their birth so that some of the family do not know when their birthdays are. They confiscated their property.[206]

> … they were taken back to Zanján with heavy chains about their necks and their feet in stocks. The governor of Zanján spoke with them and asked if they were Bahá'ís. 'Alí Muḥammad Varqá spoke first and said, "Yes." Little Rúḥu'lláh when questioned said, "Yes, I am a Bahá'í." But one old man denied the Faith saying "No, I am not a believer." The Governor in disgust struck him saying, "Everyone knows you call yourself a Bahá'í and now you deny it; but this little boy who is just at the beginning of his life and has so many hopes in the world, has had the courage to say he is a Bahá'í."[207]

According to Ḥasan Balyuzi:

> On his first encounter with Varqá, he [Ahmad Khán] began a harangue of abuse, to which Varqá replied that such language was demeaning and not meet for such an assemblage. Whereupon Varqá was sent to prison.[208]

Gloria Faizi adds

> It was Ramaḍán,[209] the month of the fast, and people sat up late into the night. In the smaller towns and villages of Persia, where life was monotonous and nothing of great interest took place from year to year, there was not much to occupy the long nights of Ramaḍán except making the usual round of visits and reading the Qur'án.

---

[206] Root, "White Roses of Persia (Part 4)," 255-56.
[207] Root, "White Roses of Persia (Part 4)," 255.
[208] Balyuzi, Eminent Bahá'ís in the Time of Bahá'u'lláh, 86.
[209] The month of Ramaḍán in 1896 took place between between 15 February and 15 March 1896.

> The town of Zanján, being one such a place, was pleasantly surprised to hear one day that a few Bahá'ís had been caught, chained and placed in a cell for people to go and see behind the prison bars. They came in dozens, wondering what Bahá'ís really looked like, and went away greatly disappointed to see that really, they were ordinary human beings.[210]

10.3 Meetings Arranged with Divines

In prison, Varqá began the process of explaining the aims and principles of the Bahá'í Faith to the Governor Ahmad Khán who within a short time developed a better impression of his Bahá'í prisoners.

The Governor arranged meetings where the main mullás were present, and invited Varqá and Rúḥu'lláh with the others imprisoned so that they could demonstrate before all the truth of the Cause they professed. He explained that they should base their arguments on the Holy Scriptures. The meetings were at night, after the Muslim community broke fast, and the gatherings sometimes went into the early hours of the following day.

Varqá, Rúḥu'lláh and Mírzá Ḥusayn Zanjání were seated before the inquisitorial gaze of the religious dignitaries, who came in such large numbers that sometimes there were not enough seats for all. The priests wished to prove that the Bahá'ís were infidels and apostates and therefore a death sentence was warranted. A death sentence could be issued by the clerics but must be ratified by the Governor. In prison they were offered freedom if they denied their belief in Bahá'u'lláh.

The three of them decided not to act in that way. In their love for the Blessed Perfection they preferred martyrdom before recanting. They were threatened with death if they did not curse Bahá'u'lláh. Rúḥu'lláh once said when threatened: "I have seen Bahá'u'lláh. I cannot deny Him."[211] And when asked if he was a

---

[210] Faizi, Fire on the Mountain Top, 79.
[211] Root, "White Roses of Persia (Part 4)," 256.

Bahá'í, Rúḥu'lláh proudly stated: "Yes, I am a Bahá'í."[212] Such was the faith of that child!

During those nights of debate with the priests, it was Varqá and his companions who provided clear and convincing arguments. No question remained without a satisfactory response. When defeated, the dignitaries either began interrupting the Bahá'ís or hurling insults at them. There were times when the Governor joined them.[213] Sometimes Varqá asked Rúḥu'lláh to answer the questions. Everyone was amazed at the capacity of that precocious child and considered him a living miracle. "This child's strange power of argument is a miracle in itself," the Governor remarked.[214]

10.4 Mírzá Ḥusayn Zanjání

Mírzá Ḥusayn Zanjání was among the Bahá'ís arrested in Zanján and sent to the Tehran gaol with Varqá and Rúḥu'lláh. His son-in-law worked as an interpreter for the Russian consulate.[215] At that time the Russian Empire was one of the two dominating superpowers of the region and the Persian government was very afraid of upsetting it.

While Mírzá Ḥusayn Zanjání was living in 'Ishqábád (Ashkhabad), Russia, he was instructed by 'Abdu'l-Bahá to move back to Zanján.[216] Ḥasan Balyuzi writes that Mírzá Ḥusayn Zanjání returned to Persia from 'Ishqábád, Russia, under the protection of Naṣiri'd-Dín Sháh himself and the Russian consul-general.[217]

Gloria Faizi writes about this strong believer:

> Among the visitors to the prison was a Muslim priest whose brother, Mírzá Ḥusayn, had been arrested with other Bahá'ís of Zanján. The priest had often told his brother that he would

---

[212] Root, "White Roses of Persia (Part 4)," 255.
[213] Balyuzi, Eminent Bahá'ís in the Time of Bahá'u'lláh, 87.
[214] Faizi, Fire on the Mountain Top, 80.
[215]Darius Shahrokh, Varqá and Son: The Heavenly Doves, 21.
[216] Momen, The Bahá'í Communities of Iran 1851-1921: The North of Iran, 461.
[217] Balyuzi, Eminent Bahá'ís in the Time of Bahá'u'lláh,8 8.

> come to no good if he did not give up his allegiance to the new Cause. Now he came to see if this imprisonment had brought his brother to his senses and prepared him to recant his Faith. Much to his surprise, he found Mírzá Ḥusayn steadfast in his beliefs, and ready to defend the Bahá'í Cause no matter what the consequences. When neither his exhortations nor his many threats produced any result, the priest left the prison in a rage, using the foulest language.[218]

One evening the Governor asked Mírzá Ḥusayn Zanjání:

> "You claim that you have accepted the Bahá'í Faith after long investigation, but tell me how it is that you went to the Bahá'ís for your investigations. Were there not enough learned Muslims for you to enquire from?"[219]

The priests arrogantly made themselves comfortable, anticipating that Mírzá Ḥusayn Zanjání would struggle with their question. Mírzá Ḥusayn Zanjání replied:

> "If a person wishes to find out about Islam, would you advise him to go to a Christian clergyman?"[220]

From this simple explanation, the mullás' composure deteriorared. One of them, inflamed with anger, came forward to strike Varqá's face with his stick. Another, even more agitated, was going to stab him in the sight of all, but the governor interposed and warned him not to do so. He promised that he, himself would do it with his own hands slowly over the course of a week.

The clerics removed Mírzá Ḥusayn Zanjání's religious turban, which he wore because he came from a family of high religious reputation. They placed an old dirty cap on his head, and twisted his eyebrows in order to ridicule him.[221]

---

[218] Faizi, Fire on the Mountain Top, 79.
[219]Faizi, Fire on the Mountain Top, 80.
[220] Faizi, Fire on the Mountain Top, 80.
[221] Faizi, Fire on the Mountain Top, 81.

10.5 Revealing Verses like Bahá'u'lláh

Sometimes Varqá had the opportunity to defend himself. On one occasion a mullá arrogantly said to the poet:

> "If you consider Bahá'u'lláh's sayings as a proof of prophethood, I too can bring words as beautiful as his."

Varqá replied:

> "At the time of Muḥammad too, there were those who made the same claim. Neither were they, nor are you, able to accomplish such a task. But even if you were capable of producing the beautiful sayings you boast of, whose would you claim them to be?"

The priest answered:

> "I would say they were my own words, of course."

The poet then took the lead:

> "Here lies the difference. Bahá'u'lláh claims that He has nothing to say of His own. All His sayings He claims to be of God. Not only does He make such a stupendous claim, but thousands of people from the different religious backgrounds of the world have accepted His words as the words of God, and hundreds upon hundreds of great scholars, men of letters and religious dignitaries have laid down their lives as a proof to the power of these words. Now tell me, can you too, after having produced your wonderful works, claim that a single person will go so far as to say you are the greatest clergyman alive?"[222]

Another version of that same conversation states that Varqá asked,

---

[222] Faizi, Fire on the Mountain Top, 80.

"What other proof is there for the truth of Islam except for the holy words of the Qur'án and their influence?"

The mullá retorted, "We have other proofs".

Varqá said, "Such as?"

The mullá said, "The traditions of the Ímáms and the like".

Another mullá in the group shouted, "Mullá, you really messed it up. You don't accept the words of Muḥammad Himself as primary proof and claim the words of His subordinates to prove the validity of Islam."[223]

Kazem Kazemzadeh relates the confusion among the clergy created by this theological defeat:

> The priests were in an uproar. One was accusing another of incorrectly phrasing his question. The other shouted that the first one did not understand the substance of the argument. "What?" the first roared. "You dare say that I do not understand and err while the Bahá'ís understand and are right?"[224]

10.6 Mullás' Disturbing Noise in Meetings

The clerics, in the presence of the governor, found themselves frustrated and ashamed of not being able to respond adequately to the statements made by the Bahá'ís which were all supported by verses from the Qur'án, the sacred book of Muslims. In their desperation they began hurling insults and making false accusations.

Their exasperation increased night after night. Eventually, they devised a way to silence Varqá's interventions. One of them asked a

[223] Darius Shahrokh, Varqá and Son: The Heavenly Doves, 20.
[224] Kazemzadeh, Varqá and Rúhu'llah: Deathless in Martyrdom, 38.

question and when the poet was ready to reply, the others interrupted with great noise and shouting.

Despite resorting to such behaviours, one of the divines involved in the evening discussions later wrote a book called *Irshad ul-Iman* (Guidance from the Ímám[225]) or *Rajm ud-Dajjal* (Stoning the False Messiah) asserting that he had defeated Varqá in the public debates.[226]

The Governor began to realize how empty of knowledge the clergy surrounded his court were. Gradually he became disgusted by the screams raised in each meeting. At the same time, Ahmad Khán did not want to confront the mullás as they were very influential among the ignorant populace, who blindly and fanatically followed their lead. A disruption in his relationship with members of that powerful institution could therefore have caused him serious difficulties. He put an end to their disruption by telling the priests: "You have come here to find out what Varqá has to say. If you have questions to put to him, you can ask them one by one, so that he can answer you."[227]

10.7 Discussion about the Old and New Testaments

On one occasion Varqá quoted a passage of the Bible to support his arguments in response to a question from one of the mullás about the authenticity of the Old and New Testaments. His doubt arose from certain verses of the Qur'án. The divine believed that the Christian and Jewish holy books had been tampered with. The mullá said: "These books of Christians and Jews are false and altered. The original books disappeared in the sky".[228] This comment upset the Governor who exclaimed, "Enough of such absurd talk".[229] A mantle of silence suddenly covered the hall.

Varqá responded to the assertion by drawing on the Kitáb-i-Íqán:

---

[225] The term Imám stands for a Muslim religious preacher.
[226] Momen, The Bahá'í Communities of Iran 1851-1921: The North of Iran, 464.
[227] Faizi, Fire on the Mountain Top, 81.
[228] Darius Shahrokh, Varqá and Son: The Heavenly Doves, 21.
[229] Darius Shahrokh, Varqá and Son: The Heavenly Doves, 21.

> We have also heard a number of the foolish of the earth assert that the genuine text of the heavenly Gospel doth not exist amongst the Christians, that it hath ascended unto heaven. How grievously they have erred! How oblivious of the fact that such a statement imputeth the gravest injustice and tyranny to a gracious and loving Providence! How could God, when once the Day-star of the beauty of Jesus had disappeared from the sight of His people, and ascended unto the fourth heaven, cause His holy Book, His most great testimony amongst His creatures, to disappear also? What would be left to that people to cling to from the setting of the day-star of Jesus until the rise of the sun of the Muḥammadan Dispensation? What law could be their stay and guide? How could such people be made the victims of the avenging wrath of God, the omnipotent Avenger? How could they be afflicted with the scourge of chastisement by the heavenly King? Above all, how could the flow of the grace of the All-Bountiful be stayed? How could the ocean of His tender mercies be stilled? We take refuge with God, from that which His creatures have fancied about Him! Exalted is He above their comprehension![230]

10.8 Discussion to Send Varqá and Bahá'ís to Tehran

The Governor was reluctant to send the prisoners to Tehran. He admired Varqá and Rúḥu'lláh, not only because of their intellectual abilities, but also because he had never seen prisoners of such innocence and piety.

In the last hearing where the validity of the Bible —both the Old and the New Testaments— was discussed, offers of material benefit were made to Varqá should he recant his faith:

> Varqá, I swear by the crown of His Majesty and the soul of Amir Nizam [commander-in-chief] that if you stop

[230] Bahá'u'lláh, The Kitáb-i-Íqán: The Book of Certitude (Wilmette, IL: Bahá'í Publishing Trust, 1989), 89-90.

> propagating this Faith, I will obtain for you a proper title from the Sháh, pay you a handsome salary, and make you my personal physician.[231]

However, as with previous threats and promises, Varqá paid this offer no heed. There could be no question of denying their Beloved or converting to the governor's interpretation of Islam.

One source reported that Varqá wisely replied: "Am I a Jew or Zoroastrian to convert to Islam? For the past sixteen days I have been proving to you the truths of Muḥammad's prophecies and you still want me to convert to Islam. I am a true Muslim. As for your promise of a stipend could a wise man renounce his faith for money?"[232]

"Do you really think," Varqá told him, "that I would renounce the Messenger of God for the titles and riches this world can offer?"

In his desire to save the Bahá'í prisoners, Ahmad Khán argued:

> "But you can dedicate your life to God's Cause and serve Islam."

To which Varqá replied:

> "This is what I am doing now. God's eternal Faith is one. What I believe is in what all the Messengers have taught. It is they who have told us in the Holy Books to watch for the advent of the Promised One. If I, as a believer in God and His Holy Books, have come to recognize the Promised One we have been waiting for, can I forsake Him and turn my back on Him for the sake of material benefits?"

Continuing to press the Governor urged Varqá:

> "Denounce this Faith in front of others, at least, even if you believe in it at heart".

---

[231] Faizi, Fire on the Mountain Top, 81.

[232] Kazemzadeh, Varqá and Rúhu'llah: Deathless in Martyrdom, 39.

To which Varqá responded:

> "It would be impossible for me to live the life of such a hypocrite."

The governor thus exclaimed:

> "Alas! You leave me no choice. I must send you and your son to the capital to be dealt with by others there, but Mírzá Ḥusayn will be blown from the mouth of a cannon here in Zanján tomorrow."

Everyone was stunned at the governor's pronouncement. When Varqá had the opportunity to speak to the governor alone, he begged the governor to send Mírzá Ḥusayn Zanjání to the capital, along with Varqá and his son:

> "Do not stain your hands with the blood of the Bahá'ís", was Varqá's supplication.[233]

The Governor was reminded of Mírzá Ḥusayn Zanjání's links with the Russian Embassy. He also consulted the Prime Minister, and after a telegram with instructions arrived from the Prime Minister himself, the governor ultimately agreed to send Mírzá Ḥusayn Zanjání to Tehran. Ahmad Khán realized that killing Mírzá Ḥusayn Zanjání would lead to enquiries about his proficiency and practice as governor, which he wished to avoid. Thus, it was decided that Mírzá Ḥusayn Zanjání be sent to the capital in chains.

There were two conditions connected with Ahmad Khán's decision. Firstly, Varqá's Bahá'í archives were to be sent to Tehran as evidence to support the religious allegations against him. He was to take an inventory of his possessions, put them in locked boxes and deliver them to the Prime Minister in Tehran. Secondly, Mírzá Ḥusayn Zanjání's family was to cover the cost of hiring a horse for his transportation to Tehran.[234]

---

[233] Faizi, Fire on the Mountain Top, 82.
[234] Balyuzi, Eminent Bahá'ís in the Time of Bahá'u'lláh, 88.

The prisoners were accompanied by a cavalry of Jahansháh Khán, a Zanján tribal leader, high-ranking officer in the Sháh's army, and one of the magnates of the region. His cavalry was going to the capital for the celebrations of the 50th anniversary of Naṣiri'd-Dín Sháh's coronation.

At this time Mírzá Ḥusayn Zanjání's home was destroyed and all Bahá'í houses were pillaged. Laqá'íyyih, Varqá's new wife along with Mírzá Ḥusayn Zanjání's wife had the opportunity to see their husbands before departing for the capital. Here is Laqá'íyyih's account:

> It was a small but relatively clean room. Varqá, Rúḥu'lláh, and Mírzá Ḥusayn sat on a rug. Rúḥu'lláh looked thinner [than before his arrest]. Addressing me, Varqá said: "See how they turned us back on the road," and added in a whisper so that the guards would not hear, "It would be good if friends could take Rúḥu'lláh from us". Then he said: "Every evening this room fills with visitors. Some come from sheer curiosity to stare at us, others come to argue and insult, but there are also those who listen carefully. When I do not want to reply to attacks of some of our visitors, I let Rúḥu'lláh answer them." When we [Laqá'íyyih Khánum and Mírzá Ḥusayn Zanjání's wife] came home, we learned that Ḥájí Ímám had been arrested on the way back to Zanján and was in jail, being tortured so he would reveal where he had been and why he was not with Varqá and Rúḥu'lláh when they were arrested.[235]

The final reflection of this chapter is about Rúḥu'lláh. Although a mature child, he was still in the process of transitioning into adulthood. The whole prison experience confined in a dungeon with chains must have been very scary. Most likely, he may have realized that the world can get very cruel and that at those dark times prayer was the best resort for anxiety and uncertainty. But above all, he may have realized that Varqá was not only his father and great role model, but also his best mate.

---

[235] Kazemzadeh, Varqá and Rúhu'llah: Deathless in Martyrdom, 39.

XI – The Mystery of Martyrdom

11.1 What is a Martyr?

The life of Varqá and Rúḥu'lláh ended in martyrdom in 1896. Two languages, Arabic and Greek, provide a semantic structure to understand the word and thus the concept, *martyr*. In its broadest definition, a martyr is one who gives up his or her life for a cause.

The word martyr comes from the Greek word μάρτυς, *mártys*, meaning a witness of an event or a personal observer who testifies to the truth of a matter. In ancient Greece the term was used in legal cases for an individual who was called to render testimony in a case. Later the term evolved to signify one who died to uphold the truth of a principle, including religious principles. When the New Testament was written in Greek, in the first centuries of the Christian era, the word martyr found its way into the Western languages. The corresponding word in Arabic is شاهد, Sháhid, meaning either a witness or a person who dies for his or her religious beliefs.

In all known religious dispensations there are individuals who gave their lives for the sake of their faith, thus becoming martyrs. In this context martyrs are those who testify with their lives the divine legitimacy of a prophet. Some chose to die rather than recant their faith while others were murdered after being accused of heresy, without opportunity to make a choice.

With their precious blood, Bahá'í martyrs bear witness to the truth of the Cause, and to their love for it. Through this act they testify to the insight, hidden from most, that spiritual life is of greater value than physical life.

Writing to a cruel and powerful religious leader, Bahá'u'lláh proudly describes His followers' commitment to truth:

> O Shaykh! This people have passed beyond the narrow straits of names, and pitched their tents upon the shores of the sea of renunciation. They would willingly lay down a myriad lives, rather than breathe the word desired by their enemies. They have clung to that which pleaseth God, and are wholly detached and freed from the things which pertain unto men. They have preferred to have their heads cut off rather than utter one unseemly word. Ponder this in thine heart. Methinks they have quaffed their fill of the ocean of renunciation. The life of the present world hath failed to withhold them from suffering martyrdom in the path of God.[236]

11.2 Martyrdom Seen Historically

The apostolic stages of the great religious systems now established have previously witnessed the sacrifice of countless detached souls in order to vindicate their beliefs before powerful and bitter adversaries. Thus this willing sacrifice in the path of God has its counterpart in the oppressions suffered by the Hebrew people in Egypt. Similarly in the Christian Dispensation many were called to give their lives, as manifest in the Acts of the Apostles, the martyrdom of Stephen, Paul's bravery as he defended his faith in the synagogues, and the believers massacred in the first years of the Christian Faith. Indeed, it is claimed that Decius killed as many as 3,000-3,500 Christians. The early adherents of Islam were likewise subject to harassment, persecution and martyrdom. Such shedding of blood appears to be an essential part of renewal of religion and the mark of a new prophetic appearance.

The early adherents of the Bábí and Bahá'í religions also demonstrated their faith through martyrdom. Anticipating this time Isaiah repeatedly warned: "I will make the heavens tremble, and the earth will move out of her place and the foundations of the earth will shake ... the inhabitants of the earth will be burned and few will escape

---

[236] Bahá'u'lláh, Epistle to the Son of the Wolf (Wilmette, Illinois: Bahá'í Publishing Trust, 1988), 148.

… the earth would sway from side to side like a drunkard ….”[237] These prophecies were realised in the tumult released by the Iranian religious leaders' massacring scores of early believers.

The Day of the Lord, as Saint Peter in highly mystical and symbolic language stated, would “come as a thief in the night; in which the heavens shall pass away with a great noise, and the elements shall melt with fervent heat, the earth also and the works that are therein shall be burned up.”[238] “When the sky is cleft asunder”, Muḥammad predicted, “when the stars have fallen, and when the seas will burst forth, when the graves turn upside down, each soul will recognize its first and last actions.”[239] “On that day no one who is on the housetop,” Jesus warned, “with possessions inside, should go down to get them. Likewise, no one in the field should go back for anything.”[240]

Referring to this recurring phenomenon, Bahá'u'lláh wrote:

> Behold how in this Dispensation the worthless and foolish have fondly imagined that by such instruments as massacre, plunder and banishment they can extinguish the Lamp which the Hand of Divine power hath lit, or eclipse the Day Star of everlasting splendor. How utterly unaware they seem to be of the truth that such adversity is the oil that feedeth the flame of this Lamp! Such is God's transforming power. He changeth whatsoever He willeth; He verily hath power over all things…[241]

11.3 An Act of Barbarism

Martyrdoms occur particularly in barbaric societies. In the 19th century Iran where Varqá lived, that place was the most backward country on earth where, according to the historian George Townshend, “Corruption, fanaticisms and cruelty gather against the

---

[237] Isaiah 13:13, 24:6, 24:20.
[238] II Peter 3:10
[239] Qu'rán 82:1-5
[240] Lucas 17: 31
[241] Bahá'u'lláh, Gleanings from the Writings of Bahá'u'lláh, 72.

cause of reformation to destroy it." Townshend elaborated upon the condition of Persia 200 years ago:

> All observers agree in representing Persia as a feeble and backward nation divided against itself by corrupt practices and ferocious bigotries. Inefficiency and wretchedness, the fruit of moral decay, filled the land. From the highest to the lowest there appeared neither the capacity to carry out methods of reform nor even the will seriously to institute them ... A pall of immobility lay over all things, and a general paralysis of mind made any development impossible. [242]

As in the Inquisition of the Dark Ages, or in the Roman persecution of the Christians, physical violence was used to challenge, repress and uproot religious belief. The manifestations of religious intolerance moved from intelligent argument to physical repression as the dominating class was unable to hamper the advancement of an emerging faith. It was a desperate attempt from the ecclesiastic hierarchy, usually allied with the state, to manage a social phenomenon over which they had no control and which threatened their power. Unable to deal with the matter in a civilized manner the establishment turned to executions, imprisonment, torture, genocide, pillage and exile. This was the nature of the society in which Varqá lived.

11.4 The Legacy of the Martyrs

Martyrdom and massacre were deployed to eliminate the early believers and limit the spread of their new ideas. However, as evidenced by history these persecutions had the opposite effect, as early believers developed more resilience and grew stronger gradually winning the hearts of the public with their steadfastness and virtue. Far from extinguishing the flame of devotion in the mass of believers, martyrdom served to inspire one to greater heights of detachment. A number of spectators of public martyrdoms were outraged by the

[242] Nabíl-i-A'zam, The Dawn-Breakers: Nabíl's Narrative of the Early Days of the Bahá'í Revelation, xxiv.

savagery displayed in the executions. Upon investigation, many came to condemn the oppressor and some converted to the new Faith, from both Muslim and Zoroastrian backgrounds.[243] [244]

On at certain occasion a Bahá'í was blown from the mouth of a cannon in front of a multitude in Shíraz, after reciting his obligatory prayer publicly. A number of witnesses to that event were touched by the faith, sanctity and courage of the martyr and subsequently became believers. Siyyid 'Alí- Akbar, the cleric responsible for the execution, was told by a principled colleague after the murder:

> Siyyid, do you discern what you have done today? The cannon's roar caused half the city to become Bábí! Indeed, you served the sacred religion of Islam and these people![245]

Speaking about the legacy of the martyrs the Hand of the Cause Dr Raḥmatu'lláh Muhájir related:

> I know a believer, a family of believers, they call it Sarvestani. This Sarvestani family, they are well scattered in Persia —they are pioneers in Arabia, a very, very wonderful family, a great family of the Bahá'ís. And I asked them, how, what happened that you come to the Faith? They have a beautiful story. The story is that, "My grandfather", the young man telling me, "My grandfather was in Sarvestan, it's near Shíráz. And one day, it was a Naw-Rúz, he had put a very nice dress and very beautiful shoes on, and white everything, and went to the street. And he saw that they are killing a man. And, he said, 'What is this man?' They said, 'He is a Bábí. We are killing him.' He said, 'When they cut his neck, blood, you know, blood spread everywhere. One drop of blood fallen on my shoes.' And he said, 'In that, it's shaken me. What is this? What is this

[243] Momen, The Bahá'í Communities of Iran 1851-1921: The North of Iran, 494.
[244] Moojan Momen, Bahá'í Communities of Iran, vol. II, 100-101 (Oxford: George Ronald, 2015).
[245] Sholeh A Quinn, "The Genesis of the Bábí-Bahá'í Faiths in Shíráz and Fárs: By Mírzá Habíb'u'lláh Afnán (Tr. And Annotated by Ahang Rabbani)(Leiden: Brill, 2008. 404 Pages.)," American Journal of Islam and Society 27, no. 2 (2010): 125.

> religion? And I became a believer.' He said, 'That one drop of blood made me a believer.' ... and his family became believer and everybody became." Now their children traveling all over the world, pioneering in Arabia. One drop of blood of the martyrs [caused this]...[246]

11.5 The Tree of the Faith

The martyrs are in a way victorious in both the short and long term. Masses become aware of their beliefs in largely populated execution spectacles and become curious. What is it that leaders of a religion, in the name of God, are murdering followers from another religion? Interestingly, the martyrs' movement then began gaining momentum, going from strength to strength and spreading far and wide throughout the country. The martyrs' beliefs began attracting public attention not only for their brilliant discourse and exemplary citizenship but also for their indomitable courage and bravery at their time of violent death. For instance, after listening about the terrible details of the genocide of the Bahá'ís in a city, a famous Iranian divine and at the same time the Crown Prince's tutor, "wrung his hands in horror and despair" and exclaimed: "How strange, how very strange, is this Cause!".[247]

It has been said that the blood of the martyrs nourished the tree of the emerging Faith. For example, twenty thousand martyrs made possible the rapid growth of the tree of the Cause which quickly extended its branches to all regions of the world. In the words of the Báb:

> Great is the blessedness of those whose blood Thou hast chosen wherewith to water the Tree of Thine affirmation, and thus to exalt Thy holy and immutable Word.[248]

---

[246] Raḥmatu'lláh Muhájir, "The Legacy of the Martyrs," 2020, https://bahai.works/Audio:Rahmatu'llah_Muhajir/About_the_legacy_of_the_martyrs.

[247] Nabíl-i-A'zam, The Dawn-Breakers: Nabíl's Narrative of the Early Days of the Bahá'í Revelation, 621.

[248] The Báb, Selections from the Writings of the Báb (Bahá'í World Centre, 1978), 190.

And in those of Bahá'u'lláh:

> Do not be sad, do not be downcast, do not let your hearts bleed. The sacred tree of the Cause of God is watered by the blood of the martyrs. A tree, unless watered, does not grow and bear fruit . . .[249]

Martyrdom is an affirmation of faith. When the new religion emerged from its early obscurity and became accepted, and as the period of violent persecution came to an end, an outer form of martyrdom surfaces. From being an event in a lifetime, martyrdom comes to take an internal form through constant sacrifice in the path of service. In this transformative view of martyrdom, believers are therefore encouraged to dedicate their life to the spread of the new teachings. Shoghi Effendi wrote:

> Every day has certain needs. In those early days the Cause needed Martyrs, and people who would stand all sorts of torture and persecution in expressing their faith and spreading the message sent by God. Those days are, however, gone. The Cause at present does not need martyrs who would die for the faith, but servants who desire to teach and establish the Cause throughout the world. To live to teach in the present day is like being martyred in those early days. It is the spirit that moves us that counts, not the act through which that spirit expresses itself; and that spirit is to serve the Cause of God with our heart and soul.[250]

Further, Bahá'u'lláh Himself has promised the station of martyrdoms to pioneers who die in their teaching posts:

---

[249] Roger White, "Bahá'u'lláh and the Fourth Estate," The Bahá'í World (1979-1983), 1986, 977, https://bahai-library.com/pdf/w/white_bw18_bahaullah_press.pdf.

[250] Bahá'í World Centre, The Compilation of Compilations, vol. II (Maryborough, Victoria: Bahá'í Publications Australia, 2000), 5.

> They that have forsaken their country in the path of God and subsequently ascended unto His presence, such souls shall be blessed by the Concourse on High and their names recorded by the Pen of Glory among such as have laid down their lives as martyrs in the path of God, the Help in Peril, the Self Subsistent.[251]

11.6 Steadfastness with Love

Martyrs are probably the antithesis of conventional citizens. They accept their sacrifice with endurance and firmness and even joy. Therefore martyrs do not hesitate to surrender themselves with exemplary stoicism to their opponents instead of recanting their faith. The account of the martyrdom of Sulaymán Khán in 1852 is a poignant case in point:

> [Sulaymán Khán] was asked the manner in which he wished to die. "Pierce holes in my flesh," was the instant reply, "and in each wound place a candle. Let nine candles be lighted all over my body, and in this state conduct me through the streets of Tehran. Summon the multitude to witness the glory of my martyrdom, so that the memory of my death may remain imprinted in their hearts and help them, as they recall the intensity of my tribulation, to recognize the Light I have embraced. After I have reached the foot of the gallows and have uttered the last prayer of my earthly life, cleave my body in twain and suspend my limbs on either side of the gate of Tehran, that the multitude passing beneath it may witness to the love which the Faith of the Báb has kindled in the hearts of His disciples, and may look upon the proofs of their devotion.[252]

While the conventional citizen seeks to acquire money, property, material possessions, fame, prestige, and security, the martyr rejects

---

[251] The Universal House of Justice, *Wellspring of Guidance: Messages 1968-1973*, p. 102.

[252] Nabíl-i-A'zam, The Dawn-Breakers: Nabíl's Narrative of the Early Days of the Bahá'í Revelation, 617-18.

them all. Instead, the martyr willingly accepts torture, rejection, ridicule, imprisonment and finally execution. In this regard, Bahá'u'lláh has attested in the Kitáb-i-Íqán:

> With what love, what devotion, what exultation and holy rapture, they sacrificed their lives in the path of the All-Glorious! To the truth of this all witness. And yet, how can they belittle this Revelation? Hath any age witnessed such momentous happenings? If these companions be not the true strivers after God, who else could be called by this name? Have these companions been seekers after power or glory? Have they ever yearned for riches? Have they cherished any desire except the good-pleasure of God? If these companions, with all their marvellous testimonies and wondrous works, be false, who then is worthy to claim for himself the truth? I swear by God! Their very deeds are a sufficient testimony, and an irrefutable proof unto all the peoples of the earth, were men to ponder in their hearts the mysteries of divine Revelation.[253]

> Consider these martyrs of unquestionable sincerity, to whose truthfulness testifieth the explicit text of the Book, and all of whom, as thou hast witnessed, have sacrificed their life, their substance, their wives, their children, their all, and ascended unto the loftiest chambers of Paradise. [254]

11.7 The Mystery of Sacrifice

The Prophet is the embodiment of the martyr in each dispensation. Abraham intended to sacrifice his son [255] in response to the test of His obedience and in order to sanctify the sacrifice of lambs as an offering to the Divine.[256] In the case of Jesus' crucifixion the prophet Himself was sacrificed: "Behold, the Lamb of God, who takes away the sin of the world!", are His words. [257] In the Islamic Faith it was

---

[253] Bahá'u'lláh, The Kitáb-i-Íqán: The Book of Certitude, 182.
[254] Bahá'u'lláh, The Kitáb-i-Íqán: The Book of Certitude, 182-83.
[255] Genesis 22.
[256] Genesis 10:13 and 22:7-8.
[257] John 1:29.

Muḥammad's grandson, the Ímám Ḥusayn, who was martyred in Iraq. And finally, the Báb was martyred on 9 July 1850, shot dead by a squad of 750 soldiers.

Bahá'u'lláh also longed for martyrdom, as revealed in this conversation with His soul:

> My blood, at all times, addresseth me saying: 'O Thou Who art the Image of the Most Merciful! How long will it be ere Thou riddest me of the captivity of this world, and deliverest me from the bondage of this life? Didst Thou not promise me that Thou shalt dye the earth with me, and sprinkle me on the faces of the inmates of Thy Paradise?' To this I make reply: 'Be thou patient and quiet thyself. The things thou desirest can last but an hour. As to me, however, I quaff continually in the path of God the cup of His decree, and wish not that the ruling of His will should cease to operate, or that the woes I suffer for the sake of my Lord, the Most Exalted, the All-Glorious, should be ended. Seek thou my wish and forsake thine own. Thy bondage is not for my protection, but to enable me to sustain successive tribulations, and to prepare me for the trials that must needs repeatedly assail me. Perish that lover who discerneth between the pleasant and the poisonous in his love for his beloved! Be thou satisfied with what God hath destined for thee. He, verily, ruleth over thee as He willeth and pleaseth. No God is there but Him, the Inaccessible, the Most High.[258]

Bahá'u'lláh's life extended until His death in 1892 and therefore His earnest desire for martyrdom in the form of sacrifice in the pathway of the Cause, never materialised. However, forty years of exile and imprisonment were the form His martyrdom took:

> The Ancient Beauty hath consented to be bound with chains that mankind may be released from its bondage, and hath accepted to be made a prisoner within this most mighty Stronghold that the whole world may attain unto true liberty.

[258] Bahá'u'lláh, Prayers and Meditations (Bahá'í Publishing Trust, 1978), 7.

> He hath drained to its dregs the cup of sorrow, that all the peoples of the earth may attain unto abiding joy, and be filled with gladness. This is of the mercy of your Lord, the Compassionate, the Most Merciful. We have accepted to be abased, O believers in the Unity of God, that ye may be exalted, and have suffered manifold afflictions, that ye might prosper and flourish. He Who hath come to build anew the whole world, behold, how they that have joined partners with God have forced Him to dwell within the most desolate of cities![259]

Importantly, Mírzá Mihdí's death on 23 June 1870 in the prison of 'Akká constitutes the offering up of a precious life in the Bahá'í Dispensation. Bahá'u'lláh exalted Mírzá Mihdí's sacrifice "to the rank of those great acts of atonement associated with Abraham's intended sacrifice of His son, with the crucifixion of Jesus Christ and the martyrdom of the Imám Ḥusayn."[260] In addition, Mírzá Mihdí's sacrifice was the spiritual ransom for Bahá'u'lláh's liberation from the prison barracks, which in turn allowed the pilgrims to more readily access their Lord. Further, Mírzá Mihdí's grave on Mount Carmel, along with those of his sister, Báhíyyih Khánum, his mother, Navváb, and the wife of 'Abdu'l-Bahá, Munírih Khanum, under the shadow of the Shrine of the Báb, constitute the focal centre of the Bahá'í administrative institutions in the Faith's World Centre in the Holy Land.[261]

There are numerous metaphors that give insight into sacrifice and martyrdom. The candle that consumes itself in order to provide light or the seed that is destroyed to make way for a tree bearing fruit are both metaphors that illustrate the fact that by sacrificing something beautiful but lesser, something far greater is achieved. The imagery of old cathedrals and churches depict Jesus as a pelican and He was called the "Good Pelican" by early theologians. A mother pelican will wound herself with her own beak to obtain blood from her body to

---

[259] Bahá'u'lláh, Gleanings from the Writings of Bahá'u'lláh, XLV, 99.
[260] Shoghi Effendi, God Passes By, 188.
[261] Shoghi Effendi, Messages to America, 31-3.

appease the thirst of her pelican chicks when there is no food or water available. A version of this narrative is that the pelican even bleeds to death so that her young can survive. This association between the pelican and the concept of sacrifice predates Christianity and is found in Roman and Greek lore. It is a powerful metaphor for the way in which the Prophet offers His life or the life of one of His kin as an act of redemption in order that humanity be spiritually revivified.[262]

11.8 Giving their Lives

Martyrs do not offer themselves as a sacrifice in order to occupy themselves an important place in history or to become heroes. Their purpose is much higher, as Shoghi Effendi has written:

> The Martyrs — most of them died because of their love for the Báb, for Bahá'u'lláh, and through Them for God. The veil between the inner and outer world was very thin, and to tear it, and be free to be near the Beloved, was very sweet. But it takes love, not reason to understand these things. We must also remember the Martyrs were called upon to deny their faith or die, as men of principle they preferred to die.[263]

Notwithstanding the acceptance with which a believer receives the mantle of martyrdom, nonetheless she or he should not deliberately expose to danger in order to become a martyr. This could be considered suicide which is forbidden in the Bahá'í Faith. "In most cases," Adib Taherzadeh wrote, "Bahá'u'lláh discouraged the friends [to seek martyrdom], and in His Tablets urged the believers to protect their lives so they could teach the Cause".[264] Bahá'u'lláh Himself

---

[262] Handal, El Concurso En Lo Alto, 337.
[263] Shoghi Effendi, The Unfolding Destiny of the British Bahá'í Community (London: Bahá'í Publishing Trust, 1981), 406.
[264] Taherzadeh, The Revelation of Bahá'u'lláh. Vol 4: Mazra'ih & Bahji 1877-92, 57.

admonished the believers to avoid unsafe situations and to exercise wisdom in all circumstances.[265 266]

> O ye loved ones of God! Drink your fill from the wellspring of wisdom, and soar ye in the atmosphere of wisdom, and speak forth with wisdom and eloquence.[267]

> In this Day, We can neither approve the conduct of the fearful that seeketh to dissemble his faith, nor sanction the behaviour of the avowed believer that clamorously asserteth his allegiance to this Cause. Both should observe the dictates of wisdom, and strive diligently to serve the best interests of the Faith.[268]

Most martyrs were killed after refusing to recant their faith and curse the name of Bahá'u'lláh. The life of the immortal Táhirih[269] is an example of this. Others were killed without warning in their home or on the street, while still others were executed after mock trials. More than 200 believers perished in this way after the Iranian Islamic revolution of 1979. However, in the Bahá'í Faith, martyrdom does not necessarily entail physical death, nor does the murder of a Bahá'í necessarily constitute martyrdom. Some of the Bahá'ís killed as a direct consequence of their relationship to the Faith were not referred to by Shoghi Effendi as martyrs.[270]

There were believers who, due to their valiant teaching efforts, were named martyrs. For example, the Hand of the Cause Mullá Muḥammad-Ṣádiq-i-Khurásání,[271] and his son Ibn-Asdaq, were both referred by Bahá'u'lláh as martyrs even though both died of natural

---

[265] S. Stiles-Maneck, "Wisdom and Dissimulation: The Use and Meaning of Hikmat in the Bahá'í Writings and History," Bahá'í Studies Review 6, 11-23, (1996).
[266] Taherzadeh, The Revelation of Bahá'u'lláh. Vol. 2: Adrianople 1863-68, 97.
[267] Bahá'u'lláh, Epistle to the Son of the Wolf, 99.
[268] Bahá'u'lláh, Gleanings from the Writings of Bahá'u'lláh, 342.
[269] Táhirih was the most outstanding woman in the Faith of the Báb as well as being a great poetess. She was executed in August 1852 in Tehran for being a Bábí.
[270] Rúḥíyyih Rabbani, The Priceless Pearl, 204 (London: Bahá'í Pub. Trust, 1969).
[271] Handal, A Trilogy of Consecration: The Courier, the Historian and the Missionary, 97-123.

causes in 1889 and 1928, respectively. Likewise, Shoghi Effendi conferred upon May Maxwell the crown of martyrdom though she died of a heart attack in her pioneering post. Keith Ransom-Kehler was another who was designated as the "First and distinguished"[272] American Bahá'í martyr, though she died of smallpox in Irán while on a mission for the Guardian. Similarly, Shoghi Effendi addressed the Hand of the Cause Dorothy Baker as his "martyr pilgrim" when she visited the Holy Land but she died later in an airplane accident. From the above it can be inferred that martyrdom is not defined by the shedding of blood. There is also the case of Bahá'u'lláh elevating His son Mírzá Mihdí —The Purest Branch— to the station of martyr, after his death as a consequence of an accident in the prison of 'Akká.

There were believers who sought from Bahá'u'lláh the honour of being a martyr, because those who perceived reality with spiritual discernment did not regard it as a sacrifice, but a blessing to proclaim the truth of the Faith with their own blood. For these men and women martyrdom constituted the most pure demonstration of loyalty and love to the Manifestation of God. Bahá'u'lláh referred to a true seeker as one who would "not hesitate to offer up his life for his Beloved, nor allow the censure of the people to turn him away from the truth". [273]

Some martyrs received special designations. For example, the immortal Badí was called the "Pride of Martyrs". In turn, Siyyid Ismá'íl was named the "Beloved and Pride of Martyrs".[274] Upon Mírzá Muḥammad-Ḥusayn was conferred the title of "Beloved of Martyrs" while his younger brother Mírzá Muḥammad-Ḥasan was referred to as the "King of Martyrs" when they were publicly beheaded in the city of Iṣfahán in 1879. On their deaths, Bahá'u'lláh wrote to Varqá about the sublime station of these two

[272] The National Spiritual Assembly of the Bahá'ís of the United States and Canada, Bahá'í News, June, 1934.
[273] Bahá'u'lláh, Gleanings from the Writings of Bahá'u'lláh, 264-65.
[274] Adib Taherzadeh, The Revelation of Bahá'u'lláh. Vol. 1: Baghdad 1853-63, vol. 1980, 2 vols. (Oxford: George Ronald, 1974), 103.

brothers to whom He called Núrayn-i-Nayyirayn (in Arabic, "Twin Shining Lights"):[275]

> O Varqá! Thy call was heard and thy letter was presented before the Throne. Praise be to God! By it the fire of divine love blazed up . . . Some of the believers are seen to be sorrowful, even fearful at the events in the Land of Ṣad [Iṣfahán]; whilst it was the Hand of Divine Might which graciously singled them out and, from the heaven of His mercy and the clouds of His generosity, caused the overflowing rains of affluence and abundance to shower upon them. The consummate power of God adorned them with honour among the people, so that the tongues of the sincere who enjoyed near access unto Him spoke forth their praise. They reached such heights that their adversaries bore witness to the elevation of their high rank. Then, at the end of their days, they attained the most exalted station which is that of supreme sacrifice; this is a station which God's chosen ones and His loved ones have at all times desired and everlastingly sought. Notwithstanding, some are sad and sorrowful. It is hoped that this grief hath appeared because of the love entertained for them. I swear by the ocean of divine mysteries that should the station of but one of the servants now engaged in their service be made manifest, the people of the world would be shaken asunder. Great is the blessedness of him who pondereth over that which hath transpired, that he may be informed of the greatness of this Cause and its sovereignty. This station which they attained was that which they themselves implored God—exalted be His glory— to grant them, and which they wished and desired with the utmost eagerness.[276]

11.9 The Mystical Dimension of Martyrdom

[275] Taherzadeh, The Revelation of Bahá'u'lláh. Vol 4: Mazra'ih & Bahji 1877-92, 73-80.

[276] Balyuzi, Eminent Bahá'ís in the Time of Bahá'u'lláh, 49-51.

As indicated earlier Bahá'u'lláh explained that there is physical martyrdom and spiritual martyrdom. According to Hand of the Cause George Townshend there are three kinds of martyrdom:

> One is to stand bravely and meet death unflinchingly in the path of God without wavering or under torture denying for an instant their faith. The second is little by little to detach one's heart entirely from the world, laying aside deliberately and voluntarily all vanities and worldly seductions, letting every act and word become a speaking monument and a fitting praise for the Holy Name of Bahá'u'lláh. The third is to do the most difficult things with such self-sacrifice that all behold it as your pleasure. To seek and to accept poverty with the same smile as you accept fortune. To make the sad, the sorrowful your associates instead of frequenting the society of the careless and gay. To yield to the decrees of God and to rejoice in the most violent calamities even when the suffering is beyond endurance. He who can fulfill these last conditions becomes a martyr indeed.[277]

Whether martyrdom takes the form of a barbaric physical act, or the elimination of self in the pathway of consecrated service to God and humanity, or pioneering to foreign lands, martyrdom is fundamentally mystical and its station and value can only be perceived with the inner eye.

Of what spiritual reality then, did these dedicated souls catch a glimpse to make them beg of God that the hour of sacrifice be hastened? From what source came the strength which moved these distinguished theologians, prosperous merchants, noblemen and women, and people of exemplary reputation to choose this path? Four Hidden Words might shed light on these fundamental questions:

> O SON OF MAN!
> Ponder and reflect. Is it thy wish to die upon thy bed, or to shed thy life-blood on the dust, a martyr in My path, and so become

[277] George Towshend, "Three Kinds of Martyrdom," The Bahá'í World, 1956, S. 865 ff.

> the manifestation of My command and the revealer of My light in the highest paradise? Judge thou aright, O servant![278]
>
> O SON OF BEING!
> Seek a martyr's death in My path, content with My pleasure and thankful for that which I ordain, that thou mayest repose with Me beneath the canopy of majesty behind the tabernacle of glory.[279]
>
> O SON OF MAN!
> By My beauty! To tinge thy hair with thy blood is greater in My sight than the creation of the universe and the light of both worlds. Strive then to attain this, O servant! [280]
>
> O SON OF MAN!
> Write all that We have revealed unto thee with the ink of light upon the tablet of thy spirit. Should this not be in thy power, then make thine ink of the essence of thy heart. If this thou canst not do, then write with that crimson ink that hath been shed in My path. Sweeter indeed is this to Me than all else, that its light may endure for ever.[281]

For both early and contemporary believers, the concept and practice of martyrdom is founded on an understanding that this earthly world is only temporary, a source of imperfections and can be exchanged for an inner realm that is characterized by heavenly happiness.

The apparent paradox of physical sacrifice bringing happiness is illustrated by the experiences of a group of Bahá'ís who were sentenced to Tehran prison. The prison had been a place of confinement and torture for several Bahá'ís but they told the guards they were happy to be incarcerated in the same prison that had previously held Bahá'u'lláh. One of the Bahá'ís cleaned his shoes in

---

[278] Bahá'u'lláh, The Hidden Words, trans. Shoghi Effendi (Wilmette, Ilinois: Bahá'í Publishing Trust, 1985), The Hidden Words, 14.
[279] Bahá'u'lláh, The Hidden Words, 14.
[280] Bahá'u'lláh, The Hidden Words, 14-15.
[281] Bahá'u'lláh, The Hidden Words, 21.

front of the guards. The guards were astonished and sought explanation for such a positive attitude upon entering the horrible prison. The Bahá'í prisoner responded that they could not enter the prison with dirty shoes because for him the prison was a holy place, which had been purified by the saints, martyrs and prophets who had inhabited it.[282] That night Ḥájíbu'd-Dawlih, the chief of the prison, who would become the murderer of Varqá and Rúḥu'lláh thirteen years later, came into the prison and ordered that the Bahá'í prisoners be flogged. One of the prisoners, who received 500 lashes, said of the prison, "This is our true home —while we lived elsewhere, we were foreigners." [283]

[282] Momen, The Bahá'í Communities of Iran 1851-1921: The North of Iran, 43.
[283] Momen, The Bahá'í Communities of Iran 1851-1921: The North of Iran, 43.

XII – The Poetry in the Dove

Regarding Varqá's literary abilities, 'Abdu'l-Bahá said that "In verse and prose he was unique in Iran in that era".[284] He composed over 6,000 verses of poetry in diverse Persian styles.[285] He was called the Silver-Tongued Nightingale by Hand of the Cause of God Ḥasan Balyuzi.[286]

It is noteworthy that, although the term Varqá is rendered normally as *dove*, Shoghi Effendi translated it also as *nightingale*[287] as in the Tablet of Ahmad (وَرْقَةُ الفِردَوْسِ , Varqá al-Firdaws, "Nightingale of Paradise")[288] and in the Kitáb-i-Íqán[289] (ورقاء هويّه, Varqá-i-Huwíyyih, "Nightingale of Holiness")

where Bahá'u'lláh identifies symbolically Himself with that mystical bird of enchanting singing.

12.1 A Mystical Name

The inspiration derived from Varqá's life has motivated thousands of Bahá'ís around the world in various generations to bear Varqá as their first name with pride and love. Similarly, believers have initiated various important educational initiatives around the world under such an illustrious and spiritual name. Examples are the Varqá Foundation in Guyana, Varqá International Children's Magazine and the Varqá School in Maharashtra, India. The question therefore stands, *What is in the Varqá name?*

---

[284] Bahá'í News Service, 1913, 362-364.
[285] Encyclopædia Iranica.
[286] Balyuzi, Eminent Bahá'ís in the Time of Bahá'u'lláh, 76.
[287] Balyuzi, Eminent Bahá'ís in the Time of Bahá'u'lláh, 49.
[288] Bahá'u'lláh, The Báb, and 'Abdu'l-Bahá, "A Selection of Prayers Revealed by Bahá'u'lláh, the Báb, and 'Abdu'l-Bahá" (Wilmette, Illinois: Bahá'i Publishing Trust, 2002), 209.
[289] Bahá'u'lláh, The Kitáb-i-Íqán: The Book of Certitude, section 16, I part.

The term *dove* has multiple meanings in literature. In history, for example, doves are used as symbols of peace and concord. After the flood, the first bird Noah sent out was a dove which returned with an olive branch in its beak representing hope and final safety in the hands of the Providence. Also in religious terms, a dove symbolises a revelation from God as described in the Bible: "And the Holy Spirit descended on him [Jesus] in bodily form like a dove. And a voice came from heaven: "You are my Son, whom I love; with you I am well pleased."[290]

Mystically, doves are creatures of both air and earth linking those dimensions like our divergent physical and spiritual natures. When flying, a dove is a symbol of the soul being released from its soil-bound time. While on ground, doves entertain us with their cooing and beautiful presence providing us with a sense of calm, relief and tranquillity.

The Manifestation of God also called Himself a *dove*. In various of His Writings, Bahá'u'lláh calls Himself a "Dove of Heaven", [291] "Celestial Dove", [292] "Dove of divine Revelation", [293] "Dove of Holiness", [294] "Dove of The oneness" and "Dove of Thy transcendent oneness".[295] He also refers to Himself as the "Dove of Truth on the boughs of the Divine Lote-Tree" [296] and the "Dove of Servitude" that "singeth in the Heaven of the Divine Cloud".[297]

---

290 Luke 3:22
291 Bahá'u'lláh, The Hidden Words, 61.
292 Bahá'u'lláh, Prayers and Meditations, 337.
293 Bahá'u'lláh, Tablets of Bahá'u'lláh: Revealed after the Kitáb-i-Aqdas, 240.
294 Bahá'u'lláh, The Hidden Words, 30.
295 Bahá'u'lláh, Prayers and Meditations, 337.
296 Bahá'u'lláh, Epistle to the Son of the Wolf, 141. In this statement, Bahá'u'lláh uses the Arabic word "ḥamámih" (حمامة) meaning dove instead of Varqá (ورقاء).
297 Stephen Lambden, "The Sinaitic Mysteries: Notes on Moses/Sinai Motifs in Bahá'í Scripture," in Studies in Honour of the Late Hasan M. Balyuzi, ed. Moojan Momen (Los Angeles: Kalimat Press, 1988), 110.

Further, the Manifestation of God alludes to Himself as the "Mystic Dove" living in the "Sanctuary of Praise",[298] on its "blissful bower",[299] "in the midmost heart of Paradise"[300] and "singing upon the twigs of this snow-white Tree".[301] The Blessed Beauty is the "Dove of Eternity" sitting "on the branches of the Lote-Tree beyond which there is no passing";[302] the "Heavenly Dove" that warbles forth "upon the branches of the Lote-Tree of Immortality",[303] "upon the twigs of the Divine Lote-Tree",[304] "in the heaven of immortality";[305] and the "Dove of Truth" standing "on the boughs of the Divine Lote-Tree".[306]

12.2 His Poetry of Love to Bahá'u'lláh and 'Abdu'l-Bahá

To Bahá'u'lláh, Varqá wrote:

> There are so many songs of love for You
> that overflow from Varqá's love-sick heart,
> that were he for even a moment to part his lips,
> they would burn to ashes this body of water and clay.[307]

An in another poem he composed about his relationship with the Beloved:

> The Beloved dwells in the privacy of my heart:
> I shall not fear the tyranny of my foes.
>
> My heart, my soul, my life, all have I given for one
> glimpse of the True Friend —and it was enough.

---

[298] Bahá'u'lláh, The Kitáb-i-Aqdas: The Most Holy Book, n174.
[299] Bahá'u'lláh, Gleanings from the Writings of Bahá'u'lláh, 36.
[300] Bahá'u'lláh, Gems of Divine Mysteries (Haifa, Israel: Bahá'í World Centre, 2002), 46.
[301] Bahá'u'lláh, Gems of Divine Mysteries, 39.
[302] Shoghi Effendi, The Promised Day Has Come, 41.
[303] Bahá'u'lláh, Prayers and Meditations, 330.
[304] Bahá'u'lláh, The Summons of the Lord of Hosts (Haifa, Israel: Bahá'í World Centre, 2002), 63.
[305] Bahá'u'lláh, Gems of Divine Mysteries, 51.
[306] Bahá'u'lláh, Epistle to the Son of the Wolf, 141.
[307] Hatcher, and Hemmat, Reunion with the Beloved: Poetry and Martyrdom, 64.

I neither desire heaven nor fear hell, for reunion
with Thee is my heaven, and remoteness from Thee my hell.

These gifts outshine the sun and moon; with such blessings,
what need have I for silver and gold.

I am a lover who circleth around his Beloved, my words
Miraculous, like the snow-white palm of Moses.[308]

A poem to 'Abdu'l-Bahá reads as follows:

O Thou! Whence God's Beauty shineth,
I know Thee.
Would my being, my soul Thy ransom be,
I know Thee.
Shouldst Thou behind a hundred-thousand veils cover seek,
By God, O Thou, the Visage of God,
I know Thee.
Shouldst Thou a King choose, or a Servant appear to be,
Apart —at the crest of each Station— apart,
I know Thee.
O Thou, the Root, Thou the Limb of Revelation,
In any garb, any garment, with any mantle,
I know Thee.[309]

It has been said that Varqá was lovingly reprimanded by 'Abdu'l-Bahá for extolling the Master, to which he responded with further verses such as:

Cease either, O shinning Orb, shedding Thy rays on the world,
to flare,
Or strike blind the eyes of those of insight, who witness

---

[308] Translated with the assistance of Hoda Seioshansian and Mary Victoria.
[309] Balyuzi, Eminent Bahá'ís in the Time of Bahá'u'lláh, 74.

dare.[310]

12.3 The Walk to Perfection

Varqá in his poems, Hatcher and Hemmat comment, "reminds one to respond to God's call and delineates in some detail how the wayfarer should tread this path. In the next poem, Varqá gives examples of the many lovers of Truth by alluding to the saints and prophets who responded to God's call by offering up their undefiled lives in the path of God. Varqá thus sees responding to God's call as a universal phenomenon:

> There is no heart that is not feverish in Your path;
> there is no eye that is not crying in longing for You.
> Anywhere there exists a heart, it is heavy with blood because of You;
> Anywhere there exists a mind, it is perplexed, bewildered because of You."[311]

Varqá's metaphors are enriching and empowering of the human soul. For example, the aforementioned authors write that for him, the "old and outworn beliefs are like an old garment. One should take this old garment off and swim in the limitless ocean of the Revelation. The old garment symbolizes the sciences, laws, and vain imaginations." [312]

Varqá's poems were hymns calling the reader to "die in the world of animal passions", enter "the realms of paradise" and "abandon the province of hell" by overcoming "all traces of self" to become "a lamp in the dark night", "a sea of benevolence on the dry land", and "an ensign in the path of love" approaching "the dawning place of victory".[313]

12.4 "O Beloved, I have nothing fitting to offer at Your feet..."

---

[310] Balyuzi, Eminent Bahá'ís in the Time of Bahá'u'lláh, 84.
[311] Hatcher, and Hemmat, Reunion with the Beloved: Poetry and Martyrdom, 32.
[312] Hatcher, and Hemmat, Reunion with the Beloved: Poetry and Martyrdom, 163.
[313] Hatcher, and Hemmat, Reunion with the Beloved: Poetry and Martyrdom, 61-63.

A central theme of Varqá's verses was martyrdom. A number of mystical planes emerge from this poetry.

For Varqá, martyrdom was like being murdered by the Beloved:

> Although murder is sinful
> for those with learning and wisdom,
> for an assassin like You
> to take my life is perfectly lawful.

Martyrdom was also like plunging forever into the Ocean of God's love:

> For while there is no one in this world
> eager for his own drowning,
> I have no desire for the shore
> here in the depths of the ocean of Your love.

In Varqá's eyes, the shedding of blood cleansed the believer in preparation for true worship:

> What? Did you think my obligatory prayer
> was lacking proper ablutions?
> Did you not know that the lover's ablution
> is incomplete without the heart's blood?

Likewise, for Varqá martyrdom was a gift offered to his Beloved:

> O Beloved, I have nothing fitting
> to offer at Your feet,
> except this meager token of my life,
> an unworthy gift for You.

Martyrdom fulfilled the longing desire to encounter the Beloved:

> There is no leaven for the friends
> except reunion with Him.
> O my heart, if you desire true life,

never forget that truth.[314]

Varqá advised that martyrdom should be accepted without vacillations:

Cannot my admonishing friends see
that my eyes are fixed on His face?
O my counselors, for the sake of God,
cease these idle cautions.[315]

From Varqá's perspective, Persia was greatly blessed by the martyrdom of the Bahá'ís. He wrote that the number slain was so great that "Throughout the land there is not one particle of soil that has not been drenched with undefiled blood". In Varqá's poetry the martyrs were referred to as "saints, pure and sanctified spirits" living "undefiled lives" who "walked into the blazoning fire until they have become sanctified from all impurities ... sacrificed themselves for [Bahá'u'lláh] because of their affection ... given their lives on the gallows of [Bahá'u'lláh's] friendship" and "shed their blood on the earth in [Bahá'u'lláh's] path."[316]

12.5 The Crown of Martyrdom

The above sections serve to understand Varqá's motivations to seek martyrdom from Bahá'u'lláh. Martha Root recalled the following story about Varqá's supplication to be given the crown of martyrdom which happened during his second pilgrimage sometime between and 1890 and 1891.

> One evening in 'Akká, Bahá'u'lláh called 'Alí Muḥammad Varqá alone to His Presence and said: "I wish to speak with you alone tonight. There is something in the existence that in most of the Tablets We have named the greatest Ether. When

[314] Hatcher, and Hemmat, Reunion with the Beloved: Poetry and Martyrdom, 61-62.
[315] Hatcher, and Hemmat, Reunion with the Beloved: Poetry and Martyrdom, 63.
[316] Hatcher, and Hemmat, Reunion with the Beloved: Poetry and Martyrdom, 61-63.

> any one is endowed with that Ether all his deeds and words will be effective in the world."
>
> Then Bahá'u'lláh arose and walked a few steps and He continued: "Even this walking of the Manifestation is effective." Again sitting down, He said: "Christ declared His Mission. The Jews crucified Him and they thought what they had done was a very unimportant matter, and Christ was buried; but as Christ was endowed with that Ether, that Ether did not stay under the ground; It came up and did Its great work in the world."
>
> Then Bahá'u'lláh turned to 'Alí Muḥammad Varqá and said: "See 'Abdu'l-Bahá, the Master, what a wonderful effect His deeds and Words have in the world! See how kind and patiently He endures every difficulty." The Bahá'í, 'Alí Muḥammad Varqá felt that Bahá'u'lláh really was showing him the Station of 'Abdu'l-Bahá, that He would be the Successor spoken of as the Greatest Branch, and 'Alí Muḥammad Varqá asked to become a martyr in the path of 'Abdu'l-Bahá. The Blessed Beauty Bahá'u'lláh, accepted this sacrifice and promised the pilgrim that he should give his life in service to 'Abdu'l-Bahá...[317]

Also, Martha Root recorded that once Varqá wrote a "letter to Bahá'u'lláh asking that not only he but that one of his sons might be martyred in the path of 'Abdu'l-Bahá, the Greatest Branch. Bahá'u'lláh replied to this petition and accepted their sacrifice, which meant that they would become martyrs".[318]

Religious artists, particularly Christians, throughout centuries in their imagination have depicted the crown of martyrdom in various forms. For some, it was a beautiful jewelled crown signalling the possession a spiritual sovereign which never will end, while for others meant a wreath of laurel representing victory of life over death, or a garland or

---

[317] Root, "White Roses of Persia (Part 1)," 74.
[318] Root, "White Roses of Persia (Part 1)," 180.

flowers perhaps meaning the happiness of encountering the Beloved. Others using halos or aureolas to add sanctity to the figure. Across all these conceptualisations, the term seems to refer to the spiritual adornment of the self, as Bahá'u'lláh reveals in His own supplication:

> Magnified be Thy name, O God, the Lord of heaven! Attire my head with the crown of martyrdom, even as Thou didst attire my body with the ornament of tribulation before all that dwell in Thy land. Grant, moreover, that they whose hearts yearn over Thee may draw nigh unto the horizon of Thy grace, above which the Day-Star of Thy beauty sheddeth its radiance. Ordain, also, for them what will make them rich enough to dispense with aught else except Thee, and rid them of all attachment to such as have repudiated Thy signs.
> There is none other God but Thee, the Guardian, the Self-Subsisting.[319]

The wonderful news is that everyone can wear a crown of martyrdom in their regular lives through serving the Cause with consecration. Although there is no need anymore for giving our own lives in violent sacrifices, we are all able to mirror in our lives the devotion of a martyr through daily deeds of service and attain the same station.

[319] Bahá'u'lláh, Prayers and Meditations, 20.

XIII - The Long Horseback March to Tehran

Tehran was 330 km away from Zanján on a road connecting many villages and small towns. To reach it required a long and tiring trip on horseback. The small caravan of armed guards who escorted Varqá, Rúḥu'lláh and Mírzá Ḥusayn Zanjání to Tehran looked more like an honour guard than prison guards. All three of the prisoners were in stocks and many witnesses asked themselves why a child should be in fetters. The rugged terrain and the bitterly cold wind and snow made the trip unbearable as told in this chapter.

13.1 Leaving Zanján

At the time of the journey to Tehran the populace was in a state of agitation. Preparations were being made throughout the country to celebrate the 50th anniversary of Náṣiri'd-Dín Sháh's accession to the peacock throne[320] of Iran. The key commemorative event was only two months away and expectations were running high. It was rumoured that the Sháh was going to pardon a large number of prisoners throughout the country.

Ḥájí Ímám was sent before to the capital in a horse-drawn artillery cart with his hands and feet chained to a cannon. This must have caused terrible pain throughout the journey on the rocky road. He arrived two days before Varqá, Rúḥu'lláh and Mírzá Ḥusayn Zanjání who were sent on horses in stocks and chains.

The populace was desperate to see the faces of the Bahá'í prisoners emerging from the fifteen days in the Zanján gaols. The fanatics in the crowd wanted to see the so-called *infidels*, (in Persian, *kafar*) who had joined a new religion, abandoning their own. Also keen were the

---

[320] Reference to the Sháh's jewelled and golden throne sitting in the Royal Palace Tehran.

ecclesiastical leaders, blood-thirsty, powerful, yet powerless to hurt the three believers due to the Prime Minister's intervention by summoning them to the capital. The clergy drew on the only means of harm available to them — inciting an ignorant crowd to hurl insults at the Bahá'ís. Like the Pharisees of a previous dispensation these divines tore their garments and invoked God's wrath on the "infidels".

Of a certainty, there was also a sector of the populace who sought to catch a glimpse of the prisoners out of genuine curiosity, for they had grown sceptical of the clergy and had seen with their own eyes everyday the clergy's corruption and defilement. At the very least there was a clear discrepancy between the ecclesiastical rhetoric and what was known of Varqá as a man of letters, a known physician, and one who had successfully defeated the arrogant theologians and priests in debate.

Mírzá Ḥusayn Zanjání years later put on paper the emotions of that day:[321]

> This was the Jubilee year of Naṣiri'd-Dín Sháh ... Jahansháh Khán's cavalry were going to Tihran to take part in the celebrations … grooms were holding the halters of the horses, pulling us through the bazaar. Horsemen were surrounding us. Crowds of the populace swirled around with people getting on each other's shoulders to have a good look. We were taken to the caravanserai of Ḥájí 'Alí-Naqi, and were made to dismount and wait for all the cavalry to foregather, so that all could march out of the city gate as one body. Spectators kept increasing. There was no passage left. It was impossible to move. In the end, they put us in a room and locked it. We were left in peace and sat down to eat. They had sent some dulmih (a Persian dish) from my home... Rúḥu'lláh said: 'We have been starving since last night. They would not give us anything to eat.' And Varqá added: 'The farrash-bashi displayed such miserliness ... gave us no supper last night. We were very hungry. Your bread and dulmih came to our rescue'... He then

[321] Balyuzi, Eminent Bahá'ís in the Time of Bahá'u'lláh, 89-90.

observed: 'These horsemen, without knowing it, are giving victory to the Cause of God, taking us with such pomp to Tihran. One does not know what is hidden behind the veil of the future. Whatever it may be it will redound to the victory of the Cause. We do not know, but He Who is the Master of Providence knows.' After a while they opened the door of the room and took us out. The horses were all ready and we were made, one by one, to mount. Rúḥu'lláh and I had little else on the saddle and had no difficulty in mounting, but Varqá had saddle-bags on his horse and found mounting it rather difficult. The head horseman told one of the bystanders to help Varqá mount his horse. That man, a Muslim, replied: 'Why should I defile my hands [by touching him]; let him mount by himself.' The sergeant-major was infuriated and dismounted. First he whipped that man, then bent his own knee for Varqá to step on and reach the saddle. While thus engaged, he was saying [a poem verse]:

'Now I know.
Aping and imitation cause a people to wither and die,
May a hundred curses on that imitation lie.'[322]

When we were all mounted the pressure of the crowd and the rush of increasing numbers of people, milling around, blocked all the thoroughfares. The horsemen of the government began beating back the crowds, who were like a billowing ocean. A way was opened for the horses to gallop through, and thus we reached the city gate and went out of Zanján.

13.2 Passing through Dízij

As the parade approached the village of Dízij, 11 km away from Zanján, the Bahá'í prisoners prepared to stay overnight. Although the villagers were already poisoned by the clergy's rhetoric, there was an element of curiosity about Varqá, who had gained a reputation as an

[322] From a Rumi poem.

accomplished poet, theologian and physician, and who was the archetype of the polymath for that age.

As usual, the divines stirred up the masses shouting:

> "Why aren't such heretics killed? You faithful Muslims what are you waiting for? Let us kill them"[323]

> "When will this land be purged of these infidels?[324]

However, the guards intervened. Hasan Balyuzi related:

> The Sartip[325] of Dízij had asked Jahansháh Khán's cavalry to be his guests. Shortly after their arrival, one of the Sartip's servants came to conduct the prisoners to an assemblage of the notables and divines. Soldiers with their rifles were well in evidence. Mírzá Ḥusayn Zanjání writes, 'I was sure they had brought us from Zanján to this place to kill us. Varqá had thought likewise.' They were made to sit on a dais, all eyes fixed on them. Then they were collectively arraigned. Varqá bravely withstood their assaults.[326]

From the crowd a mullá began to remonstrate with Varqá, claiming he had fallen from being a consummate figure to an apostate. Varqá replied:

> You do not understand the meaning of the term apostate. We have not turned back, we have not denied our faith, we have moved forward. Moreover, I have inherited my faith from my father. This child [Rúḥu'lláh] is a third generation Bahá'í, and I testify to the truth of my father's faith.[327]

---

[323] Darius Shahrokh, Varqá and Son: The Heavenly Doves, 22.
[324] Faizi, Fire on the Mountain Top, 87.
[325] Brigadier general
[326] Balyuzi, Eminent Bahá'ís in the Time of Bahá'u'lláh, 90.
[327] Kazemzadeh, Varqá and Rúhu'llah: Deathless in Martyrdom, 40.

Overcome by Varqá's genius, the crowd turned to Rúḥu'lláh, but Rúḥu'lláh was also invincible. He stated that he was not an apostate because he had adopted the religion of his father. "I am just like you", he said, which infuriated some divines. One person thought that Rúḥu'lláh's intended meaning was that he was also a Muslim, but Varqá went on to explain that the boy, like the others, had been born into his father's religion. Blind to the truth and impotent to affect change in the prisoners, the crowd turned their raging attention to Rúḥu'lláh's unfettered feet. They called a carpenter to make a pair of fetters for the child.

> "This child is insulting holy divines. And why he is not fettered?" the priests screamed.[328]

The carpenter who responded to the summons was surprised by the request because stocks, in his experience, were only made for adults. "Besides, what was the point of restraining an innocent child?" he asked himself, but nonetheless complied with the instructions and attended to the task.

However, the boy never complained. The next day he, together with his father and Mírzá Ḥusayn Zanjání continued the march with radiant acquiescence, elevating his spirit and that of the group by chanting prayers and reciting poems he composed.

A child prisoner in fetters riding a horse escorted by armed guards was an unusual scene and it provided an opportunity for conversations about the Bahá'í Faith with those whom they met along the 333 km stretch between Zanján and Tehran.

13.3 Soltaniyeh

After Dízij they stopped in Soltaniyeh, the old capital of the Ilkháni Mogul dominion. They passed through the majestic Soltanieh which

---

[328]Balyuzi, Eminent Bahá'ís in the Time of Bahá'u'lláh, 90.

would later inspire Louis Bourgeois, the architect of the Bahá'í Temple in Wilmette, America.[329]

This magnificent 14th century mausoleum stood on the horizon signalling to travellers that their arrival in Zanján was imminent. It was crowned with a beautiful and turquoise dome that could be seen from all directions –a blessing and a promise for the tired traveller hoping to reach his or her destination. Contrary to the reception received in Dízij, the prisoners were warmly welcomed by the population in Soltaniyeh who were aware of Varqá's fame as a poet and a medical practitioner.

Soltanieh was the domain of Jahansháh Khán, an influential tribal leader in whose service was the cavalry taking the Bahá'ís. His son made a special welcome to the prisoners and treated them respectfully.

As the journey continued the guards avoided passing through the cities of Qazvín and Kareidan —the native village of Mírzá Ḥusayn Zanjání— fearing that the Bahá'ís might attempt to free the beloved prisoners.

13.4 The Chains Might Fly Off to Heaven

The caravan continued advancing toward Tehran. Periodically the guards checked and tightened the chains and fetters, as they feared the fetters "would fly off into heaven" or that the Bahá'ís would attack them.[330]

Varqá suffered greatly. He was a large man, the travel was slow, and each time the horse moved the weight of the stocks tied to his ankles pulled on his legs creating considerable pain.

According to the historian Kazem Kazemzadeh:

---

[329] Benjamin Tiven, "Hossain Amanat," Bidoun, Spring 2013, https://bidoun.org/articles/hossein-amanat.

[330] Kazemzadeh, Varqá and Rúhu'llah: Deathless in Martyrdom, 40.

Many years later, when telling the story to his grandson, Ḥájí Ímám remembered that the guard (farrásh) who was chaining him, fumbled and took a long time, probably because of inexperience. The prisoner could not restrain himself and said to the guard, "After all the many years of service as guard, you still don't know how to chain people's feet". The guard, infuriated by this remark, grabbed an iron bard and hit Ḥájí Ímám on the head. The scar remained.[331]

13.5 Proud of their Chains

The trip to the capital was made under severe winter conditions which at that time of the year the temperature was below zero. The road was covered with snow. As the prisoners were leaving a village, Varqá noticed that Rúḥu'lláh was covering his feet with his 'abá. Later the father asked,

> "Why did you, dear son, cover your feet? Were you ashamed of the chains? You should be proud of them rather than ashamed".
>
> "No, father [áqá ján, "dear father", a form of addressing one's father]," Rúḥu'lláh said. "I covered my feet because it was cold. I am not ashamed of chains."[332]

13.6 The Scared Soldier

Upon arriving at a certain village, a young man began to have a conversation with Rúḥu'lláh. The young man's father-in-law decided to play a practical joke. He asked the guards to pretend to arrest the young man as if he were a believer.

Two of the soldiers addressed the young man and said: "Ah, you, so and so. You too are a Bábí and have to be chained with the rest." They grabbed a chain and put it on his neck.

---

[331] Kazemzadeh, Varqá and Rúhu'llah: Deathless in Martyrdom, 40.
[332] Kazemzadeh, Varqá and Rúhu'llah: Deathless in Martyrdom, 41.

The young man was so scared that he screamed and fainted instantly. One observer thought he had died but he was then revived. The guards explained the joke, and said to him, "What a coward you turned out to be. We were only playing a trick on you."

The young man replied: "What sort of joke is this? I almost died of fear."

A guard pointed to Rúḥu'lláh and asked, "Why is this child not afraid?"

Looking with admiration at the child, the surprised victim replied, "But he is a Bábí." [333]

13.7 A Cavalry Died

The officer in charge, a sergeant-major, wanted to alleviate Varqá's agony. When his horse moved suddenly, the saddle rubbed against the chains and fetters, so the sergeant-major ordered that the saddles be removed and placed on another horse.

But others were not so kind. According to Darius Shahrokh, "…the attendant at times would whip Varqá's horse for the sudden jerk to hurt him even more. Many of these ignorant people believed, and still believe, that the more vicious they could treat the Bahá'ís, the higher their reward would be in heaven."[334]

One of those merciless guards was Atakishi. According to Ḥasan Balyuzi:

> To Atakishi, one of those two, the sergeant made the observation that indeed by the way he maltreated the prisoners

[333] Kazemzadeh, Varqá and Rúhu'llah: Deathless in Martyrdom, 40.
[334] Darius Shahrokh, Varqá and Son: The Heavenly Doves, 23.

> he bore resemblance to Azraq the Syrian.[335] (Azraq-i-Shami was a man notorious for causing the captive family of Ímám Ḥusayn to suffer gravely, after the tragedy of Karbila.) To that appropriate observation Atakishi had the temerity to retort: "Not so, not so. It is these people who are Azraqs of the present day. Now we must take our revenge. They think that they are the Ímáms and we are the Syrians (Shimrs), while it is we who are the Ímáms and they who are the Syrians."[336]

Atakishi added: "These are infidels. The more they suffer, the more it pleases God." And Varqá simply replied: "Let God judge between us." [337]

Shortly after this interaction the group found Atakishi on the road. He was lying beside a water source where he had stopped to smoke and was suffering from strong convulsions. He complained of a sharp pain in his stomach and was taken immediately to Karaj. Varqá prescribed a medicine but Atakishi died the next day on arrival in Tehran.

Varqá was plagued with feelings of guilt. He lamented the fact that he called for God's judgement instead of enduring the persecution at the hands of Atakishi. Feeling remorseful, he said, "I should have forgiven him, and prayed the Lord to guide him on the path of truth."[338]

13.8 The Sergeant-Major Embraces the Faith.

Among the guards there were two who showed affection for Rúḥu'lláh. They had never seen a child so extraordinary and so charming. The sergeant-major wanted to lighten the load of the chain but Rúḥu'lláh stated that he should comply with the orders of his superiors. This officer had "listened carefully to the conversations that

---

[335] In this context, the term "Syrians" is historical specific to the 7th Century and refers to the he cruel-hearted people who killed Ímám Ḥusayn (Muhammad's grandson) in Karbilá in 680 AD.

[336] Balyuzi, Eminent Bahá'ís in the Time of Bahá'u'lláh, 91.

[337] Kazemzadeh, Varqá and Rúhu'llah: Deathless in Martyrdom, 41.

[338] Kazemzadeh, Varqá and Rúhu'llah: Deathless in Martyrdom, 41.

they [the believers] had with the Mullás and was convinced of the truth of their arguments.[339]

It has been reported that at the end of the journey, after witnessing the behaviour, spirituality and innocence of the three prisoners, this sergeant-major secretly accepted the Bahá'í Faith.[340]

13.9 The Long Journey

None of the three Bahá'ís knew the fate that awaited them in the capital. However, they were prepared to embrace martyrdom if the hour came. Although free from the claws of the Zanján clerics and the Governor's vacillations, their destiny was uncertain and at the mercy of the Prime Minister.

One is tempted to speculate, what they would be thinking traversing those desolate and barren distances for entire days where the only noise was the wind whistling as if nature was talking to them. The monotonous cadence of the horses trotting, sounding probably like mysterious echoes from past ages reverberating from the desolate mountains, transporting their thoughts in profound reflection and meditation. Would Varqá and Rúḥu'lláh be thinking of their pilgrimages to Bahá'u'lláh and 'Abdul-Bahá? Would they be sharing those stories with Mírzá Ḥusayn Zanjání eager to learn more and more about what it would be like to be in the Blessed Perfection's presence? Would Bahá'u'lláh was watching them from above, would He be proud of them? What would He be communicating to them in those rapidly-changing circumstances in their lives? Rúḥu'lláh may have also been thinking about his mother and brothers —would he be seeing them again? Where would they be staying in Tehran? Would he see his beloved grandfather one more time? Too many unanswerable questions and too much food for thought while gazing towards a horizon that kept moving ahead of them like an unreachable mirage.

---

[339] Kazemzadeh, Varqá and Rúhu'llah: Deathless in Martyrdom, 41.
[340] Kazemzadeh, Varqá and Rúhu'llah: Deathless in Martyrdom, 90.

Varqá would probably be chanting aloud his odes reminding himself that they were there for the Beloved:

I hearkened unto the arch of Your brow
and became entangled in Your jet black hair;
I know not whether to call You the Praiseworthy One,
or simply He who is Just.

With Your fathomless elegance and beauty
You are the destroyer of the gnostic lover;
With the plentitude of Your heavenly virtues,
You are the object of every pious scholar's quest.

O those of you who are insane with love,
since the pious ones are ignorant of the ecstasy
of your love for the Beloved of Hearts,
conceal if you can the secrets of your heart.[341]

For days the prisoners kept moving through the rocky road flanked on the left by the rugged slopes of the Alborz ranges and on the right by the vastness of the Iranian plateau until finally, exhausted, they sighted from the distance the imponent gate to enter the city of Tehran.

[341] Hatcher, and Hemmat, Reunion with the Beloved: Poetry and Martyrdom, 63.

XIV - The Anbár Prison

The entourage arrived in the capital around the end of March 1896.[342] On the third day they were taken to the notorious Anbár prison where they were incarcerated in chains. After approximately four weeks of their arrival, Naṣiri'd-Dín Sháh was assassinated in public by a revolutionary an event precipitating the martyrdom of Varqá and Rúḥu'lláh on 1 May 1896.

14.1 Arriving in Tehran

Upon arrival Varqá, Rúḥu'lláh and Mírzá Ḥusayn Zanjání were taken to the stable of General Jahansháh Khán whose son in Soltanieh, as seen in the previous chapter, received the three Bahá'ís well. In his service was the cavalry accompanying Varqá.

On the second day they were taken to the house of the brother of the governor of Zanján called the Mu'ínu'd-Dawlih. Like his sibling Ahmad Khán, he was an influential public bureaucrat who during his life occupied various governmental roles including Master of the Household, Court Chamberlain, and Governor of Mázindarán.

'Azízu'llah, Varqá's eldest son by then 15 years of age, who had departed from Zanján earlier than his father and younger brother, was allowed into the prison for a visit. He was of course distressed to see them in that situation. His father advised him not to come back because 'Azízu'llah could also be put in prison if recognized.

At the Mu'ínu'd-Dawlih's residence they met Ḥájí Ímám who had arrived a few days before. It was here that Varqá's property was pillaged by a group led by the brutish Náyib Nasru'lláh, the warden

---

[342] This is assuming that people are unlikely to travel on horseback during Ramaḍán because of the hardships derived from fasting. Ramaḍán finished in the middle of March 1896. Added to this is required the 10 to 15-day horseback trip to traverse 330 km.

of the Tehran prison. Among his possessions were Bahá'u'lláh's robe and a watercolour portrait of the Báb. The portrait of the Báb was seized by Ḥájíbu'd-Dawlih, an influential court minister, who showed it to the Sháh as a war trophy.[343] That the matter had reached Naṣiri'd-Dín Sháh's personal attention meant that the Bahá'í prisoners were now under special scrutiny. Though Varqá pleaded not to be separated from these relics, it was in vain. Varqá said that these were the only items precious to him and he now had to give them up as a sacrifice in the path of service to the Cause of Bahá'u'lláh.

On the third day the four Bahá'ís, Varqá, Rúḥu'lláh, Mírzá Ḥusayn Zanjání and Ḥájí Ímám were paraded through the bazaar and the main avenues to where the interrogations were going to take place. Avenue Firdawsi was full of spectators eager and curious to know what the Bábís were like. According to Ḥasan Balyuzi:

> They were marched down that avenue, surrounded by farrashes [royal footmen] and executioners dressed in red, to Maydan-i-Tupkhánih (Artillery Square) —later Maydan-i-Sipah (Army Square) — dragging their chains with them. There, governmental quarters were close by. Proceedings in the Chamber of Justice (which Mírzá Ḥusayn Zanjání called the 'Quintessence of Tyranny') were futile and inconsequential.[344]

At that time Bahá'ís were routinely charged with being infidels, with apostasy, and with conspiracy against the government. The usual judicial procedure was to send the accused for interrogation under torture. Without being convicted, the prisoners might stay indefinitely in a state of legal limbo unless a large bribe was offered in exchange for their freedom. Despite the injustice of the Qájár system, the conviction would not amount to execution, a sentence for which monarch's assent would be required given especially that the four Bahá'ís were direct prisoners of the Prime Minister.

---

343 Masumian, and Masumian The Báb in the World of Images, 346.
344 Balyuzi, Eminent Bahá'ís in the Time of Bahá'u'lláh, 92.

Consequently, the four Bahá'ís were sent to the King's prison charged with being Bahá'ís. In this, the infamous and influential Ḥájíbu'd-Dawlih played a decisive role after talking to the Sháh because of his overt hatred for the Faith of Bahá'u'lláh.[345]

14.2 The Two Ḥájíbu'd-Dawlihs

The First Ḥájíbu'd-Dawlih

Several individuals held the title of Ḥájíbu'd-Dawlih during the Qajar era, including Ḥájí 'Alí Khán Mughaddam Maraghí (1807–1867). His birth name was Ja'far-Qulí K͟hán (1863-1928). He was a native of Marág͟hih, a city 140 km south of Tabríz and the location of a famous astronomical observatory established in 1259. In Marághih, at the age of ten years he was employed by the monarch of the time. He descended from a family whose ancestors had rendered great war services to the crown.

Ḥájíbu'd-Dawlih was a courtier who soon rose through governmental ranks to reach the position of treasurer. To him were given grandiose titles such as Etemad-ol-Saltaneh (The King's Confidant) and Zia al-Molk (the Light of the Kingdom). However, Ḥájíbu'd-Dawlih was accused of misusing his position and of abuse of power including misappropriation of public funds and of private property. As a result, he was dismissed and imprisoned for one year. Eventually, he was pardoned and through royal family influences he regained his position. In 1848-9 Ḥájíbu'd-Dawlih was appointed farrásh-báshí, that is, headfootmen which was the equivalent to chief of the royal house.[346] Dr Polak, a Polish personal physician to the sovereign described him as "a man without heart and, on command, ready for

[345] Balyuzi, Eminent Bahá'ís in the Time of Bahá'u'lláh, 92.
[346] Moojan Momen, The Bábí and Bahá'í Religions 1844-1944: Some Contemporary Western Accounts, 491 (Oxford: George Ronald, 1981).

any cruelty" [347] and Shoghi Effendi called him a "bloodthirsty fiend".[348]

He is also known in history for executing the cruel Prime Minister Amír Kabír in 1852 under the direct order of the sovereign. It is because of this execution that the title Ḥájíbu'd-Dawlih was awarded to him, a rhetorical royal designation meaning "one who covers the government". This Ḥájíbu'd-Dawlih will be remembered in history for his brutality and for the murder of many believers including Ṭáhirih in 1852. [349] In 1859 the incumbent Prime Minister and Ḥájíbu'd-Dawlih were both dismissed.

With the constant support of the wife of the previous Sháh, Ja'far-Qulí Khán, the second Ḥájíbu'd-Dawlih, became as the governor of the provinces of Khuzistan, Luristan and Bakhtiari. Due to his injustice, local tribes rebelled against him and Ḥájíbu'd-Dawlih was summoned to the capital. However, he was not disciplined but given the Ministry of Justice and later the Ministry of Endowments. After those posts, he was appointed governor of the province of Hamadan.[350] Part of his power derived from his marriage to Princess Kokab Saltaneh, the eldest daughter of Mas'úd Mírzá who, in turn, was the eldest and powerful son of Náṣiri'd-Dín Sháh.

Dr Polak, a Polish personal physician to the sovereign described him as "a man without heart and, on command, ready for any cruelty"[351] and Shoghi Effendi called him a "bloodthirsty fiend". [352] Shoghi Effendi related Ḥájíbu'd-Dawlih's fate in *God Passes By*:[353]

---

[347] Momen, The Bábí and Bahá'í Religions 1844-1944: Some Contemporary Western Accounts, 491.
[348] Shoghi Effendi, God Passes By, 83.
[349] Momen, The Bahá'í Communities of Iran 1851-1921: The North of Iran, 491.
[350] Niloofar Kasra, "Haj Ali Khan Hajib Al-Dawlah," Institute of Iranian Contemporary Historical Studies News, 2015, http://www.iichs.ir/News-619/حاج--اول-اعتمادالسلطنه-ا%E2%80%8Cعلی%E2%80%8Cخان-
حاجب%E2%80%8Cالدوله/?id=619.
[351] Momen, The Bábí and Bahá'í Religions 1844-1944: Some Contemporary Western Accounts, 491.
[352] Shoghi Effendi, God Passes By, 83.
[353] Shoghi Effendi, God Passes By, 83.

> Ḥájíbu'd-Dawlih, that bloodthirsty fiend, who had strenuously hounded down so many innocent and defenseless Bábís, fell in his turn a victim to the fury of the turbulent Lurs,[354] who, after despoiling him of his property, cut off his beard, and forced him to eat it, saddled and bridled him, and rode him before the eyes of the people, after which they inflicted under his very eyes shameful atrocities upon his womenfolk and children.

The Second Ḥájíbu'd-Dawlih

The second Ḥájíbu'd-Dawlih, Ja'far-Qulí Khán (1863-1928), was responsible for the death of Varqá and Rúḥu'lláh in 1895. This individual entered to the service of the Shah as a child and accompanied to the monarch twice to Europe. In 1892 he was appointed farrásh-báshí of the court. Ḥájíbu'd-Dawlih was the nephew of the brother to the Shah's mother.

As farrásh-báshí, he also acted as the Sháh's aide-de-camp. There was much power in his hands, including overseeing servants and guards. In addition to this, he was the head of the royal executioners. These executioners, dressed in distinctive scarlet clothes, terrorised and tortured the prisoners, sometimes to death.

There was much power in his hands, including overseeing servants and guards. In addition to this, he was the head of the royal executioners. These executioners, dressed in distinctive scarlet clothes, terrorised and tortured the prisoners, sometimes to death.

Ervand Abrahamian wrote of the Qájár judiciary system:[355]

[354] An Iranian ethnic group living mostly in western and south-western Iran.
[355] Ervand Abrahamian, Tortured Confessions: Prisons and Public Recantations in Modern Iran (University of California Press, 1999), 19-20.

Although nineteenth-century Iran kept judicial torture behind closed doors, formal punishments were performed in full public view—often in the Maydan-e Falakeh (Flogging Square). They were carried out by the Mir Ghazabs (masters of Wrath) and their farrash (footmen). The Masters of Wrath were also known as the Nasaqchis—literally, those who both "mutilate the body" and "restore order to the body politic". Wearing black hats and bright red coats, the Masters of Wrath led royal processions and displayed to the public the brute power of their sovereign. In appointing provincial governors, the Sháh bestowed on them both a Mir Ghazab and a jeweled dagger to symbolize his royal prerogatives over life and death … the Masters of Wrath performed their duties in public squares—flogging feet and backs; gouging out eyes; and chopping off fingers, feet, ears, and tongues. They also executed the condemned by hanging them in public squares, hurling them from city walls, or blowing them away with cannon shots.

The condemned were paraded throughout the bazaar before ascending the public scaffold. In nineteenth century Tehran, the scaffold was an octagonal brick platform with a mastlike pole in the Maydan-e Qayek (Boat Square) adjacent to the Ark-e Sháhi (Royal Citadel). At the turn of the twentieth century, executions were moved to the expansive Maydan-e Tupkhaneh (Cannon Square) inside the Royal Citadel between the ministries, the telegraph office, and the Anbár-e Shahi (royal Storehouse), a warehouse used also as an imperial dungeon. This Anbár became synonymous first with habs (dungeon) and later with zendan (prison). It was also known colloquially as the Falakeh both because its courtyard had a circular view of the sky (falak) and because the bastinado (falak) was administered there. Victims could enjoy a heavenly view while receiving their lashes.

14.3 The Anbár

The Anbár, literally translated as warehouse or depot, was the generic term for prisons in the nineteenth century and prisoners were called Anbáris. The Anbárs were a place for criminal and ordinary prisoners, however in times of the Qájár dynasty they also became spaces for political prisoners. The Anbár to which Varqá and Rúḥu'lláh were sent was called "Anbár-i-Sháhí" (the King's Prison) referred to in the previous paragraph. Ḥájíbu'd-Dawlih was the chief of the prison.

The Anbár was situated at the south-east of the Maydan-i-Arg,[356] the public square which was part of the royal palace complex. This was a big closed enclosure controlled by the military which gives access to the main palace complex through a guarded portal. Around the square, the telegraph and the notary public offices as well as other public departments such as a "reclamation" office were located.

The Anbár was located next to the Naqqareh Portal. The word *Naqqareh* stands for kettledrums. These portals were used for announcing important news to the public accompanied by the sound of those instruments.

> The Naqqareh Khaneh [kettledrums building] portal was built opposite the big portal of Takht-e Marmar yard connected to the southern fortification of the citadel. It had a gate linking the city and the royal citadel together. On its either sides were upper and lower rooms where citadel sentinels and guards on duty were positioned. Later it served as a prison [Anbár] too. Gates were closed at night.[357]

The prison was created by Naṣiri'd-Dín Sháh in the middle of his reign to replace the infamous Síyáh-Chál (the dungeon) where Bahá'u'lláh had been chained 44 years previously. The Síyáh-Chál had been demolished in 1868 to build a splendid new royal opera house which

---

[356] Citadel plaza.

[357] Handicrafts and Tourism Organization Iranian Cultural Heritage, Nomination of Golestan Palace for Inscription on the World Heritage List (Tehran 2012), 84. https://whc.unesco.org/uploads/nominations/1422.pdf.

ironically served as the place for Naṣiri'd-Dín Sháh's funeral in 1896 that took place a few days after Varqá's and Rúḥu'lláh's martyrdom. The Síyáh-Chál and the Anbár were within a short distance.

The Anbár was a primitive prison without cells, windows, sources of light, or ventilation. The floor on which the prisoners sat was muddy and damp and riddled with vermin. The prisoners were chained to each other in groups of six or seven or individually chained standing at the wall for further punishment.[358]

Anyone whom the government wanted to die in prison was imprisoned in the Anbár. The prisoners' chains were so heavy that the prisoners could barely bear their weight. To go to the toilet they had to be unchained from the others causing a high degree of discomfort to all. Hunger was constant as their diet consisted of dry bread and water, unless family or friends were able to bring food to the prison.

Murderers, robbers, and political prisoners were assembled together in the Anbár. The Anbár was also used as a torture and execution site. It epitomised the miseries of Qájár society.

In this setting, Varqá and his companions appeared as a shining light. Many other Bahá'ís had previously been held there, including the Hand of the Cause Ḥájí Akhund and Trustee of the Ḥuqúqu'lláh, Ḥájí Amín. A group of Bahá'í women from Tehran ensured a supply of food and clean clothes for the prisoners where possible. In general, the Anbár was a place familiar to the oppressed Bahá'í community living in the capital.

Yaghoub Khazae describes the conditions of this Anbár in the following terms:[359]

---

358 Mohammad Reza Rezaeian Koochi, Ghadir Najafzadeh Shavaki, and Sajad Moradi, "Analysis of Some Punishment Practices Based on Legal-Historical Principles of Iranian Society: Qajar Dynasty Case Study," Journal of History Culture and Art Research 6, no. 2, 647-654 (2017).

359 Yaghoub Khazaei, "An Analysis of the Pre-Modern and Modern Prison Structure Case Study: Tehran's Anbár and Qasr Prisons," Journal of Historical Researches 10, no. 38, 13-30 (2018).

> … the Anbár was located southeast of the Arg Square. There was a dark corridor, four meters wide and fifty feet long, leading to the small door of the Anbár. Upon entering the warehouse door, a courtyard five meters wide and approximately eighty meters long came up. In the southern part of this narrow courtyard, there was an arched façade, the floor of which was two steps above the floor of the courtyard.
>
> To the right and left of the arches, spikes were installed on the wall. Behind these arches, there was an eight-meter-wide covered hall, the same length as the yard, which was not very bright, and prisoners were imprisoned in this large hall. When the weather was sunny, the prisoners were brought from the hall to the front arch with the chains around their necks, and the top of the chains were locked to the spikes in the arches. In addition, prisoners were in turns transferred from the hall to the arches to be ventilated and sunbathed. Throughout the back hall, spikes were mounted all over the ground and there were strong iron rings sitting in intervals. After dinner and going to the toilet, the prisoners laid on either side of the fixed wooden beam on either side of the floor, with their feet inside the middle pole.
>
> The prisoners were lying on the floor so that the prison guards could easily check on them. On top of the middle beam where the rings were installed, an iron rod was placed so that the prisoners' legs got locked. Although the prisoners' legs were locked in those stocks, as a precaution, the prisoners' heads were also locked with their chains against the wall spikes. In the prison front courtyard, there was a ruined chamber in the middle of which a deep well had been dug, and prisoners sentenced to death were beheaded at the well and their bodies dumped into the well.

Certainly, the conditions of the dungeon were so harsh that very few could bear them. According to Gloria Faizi:

> There were about sixty other prisoners in that place — murderers and thieves of every description— but none were treated as cruelly as the Bahá'ís. Five days later, two other Bahá'ís were brought to the same prison, but these men were not prepared to suffer for their Faith. They denied having anything to do with the new Cause, hoping that they would be set free. The jailer, however, was in no hurry to send them away. "As you are not Bábís," he said, "you can sit with the crowd of thieves and murderers".[360]

Martha Root wrote about the historical photograph of the four Bahá'ís in the Anbár:

> So they were sent in their chains to Tihrán and a photograph was taken as soon as they arrived. It was the custom to take photographs of prisoners and send them to the state. The description was written on the picture. Rúḥu'lláh's 'abá (coat) and kuláh (cap) had been taken away from him and the ones that appear in the photograph were hastily borrowed from another prisoner and put on the child. They were much too large for him. They are not his own clothes at all. Now the family actually has the original photograph that was filed with the prison record. (In the revolution of 1908 when all the old archives and records were thrown out, a Bahá'í official saw this photograph and took it to 'Azízu'lláh Varqá and the indictment, the crime, written is that they had become Bahá'ís, Bábís).[361]

It is noteworthy that in fact there are two photographs. The first shows only Varqá and Rúḥu'lláh whereas the second portrays the four Bahá'ís. The second photograph was published for the first time in 1912 in *Star of the West* in a single column article in the Persian language entitled "Martyrs and Prisoners in Persia 1896".[362] The

---

[360] Faizi, Fire on the Mountain Top, 88.
[361] Root, "White Roses of Persia (Part 4)," 255.
[362] Star of the West, "Martyrs and Prisoners, vol. 12, no. 4, Persian section (February 1913), 91-93. Unfortunetely, the story does not appear in the English section.

group photograph was the registration photo taken shortly after their arrival. In the other photograph where only Varqá and Rúḥu'lláh appear some interesting details come up, a fabric covering the background is held by two men to hide the brick wall. On the right side an officer is showing his face holding a baton and wearing a special ring. A piece of cloth similar to Mírzá Ḥusayn Zanjání's garments appears on the left side suggesting that the other two Baha'is might be sitting beside the fabric.

14.4 Contacting the Prisoners

The conditions in the prison were very severe. The prison authorities had strict instructions to monitor who was visiting Varqá and Rúḥu'lláh. Fortunately, Fatimih Khánum, a Bahá'í woman of Tehran, was allowed to see them and brought them food and clean clothes.[363] According to Martha Root, there appears another visit from 'Azízu'lláh to see his father and brother.

> When all this had taken place and they were settled in the prison, 'Azízu'lláh succeeded in getting permission to go and see his father and brother in the prison. "Rúḥu'lláh, what do you need, what can I bring you?" asked Azízu'lláh and the little brother said eagerly: "Please bring me a Book of Tablets and the Book of Prayers to read in the prison, for they took away all my books." The food was very bad in that prison and the child had very few clothes, but he did not ask for any material things.[364]

Gloria Faizi describes a strategy of the Tehran Bahá'ís to obtain information about the condition of the four Bahá'ís in prison:

> One day a young man was taken to prison, accompanied by a very angry father who had asked the authorities in charge to arrest him. The father complained that his son was insolent and

[363] Momen, The Bahá'í Communities of Iran 1851-1921: The North of Iran, 55.
[364] Root, "White Roses of Persia (Part 4)," 256.

disobedient and insisted that he had to be punished by being sent to prison.

The boy was kept in jail for three days, during which time he sat close to the Bahá'í prisoners and got to know them. "What have you done," they asked him, "to make your father so angry?" "I wanted to go to Hamadán," he replied, "and my father would not permit me to do so. In the end I decided to run away from home, but my father found out about it and had me imprisoned."

It was some time after the boy was released that the Bahá'ís in prison came to know that both he and his father were fellow believers who had worked out this plan so that they could get some information about their friends from Zanján.[365]

14.5 The Prison Chains

The Bahá'ís were put under the heavy chains called the Qarih-Kahar or "Black Pearl" [366] These dreaded chains were the ones that Bahá'u'lláh once wore in the Síyáh-Chál. The "Black Pearl" was used to pressure Bahá'ís to pay a bribe so that lighter chains would be used. Due to the weight of the chains, the prisoners could not hold up their heads. However, the spirits of the Bahá'ís could not be broken.

In particular Rúḥu'lláh found the chains very difficult to cope with. The Bahá'ís put wooden supports on both sides of his neck so he could rest at night, but even with these supports in place Ḥájí Ímám held them every night so that the little one could sleep.

In a talk given to the New York friends in 1912, 'Abdu'l-Bahá recalled:

---

[365] Faizi, Fire on the Mountain Top, 92.

[366] Qarih-Kahar literally means "Dark bay horse", and therefore, the expression "Black Pearl".

> While Rúḥu'lláh was in shackles, he lifted his chains and kissed them saying "Thanks God that in Thy path these chains have fallen on my head. O my God, Thou art powerful and kind. Although a child Thou have made me steadfast in Thy Cause."[367]

Mírzá Ḥusayn Zanjání wrote of a night when Rúḥu'lláh fell asleep:

> One night, when Rúḥu'lláh had fallen asleep under the chains, I saw his father caress his face and whisper: 'O God, is it possible that this sacrifice I bring to Thee will be accepted in Thy sight?' I was moved beyond words. I sat up and wept for many hours, stirred by strange emotions, though no one guessed how I passed that night ... In the morning I recounted to Varqá something I had once heard from a very good Bahá'í teacher. He had said that if he knew there was any danger threatening his life, he would run away from it as fast as he could for God has created us for a purpose and we have a duty to perform in this world. We should live and serve our fellow men. Varqá replied: 'This is true, according to the standards of reason. But in the realms of the spirit, each one of us has a different path to tread.'[368]

14.6 The Chelo Kebab

The treatment of Bahá'í prisoners was worse than the treatment of other prisoners. Frequently they were denied even the daily bread ration. Once, a rich man from Qazvín by the name of Ghiyáth Nízam was imprisoned for political reasons. He had a servant and was able to buy food and meet his needs.

Ghiyáth Nízam came to know that the four Bahá'ís did not have money and were therefore hungry. He was moved by the injustice and approached the guards explaining that he wished to purchase food for all in the prison. Consequently, *Chelo Kabab* was ordered. This is a

---

[367] Star of the West, vol. 3, No. 18 (February 1913), 362-364.
[368] Faizi, Fire on the Mountain Top, 89.

meal consisting of saffron rice and marinated meat cooked on a skewer over a fire and served along roasted onion and tomatoes with butter. Widely regarded as the national Persian dish, it is known for its taste and strong alluring smell.

The rich man arranged everything. However, the jailers did not allow the rations to reach the four Bahá'ís. "You are not counted among the others,"[369] they were told. The rich man found out that Ḥájíbu'd-Dawlih had instructed the guards not to deliver the food to the believers. Ghiyáth Nízam later said: "The fools did not realize that it was for the sake of those few roses that I watered all the thorns."[370] Shortly afterwards he distributed three silver coins to each prisoner.

14.7 Bahá'u'lláh's White Robe

Two most valued objects cherished by Varqá were confiscated on the day of his arrival in Tehran, while Varqá was held at the residence of the brother of the Governor of Zanján. Bahá'u'lláh's robe and the Báb's portrait were taken by the wicked Náyib Nasru'llah and the cruel Ḥájíbu'd-Dawlih, respectively.

The four Bahá'ís were confronted by witnessing Náyib Naṣru'lláh,[371] the main jailor wearing Bahá'u'lláh's white robe with great irreverence. According to Ḥasan Balyuzi:

> Varqá's entreaty not to dispossess him of that robe, so highly prized, did not have the slightest effect on the hard-hearted Náyib, who took it away and appeared dressed in it, to taunt Varqá. At the end, when all had gone, Varqá remarked that everything mulcted from him was of the very best, worthy to lose in the path of God."[372]

14.8 The Portrait of the Báb

---

[369] Faizi, Fire on the Mountain Top, 88.
[370] Faizi, Fire on the Mountain Top, 88.
[371] Náyib, means deputy
[372] Balyuzi, Eminent Bahá'ís in the Time of Bahá'u'lláh, 92.

Among the belongings confiscated from Varqá were photographs of Bahá'ís and the portrait of the Báb. The guards delivered these things to Ḥájíbu'd-Dawlih. He asked Varqá to identify the believers in the photos but Varqá refused. The only thing the poet did was to write on the back of the Báb's portrait: "A portrait of His Holiness The Siyyid-i-Báb".[373]

One day, Varqá requested one of the jailers to tell Ḥájíbu'd-Dawlih that he would like to talk to him confidentially. Ḥájíbu'd-Dawlih thought that finally Varqá would offer a bribe in exchange for his release.

Around the same time, 'Abdu'lláh Núrí, Varqá's former father-in-law, who resided in the capital had sent him a message asking to write a poem extolling the Sháh on the occasion of his 50th jubilee and suggesting Varqá to add a request for his release at the end of the poem. Varqá flatly refused this request: "My pen has written praises of God and His divine Messenger. Am I to pollute it now by flattering a Tyrant? Never! Let him do what he wants with me; I am prepared for the worst."[374]

Instead Varqá wrote a letter to the sovereign asking him to examine the Bahá'í books that had been confiscated and call a public meeting inviting the most prestigious religious scholars.[375] The purpose of the meeting would be to establish the difference between Bábís and Bahá'ís,[376] and to determine if there were any statements against the government or the common weal. The high priests were to be invited and pass judgement and if any fault were found, Varqá would then accept to be punished.[377]

---

[373] Kazemzadeh, Varqá and Rúhu'llah: Deathless in Martyrdom, 41.
[374] Faizi, Fire on the Mountain Top, 89.
[375] Faizi, Fire on the Mountain Top, 89.
[376] At those times, people did not understand the difference between Bábís and Bahá'ís and therefore they blamed the "Bábís". In 1852 three Bábís attempted to take the life of Náṣiri'd-Dín Sháh in 1852 in revenge for the martyrdom of the Báb.
[377] Faizi, Fire on the Mountain Top, 89.

Varqá's letter was given to the Ḥájíbu'd-Dawlih to be delivered personally to the Sháh.[378] Bitter and disappointed at not receiving a bribe, this brutal individual said:

> "What? Are you trying to convert me?" Thinking of a bribe he added "Come to the point".[379]

Filled with rage Ḥájíbu'd-Dawlih violently struck the poet on his neck with a stick —most likely in front of Rúḥu'lláh— exclaiming:

> "You are too arrogant …and your conversation today is like your presumption of yesterday when you wrote on the portrait of the Siyyid of Shíráz: 'A likeness of His Holiness The Siyyid-i-Báb'"[380]

Disillusioned, Ḥájíbu'd-Dawlih left the room. The only time he would see Varqá again was when he returned like a monster to kill him and his son.

14.9 The Murder of Naṣiri'd-Dín Sháh

As the events were unfolding, Náṣiri'd-Dín Sháh, whom Bahá'u'lláh had predicted would be "an object-lesson for the world",[381] and to whom He referred as the "Prince of Oppressors"[382] for the great harm he had committed against the Cause of God, was publicly assassinated on Friday 1 May 1896.

He was preparing to celebrate the fiftieth anniversary of his accession to the throne. It was a national holiday, the magnificence of which had never before been seen, and which had aroused much expectation. The day prior the great celebrations the Sháh went on pilgrimage to the Sháh Abdu'l-Azim shrine, located 10 km away from the Palace, to seek blessings for his diabolical reign. It was his custom to visit the

[378] Faizi, Fire on the Mountain Top, 89.
[379] Kazemzadeh, Varqá and Rúhu'llah: Deathless in Martyrdom, 42.
[380] Kazemzadeh, Varqá and Rúhu'llah: Deathless in Martyrdom, 42.
[381] Shoghi Effendi, The Promised Day Has Come, 288.
[382] Shoghi Effendi, God Passes By, 197.

shrine every Friday, which is the day for religious observance in the Islamic world.

Náṣiri'd-Dín Sháh was assassinated in the afternoon of 1 May 1896 at short range while he was circumambulating the inner shrine. It has been said that before dying he said: "I will rule you differently if I survive!"[383] He was sixty-five years old. A servant witnessing the event later recalled:

> Naser al-Din Sháh and his chancellor entered the courtyard of Hazrat Abdul Azim Holy Shrine around the noon. The courtyard's master and servants wanted to drive out people and close it to the general public, as it was the custom at that time. The king opposed and said, "Do not eject anybody from arriving. Today, I want to go on a pilgrimage like other people.' The king decided to take on a pilgrimage. The chancellor recommended, 'It is better to eat lunch before going on a pilgrimage'. The king returned, 'No, first, I go on a pilgrimage because I'm with ablution. No problem, if I eat lunch one hour later.' The king entered and circled the holy shrine. He stood on lower position of his foot and asked for a prayer rug and cloth cover for the praying seal. The chancellor went a few steps farther to bring a prayer rug. The king wore his glasses and looked at women. From the left side of the king, a person from among two women took his hand out of his cloak and stretched a big paper as a petition toward him. About a span from the king, the sound of fire of five or six shots was heard from underneath the letter. The king just had the chance to say, 'Hajj Hassan-Alí Khán hold me.' Hajj Hussein Alí Khán, I and some other servants who were near the king held him. He took five or six steps before his feet became numb. We took him to the room known as Tomb of Crown Prince, which was near the shrine. There, after

---

[383] Iranian Review, Contemporary History, 2016, http://www.iranreview.org/content/Documents/Assassination-of-Nasser-al-Din-Shah.htm.

> stretching him on the floor, he heaved a loud sigh and did not breathe any more…[384]

The news did not reach the palace immediately and the Prime Minister announced at the shrine that the now defunct monarch was only injured in order to avoid public unrest.

The assassin Mírzá Riḍá Kirmání managed to run away but was captured weeks later trying to leave the country and was subsequently tried and hanged. He was known as a person of interest as there was intelligence about his intentions. Mírzá Riḍá Kirmání was a follower of the cause of Pan-Islamism who was opposed to the corruption and immorality of the Qájár dynasty. Pan-Islamists wanted to unite the two rivalling sects of Islam, Sunni and Shí'ah, but were opposed to the Bahá'í Faith.

The corpse was taken to the royal carriage by the Prime Minister as if the monarch were alive. The Prime Minister even made a show of waving the dead Sháh's arm through the carriage windows. Thus the announcement of his death was postponed, and was communicated afterward. Upon arrival at the palace, the Prime Minister announced that the Sháh would talk to the people the following day.

Behind closed doors, the reality was different. Two weeks later the British Ambassador reported to London what had transpired at the Golestan Palace:[385]

> During this time it had got dark and candles with glass had been brought into the room and placed in a row along the floor. It was an interesting and in some ways a touching sight. The Sadr Azam [Prime Minister] reclined in his couch in the corner, dictating or listening to telegrams, and at times breaking into a sudden lament. The old telegraph clerk, who

---

[384] Shah Mirza Mohammad Khan Amin Khaqan, "Execution of Mirza Reza Kermani," 2013, http://navideshahed.com/en/news/312363/execution-of-mirza-reza-kermani.

[385] J Griffiths, "The British Role within Qajar Dynastic Succession" 52 (University of Manchester, 2011).

> had been much with the Sháh, sat clicking at his instrument, with the tears pouring down his face.

The Prime Minister had in mind to invite the Crown Prince living in Tabríz, which was 630 km away, to come to the capital and sit on the peacock throne. This task had to be attended to as soon as possible because his two ambitious brothers were making political maneuvers in the capital to usurp the throne.

In addition, throughout the country the Bahá'ís were accused of being the murderers of the king as the news about the real assassin took time to spread and political confusion was engulfing. The first victims of the political confusion were the Bahá'ís in Iran. As rumours ran fast and wide, the safety and lives of thousands of Bahá'ís were thrown in danger. The immediate response by the enemies of the Faith, was to instigate a massive campaign to discredit and repress the believers in the cradle of the Faith of Bahá'u'lláh. Sometime later the Prime Minister formally announced the facts of the regicide to a nation in shock and the persecutions diminished.

Marie René-Davy de Chavigne de Balloy, the Minister Plenipotentiary of France in Tehran reported to Gabriel Hanotaux, Minister of Foreign Affairs in Paris:

> They are seeking to agitate against the Bábís, who are very numerous ... It is unfortunate that from the first assassin was incorrectly said to be from among the members of this sect. The Bábís absolutely repudiate violence as a means of action, depending entirely on persuasion and on the purity of their doctrines, which are, in fact, much superior to those of Islam. They are now beginning to be terrorized because the murder of the Sháh has been attributed to them, and this terror is sufficiently justified by the fact that Ḥájíbu'd-Dawlih, the Farrás͟h Bás͟hí of the King, in a fury on returning from S͟háh 'Abdu'l-Azím has put to death, with his own hands and without orders from anyone, two Babis imprisoned in the Palace who had been arrested in Zanján. It is doubtful whether

> they denied their principles despite the agitation of which they were the object...[386]

Even the prestigious London newspaper *The Times* reported the next day that the culprit had been arrested and "he is supposed to be a Babi".[387] However, four days later it published a letter by the renowned orientalist Edward G. Browne advising that "the outrage of Friday last cannot be laid to be the charge of the Bábís, though it is but too probable that attempts will be made, especially by the mollahs, to fix it upon them...".[388] The Prime Minister acted quickly to identify and publicise the name of the assassin and this ameliorated the tense situation.

When the news of the assassination reached the palace, Ḥájíbu'd-Dawlih immediately entertained the idea of killing Varqá and Rúḥu'lláh at the Anbár, a place within walking distance from the palace. What he did not consider was that Varqá and Rúḥu'lláh were not ordinary convicts but actually prisoners of the Prime Minister who had called them from Zanján to Tehran about four weeks earlier. However, intoxicated by his own cruelty, Ḥájíbu'd-Dawlih acted hastily without thought of consultation with the Governor of Tehran.

Writing of Ḥájíbu'd-Dawlih's response to the assassination, the historian Moojan Momen, wrote:

> Part of his anger at the assassination must have been the knowledge that he would lose his powerful position as a result, since the post of chamberlain was a very personal appointment to the Sháh and a new Sháh would bring in someone he knew well —as indeed happened.[389]

---

[386] Momen, The Bábí and Bahá'í Religions 1844-1944: Some Contemporary Western Accounts, 361-62.
[387] Momen, The Bábí and Bahá'í Religions 1844-1944: Some Contemporary Western Accounts, 359.
[388] Momen, The Bahá'í Communities of Iran 1851-1921: The North of Iran, 359.
[389] Momen, The Bahá'í Communities of Iran 1851-1921: The North of Iran, 68.

In a government where all officials were encouraged to persecute Bahá'ís, and competed with each other to prove their loyalty to the crown, the Ḥájíbu'd-Dawlih may have wanted to show the new sovereign how committed he was to the elimination of apostates and to assure him that Ḥájíbu'd-Dawlih's reputation for murder and political assassinations was well-founded.

Moojan Momen proposed an alternative interpretation and wrote that Ḥájíbu'd-Dawlih, "thinking the Bahá'ís to be responsible for the assassination of the Sháh, took upon himself to exact retribution by killing the prisoners in the royal palace". [390] Shahrokh had hypothesized: "Now the king is dead, and he has one of the prize followers of Bahá'u'lláh in his vicious clutches"[391]. Perhaps the Sháh himself was opposed to the idea of executing the four Bahá'ís and now, eliminated, the Ḥájíbu'd-Dawlih felt free to satisfy his desire. And possibly Ḥájíbu'd-Dawlih was simply frustrated and therefore angry because he could not get a bribe from Varqá for his release as Kazemzadeh[392] and Faizi[393] suggested. Imprisoning the innocent for purposes of extortion was rampant in the Qájár administration.

The next chapter outlines the tragic death of Varqá and Rúḥu'lláh on that tragic afternoon 1 May 1896 at the Anbár prison right after the Sháh's assassination. By that time Rúḥu'lláh, according to Martha Root, "had hardly crossed the threshold of his twelfth year" and Varqá was about forty-two years of age.[394]

The martyrdom of Varqá and Rúḥu'lláh took place two and a half hours before the sunset, around 4:30 pm of the day of the king's assassination.

---

[390] Momen, The Bábí and Bahá'í Religions 1844-1944: Some Contemporary Western Accounts, 361.
[391] Darius Shahrokh, Varqá and Son: The Heavenly Doves, 26.
[392] Kazemzadeh, Varqá and Rúhu'llah: Deathless in Martyrdom, 42.
[393] Faizi, Fire on the Mountain Top, 89.
[394] Root, "White Roses of Persia (Part 1)," 72.

Figure 19: Laqá'íyyih Khánum. Courtesy: Monireh Kazemzadeh.

Figure 20: 'Alá'u'd-Dawlih, the Governor of Zanján.

Figure 21: Kámrán Mírzá, Governor of Tehran.

Figure 22: Mas'úd Mírzá, Governor of Isfahan, the Sháh's oldest son.

Figure 23: Naṣiri'd-Dín Sháh (reigned 1848 – 1896).

Figure 24: Photograph of the scene depicting the assassination of Naṣiri'd-Dín Sháh in the film Soltan-e Sahebgharan.

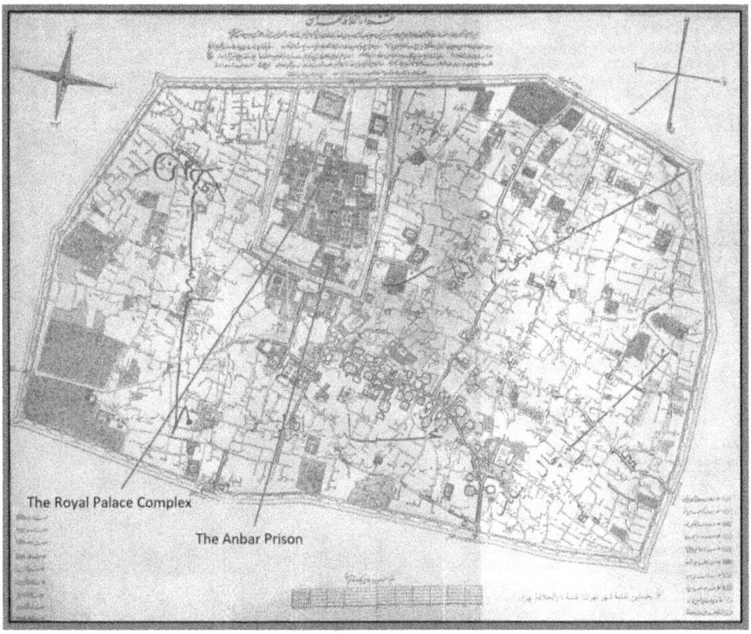

Figure 25: Map of the Royal Complex of Tehran in the 19th Century.

Figure 26: The first Ḥájíbu'd-Dawlih Ḥájí 'Alí Khán Mughaddam Maraghí (1807–1867), responsible for the assassination of Ṭáhirih in 1852 and the death of many believers.

Figure 27: Painting of the Arg Square in the 19th Century by Eugène Flandin.

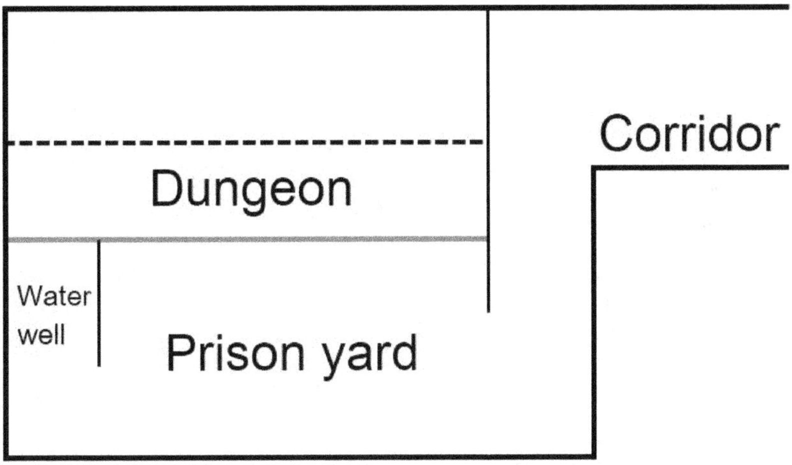

Figure 28: Plane of the Anbár prison. Adapted from: Yaghoub Khazaei (2018).

Figure 29: Political prisoners in the Anbár prison.

Figure 30: A criminal being punished with the bastinado in Iran.

Figure 31: Rúḥu'lláh Varqá in 1891.

Figure 32: View of Ferdowsi avenue (formerly, Alaé-Doulah) Tehran (1915) where Rúḥu'lláh, Varqá, Mírzá Ḥusayn Zanjání and Ḥájí Ímám Zanjání were paraded in 1896 before being sent to prison.

هو البهی الابهی

Figure 33: Facsimile of Rúḥu'lláh's Calligraphy. Source: Bahá'í World Centre.

Figure 34: Rúḥu'lláh portrait by Jill Hatcher. Courtesy: Juxta Media.

Figure 35: The Hand of the Cause ‘Alí Muḥammad Varqá. Courtesy: George Ronald.

Figure 36: Rúḥu’lláh and Varqá in chains.

XV - The Martyrdom of Varqá and Rúḥu'lláh

Not even consulting the Prime Minister or the Governor of Tehran or awaiting for the result of the investigations that had just started, Ḥájíbu'd-Dawlih, the chief of the Anbár prison, rushed to the prison with four of his executioners and a group to soldiers to commit a most horrendous crime in the afternoon of Friday 1 May 1896.

15.1 Ḥájíbu'd-Dawlih Arrives at the Prison

The sudden appearance of Ḥájíbu'd-Dawlih along with the scarlet dressed executioners at the prison and their mysterious silence made it clear to all that something horrible was about to happen. Ḥájíbu'd-Dawlih, the Anbár chief, had a terrifying look in his eyes and immediately gave orders that all prisoners should be locked in their places. There was an expectation that all the prisoners were about to be punished without reason, which had happened on previous occasions.[395]

Ḥájíbu'd-Dawlih with his four executioners stood in a row and instructions were given to the jailers to call the Bahá'ís to another building. He was shouting constantly and behaving like a wild animal. "Come with me," he ordered Varqá, Rúḥu'lláh, Ḥájí Ímám and Mírzá Ḥusayn Zanjání, "You are wanted in court."[396]

The four Bahá'ís had a sense that they were not being summoned to court at all. The presence of the four executioners, and the fact that the prisoners were not allowed to wear their 'abás,[397] indicated that the call to trial was a lie. However, Rúḥu'lláh insisted on wearing his garment.

---

395 Balyuzi, Eminent Bahá'ís in the Time of Bahá'u'lláh, 94-95.
396 Faizi, Fire on the Mountain Top, 89.
397 A type of long coat.

They were led in chains through a corridor to another chamber where Ḥájíbu'd-Dawlih gave orders that their chains be unlocked. The atmosphere was tense. The jailor's hands were shaking as he tried to open the locks. Another jailor was called to the task. The presence of armed soldiers standing on the roof of the prison gave the impression that they were there to shoot the prisoners. It was clear that this was not going to be a routine chastisement. At this time the prisoners knew nothing of the Sháh's assassination due to their total isolation and confinement.

The cold-blooded Ḥájíbu'd-Dawlih then gave orders to bring the Bahá'í prisoners into an adjacent room, in pairs. Varqá and Rúḥu'lláh were the first pair to enter the room. The door was shut behind them and Mírzá Ḥusayn Zanjání with Ḥájí Ímám stood, terrified, in the courtyard outside. They were unable to hear what was transpiring inside the room but the full story was told to them later by the jailors who witnessed the scene. This was then documented by Mírzá Ḥusayn Zanjání. The stories related about this incident by Mírzá Ḥusayn Zanjání and by Ḥájí Ímám have some variances. 'Abdu'l-Bahá and two Rúḥu'lláh's brothers, 'Azízu'llah and Valíyu'lláh, also recounted this history to Western audiences.

15.2 Varqá is Killed

Mírzá Ḥusayn wrote that Ḥájíbu'd-Dawlih shouted at Varqá: "You did at last what you did."[398] As Varqá was unaware of the monarch's assassination, he replied calmly that he was not aware that he had done anything wrong. The Anbár chief was ambiguously referring to the 1852 failed attempt on the life of Náṣiri'd-Dín Sháh by a few Bábís.

According to Martha Root, who heard the story from the Varqá family, Ḥájíbu'd-Dawlih rebuked Varqá, saying: "It is you who have murdered the Sháh." "Bahá'ís would never kill His imperial Majesty the Sháhansháh,"[399] was Varqá's response.[400]

---

[398] Darius Shahrokh, Varqá and Son: The Heavenly Doves, 28.
[399] A title for Náṣiri'd-Dín Sháh meaning king of kings.
[400] Root, "White Roses of Persia (Part 4)," 256.

Such a response angered Ḥájíbu'd-Dawlih. "Do you want me to kill you first, or your son?"[401] Varqá realized at that moment that both he and his son were definitely going to be killed. "It does not make a difference to me,"[402] was his valiant response.

Enraged by this dismissive response, the Sháh's right-hand man unsheathed his sword from its scabbard and inserted it into Varqá's stomach, saying, "How are you feeling?" The poet's last words were "Feeling better than you. Praised be God!"[403] These words manifested both defiance and joy — the martyrdom long promised by Bahá'u'lláh and 'Abdu'l-Bahá had finally been consummated.

The blood thirsty Ḥájíbu'd-Dawlih was not yet satisfied. Rúḥu'lláh had stood watching him instructing the executioners to fasten Varqá's head into a stock used to lock prisoners' feet. Then the four executioners like hyenas began ravaging the prey that Ḥájíbu'd-Dawlih had just killed. The martyr's body was hacked into pieces and literally torn it apart, limb by limb.[404] The executioners used a poniard to sever "his arms and legs piece by piece while the blood was gushing out like a fountain."[405] [406] In the meantime, the boy was shouting "Father, father, take me with you!"[407]

Valíyu'lláh, Varqá's youngest son added the chilling information that the poet was still alive while being mutilated.

In a Tablet of Visitation to Varqá, 'Abdu'l-Bahá speaks of the poet's steadfastness:

> These blood-thirsty animals tore you with darts and fangs. While in such a condition that the heavens and earth were

---

[401] Darius Shahrokh, Varqá and Son: The Heavenly Doves, 28.
[402] Faizi, Fire on the Mountain Top, 91.
[403] Faizi, Fire on the Mountain Top, 91.
[404] Balyuzi, Eminent Bahá'ís in the Time of Bahá'u'lláh, 96.
[405] Darius Shahrokh, Varqá and Son: The Heavenly Doves, 28.
[406] Mírzá Abu'l-Faḍl-i-Gulpáygání.
[407] Faizi, Fire on the Mountain Top, 91.

weeping for you ye were both happy through the favour of your Lord and ye were grateful in attaining to sacrifice and thankful in the acceptance of such a radiant gift in the Kingdom of 'Abhá.[408]

15.3 Rúḥu'lláh is Killed

Intoxicated by his own cruelty Ḥájíbu'd-Dawlih wanted even more blood. His mind was set on killing Rúḥu'lláh, Mírzá Ḥusayn Zanjání and Ḥájí Ímám. His diabolic thirst was not satiated. Guided by his animal instinct, he then turned to the 12-year old Rúḥu'lláh who had been watching in horror his father's body being dismembered. Certainly, such a carnage was among the most unimaginable butchery scene that a human being could observe, let alone a child.

Ḥájíbu'd-Dawlih ordered Rúḥu'lláh to curse Bahá'u'lláh, but the child courageously said: "No, I will never curse Him, I will go with my father…I have seen Bahá'u'lláh! I could never curse Him![409]

"Do not weep," said Ḥájíbu'd-Dawlih, "I shall take you with myself, will get you an allowance, and obtain a post for you from the king."[410] Mirroring his father's spirit Rúḥu'lláh said "I do not want your allowance or the post. I wish to join my father."[411]

Threatening the child with death Ḥájíbu'd-Dawlih said, "If you refuse to deny, we will kill you worse than your father." But the child was defiant, "You may kill me a thousand times worse. Is my life of more value than my father's? To die for Bahá'u'lláh is my supreme desire."[412] "I want to join my father, I want to be with him!"[413] was Rúḥu'lláh's constant plea.

---

[408] Thellie Lovejoy, Dwight Barstow Collection (2005), 219.
[409] Root, "White Roses of Persia (Part 4)," 256.
[410] Balyuzi, Eminent Bahá'ís in the Time of Bahá'u'lláh, 96.
[411] Darius Shahrokh, Varqá and Son: The Heavenly Doves, 28.
[412] Juliet Thompson, The Diary of Juliet Thompson (Kalimát Press, 1983). https://bahai-library.com/thompson_diary&chapter=4.
[413] Kazemzadeh, Varqá and Rúhu'llah: Deathless in Martyrdom, 43.

In a state of intense emotion, Rúḥu'lláh threw himself on the floor and while on his knees turned his heart in prayer to God. Were those prayers to release despair, or perhaps the resignation of seeing his progenitor leave him? Varqá was his companion of journey and prison, his best friend who had taught him to read and compose poetry, the father who had taught him to love Bahá'u'lláh and 'Abdu'l-Bahá and had taken him crossing country after country to see those divine Beings. His prayers had allowed him before to rise above the atrocities and miseries of the Anbár prison. At that moment, a mature perception reached him becoming aware that the end of the spiritual path trodden with his father had come and he "must give his fatal answer alone".[414] The hour of martyrdom that he had praised in his poems had arrived and reunion with the Beloved was at hand. To be reunited with his father in the spiritual realm was probably his whole prayer to God.

Defeated by the child, Ḥájíbu'd-Dawlih determined to execute the child. One obstacle restrained him. His religion prohibited the spilling of children's blood. If he wanted to remain in government Ḥájíbu'd-Dawlih had to demonstrate his commitment to upholding Shariah religious law. Ḥájíbu'd-Dawlih resorted to a legal loophole. In order to please both crown and the Mullás, and to avoid the spilling of blood, he determined to asphyxiate the child. Such a religious caricature, as Kazemzadeh characterised it,[415] represented at its best the extent of his criminal and at the same time delusional nature.

A rope was needed to strangle the child but nothing akin was available. Ḥájíbu'd-Dawlih then sent an executioner to get a bastinado. The bastinado consisted of a long pole with a rope hanging from its ends. These ends were in the shape of knots where the victim's feet were placed and then adjusted. Two people held each side of the stick, while a third strongly whipped the soles of the feet of the victim until they bled.

---

[414] John S. Hatcher, "A Sense of History," in Response to the Revelation: Poetry by Bahá'ís (Ontario: The Canadian Association for Studies on the Bahá'í Faith,, 1980), 16.
[415] Kazemzadeh, Varqá and Rúhu'llah: Deathless in Martyrdom, 43.

While this was unfolding Mírzá Ḥusayn Zanjání and Ḥájí Ímám were on the other side of the closed door, hearing only shoutings from inside the room. Full of anxiety and praying fervently, they desperately wanted to know what was going on inside. When one of the guards returned to the room with a bastinado, Mírzá Ḥusayn Zanjání and Ḥájí Ímám thought that Ḥájíbu'd-Dawlih wanted to bastinado Varqá. Mírzá Ḥusayn Zanjání said: "I dread this beating. I hope they will cut my throat or shoot me and get it over with quickly".[416]

With the doors closed it was hard to decipher the noises coming from inside the room. Suddenly another executioner left the room with a blood-stained dagger in his hands and went straight to the small courtyard pool to wash it. Petrified by what they were observing Mírzá Ḥusayn thought that the worst had happened to Varqá. By then both Bahá'ís were full of anxiety and wondering what had happened to Rúḥu'lláh. Soon another executioner came out, carrying Varqá's clothes in his arms.

Inside the chamber, Rúḥu'lláh's martyrdom was taking place. His head was put through the bastinado loops and his neck was fastened. Rúḥu'lláh's last words were "Yá Bahá'u'lláh". [417] As the executioners lifted the stick the child began gasping for air until eventually, he stopped breathing and passed out.

Thinking that Rúḥu'lláh was dead, Ḥájíbu'd-Dawlih ordered that Mírzá Ḥusayn Zanjání and Ḥájí Ímám be brought inside to be killed. As the executioners opened the door and summoned the two Bahá'ís standing outside, the inert body lying on the floor suddenly stood up, walked about a meter and collapsed again. Rúḥu'lláh's spirit was finally free to meet his father in the abode of the Beloved.

---

[416] Faizi, Fire on the Mountain Top, 90.
[417] Star of the West, vol. 3, No. 18 (February 1913), 362-364.

15.4 Ḥájíbu'd-Dawlih Runs Away

Mírzá Ḥusayn Zanjání had recorded that, unaware of what was happening, as the door was being opened, "we heard strange noises and hurried talking, but nothing seemed to make sense to us anymore".[418] They thought their end had come. However, Rúḥu'lláh's sudden movement after he was deemed dead had frightened Ḥájíbu'd-Dawlih more deeply than anything he had experienced in his bloody career.

Ḥájíbu'd-Dawlih might have wondered whether Rúḥu'lláh's supernatural occurrence was a sign from God telling that, though he had followed the letter of the religious law with regard to killing minors, he had yet committed homicide which was condemned and unforgivable. Ḥájíbu'd-Dawlih was the father of five children and the family was still mourning the sudden death of his eldest son exactly one month ago.[419] [420] This son had died around the time Varqá and Rúḥu'lláh reached Tehran.

Perhaps Ḥájíbu'd-Dawlih realised that the atrocity of his crime was too great to be justified to the new king and the court. In a moment of lucidity Ḥájíbu'd-Dawlih recognised that father and son had nothing to do with the regicide —they had been in custody for three months in both Zanján and Tehran gaols. Not even the all-powerful Governor of Zanján had dared to stain his hands with their innocent blood. Who was then he, a courtier, to assume judiciary roles and to kill without sentence? Could he not have waited and sought guidance from the government? Suddenly, Ḥájíbu'd-Dawlih realised for the first time that his entire life had been a series of criminal acts. He was horrified by his own macabre brutality. In a state of torment, he lost his mind and fled like a deranged man.

---

418 Faizi, Fire on the Mountain Top, 90.

419 18 Shavval 1313 AH -2 April 1313 AH

420 Rahman Fattahzadeh, "Mohammad Hassan Khan Etemad Al-Saltanah," Computer Research Center of Islamic Sciences, 2014, http://farabiasl.ir/portal/72-محمدحسن%E2%80%8C-خان%E2%80%8C-(اعتمادالسلطنه)%E2%80%8C.html.

The only words Ḥájíbu'd-Dawlih could murmur to his minions were "They can wait until tomorrow"[421] as heard by Mírzá Ḥusayn Zanjání and Ḥájí Ímám. Leaving his dagger with another jailor in the room he ran away like a crazy man. He did not return the next day. Probably because the next day it was announced that the crime was the result of a political plot nothing to do with religious matters and he had realised his grave misdeed.

In an ode to Varqá and Rúḥu'lláh the poets Nayyir and Siná lamented this gross injustice:

> If Háhjib thought this slaughter just,
> where was the trial held?
> Where were the judges?
> Where was an authentic decree?[422]

[421] Faizi, Fire on the Mountain Top, 90.
[422] Hatcher, and Hemmat, Reunion with the Beloved: Poetry and Martyrdom, 80.

XVI - After the Martyrdom

The Bahá'ís of Tehran may have known about the martyrdoms the next day through the ladies, who pretending being Mírzá Ḥusayn Zanjání's and Ḥájí Ímám's sisters, used to regularly bring food to the prisoners.[423] The devastating news were soon reached out in horror the believers in the interior of their country as well as the family in Tehran, Yazd, Zanján and Tabríz.

Varqá's and Rúḥu'lláh's bodies were secretly buried in an unknown place by the prison guards.[424] The two martyrs were buried in a hurry with no prayers, flowers or tears. For a period of time the location of the remains was unknown. The brothers and poets Nayyir and Siná lamented in verse the whereabouts of their bodies:

> And if he was not devoured by the wolf
> but was thrown into a well,
> what happened to the story of the bucket
> when the wayfarer said: "Ah there! Good news!"?
>
> And if like John his blood
> was poured upon a tray,
> where is his head and
> where his beauteous body?
>
> If his head was severed
> like that of Ḥusayn,[425]
> where is the pure
> and radiant body?
>
> And if by the sword and dagger
> he was hacked into pieces,
> why does no one ask

[423] Momen, The Bahá'í Communities of Iran 1851-1921: The North of Iran.
[424] Mírzá Abu'l-Faḍl-i-Gulpáygání, Bahá'í Proofs, 100, 1902.
[425] Prophet Muhammad's grandson who was martyred in Karbilá, Iraq, in 680 AD.

"What happened to those limbs?"[426]

Later the family accessed the remains and one of Varqá's sons [427] moved the remains to a beautiful mausoleum in a place which became known as the "Vargayieh".[428] [429] The mausoleum consisted of a nine-sided building where an English version of the Tablet of Visitation revealed by 'Abdu'l-Bahá for Varqá and Rúḥu'lláh was on the wall.

16.1 The Mausoleum

Several years later Martha Root visited the graves and explained:

> I had longed to visit the graves of these two great martyrs, to bow my head in humblest, tenderest reverence where their dear hurt bodies are laid to rest. One day the opportunity came very unexpectedly. We were driving out to see the Bahá'í cemetery and friends said "There in the distance where you see the trees and the garden is the mausoleum of 'Alí Muḥammad Varqá and his son Rúḥu'lláh; we are going to take you there after we visit the Bahá'í cemetery." I had expected to go there with the Varqá family, but in the busy days of speaking and writing there had never been a free hour, so it seemed good to go now and we went. In the days of the passing of these martyrs there was no Bahá'í cemetery and in fact their bodies were hid for a number of years. Then 'Azízu'lláh Varqá and his younger brother Valíyu'lláh bought a little estate near Tihrán (about twenty minutes ride by motor car from the Yusssef Abad Gate of the city). It is enclosed by high walls and divided into two parts by another high wall. The first part

[426] Hatcher, and Hemmat, Reunion with the Beloved: Poetry and Martyrdom, 80-81.

[427] Lovejoy, Dwight Barstow Collection, 219.

[428] The old cemetery was destroyed many years ago by the authorities of the previous regime due to their plan for a new road. Many families transferred the remains of their loved ones to the new Bahá'í cemetery which was purchased and prepared by the Bahá'í community. However, the remains of Varqá and Rúḥu'lláh were transferred to a building in the vicinity of the old cemetery.

[429] Luṭfu'lláh Ḥakím. "The Divine Traces in Persia," The Star of the West, vol. 21, no. 3, (June 1930), 94.

is like a miniature farm or very large garden with little houses for the caretaker and his family. Each member of this peasant family was so clean, so sweet, so spiritual, one could but feel that they had been refined and ennobled by their cherished task of caring for the garden where such glorious saints are resting.

Going through the first garden into the second was like stepping into paradise. It was still winter, but the trees, the vines, the rose bushes showed plainly that in the spring and summer the place is a haven of shade and perfume. It was a typical Persian garden with a stately little lake and the birds were singing softly. The mausoleum is a beautiful nine-sided building approached with nine paths through the garden and within are nine sides and the whole is in pure white.

O, what a real peace in that place! The sun poured through the windows as if it loved to come and dwell there! I knelt to pray and whispered first: "O Bahá'u'lláh Thou art here with them! It is the same kind of peace that I experienced in Bahjí at Thy Tomb! Thou hast never left them, living and dead Thou art with them always!" Truly it was a spiritual communion to pray in this holy spot!

Silently we passed out from that holy shrine, pressed the hands of the kind caretakers, and came back into the world of service in Tihrán.[430]

16.2 Tablet of Visitation

There is a beautiful Tablet of Visitation[431] revealed by 'Abdu'l-Bahá for father and son translated by Valíyu'lláh Varqá:[432]

---

[430] Root, "White Roses of Persia (Part 4)," 257-58.
[431] Provisional translation prepared by the Hand of the Cause of God Valíyu'lláh Varqá
[432] Lovejoy, Dwight Barstow Collection, 219.

A visitation to the one who has been martyred in the path of God, the blessed Wargha[433] with a portion of his liver[434] (e.g., the essence of his life and the light of his eyes), Ruhollah.

Upon them be Baha' El 'Abha'.
He is God!
O thou two attracted ones to the fragrances of God and enkindled by the fire of the love of God, thou two sincere ones in the Cause of God and heralds of the Name of God!
I testify verily that ye are both believers in God and that ye are accepting the Word of God.
Under the swords drawn across your throats, there arose from you the loud cry: "Ya Baha' El-Abha!"
Ye endured all catastrophies in the path of God and underwent all trials in the love of God. Verily ye both roamed the fields, the mountains and the seas and were honoured at the Holy Shrine whose light is ever shining.
Ye tarried in the Holy Radiant Threshold and begged for sacrifice in the love of Baha and hastened to the altar of the greater martyrdom with an attraction by which the faces in the Supreme Concourse were made joyful. Then ye were put under the claws of the blood-thirsty wolves and under the sickles of most cruel and savage beasts. These blood-thirsty animals tore you with darts and fangs.
While in such a condition that the heavens and earth were weeping for you ye were both happy through the favour of your Lord and ye were grateful in attaining to sacrifice and thankful in the acceptance of such a radiant gift in the Kingdom of Abha. Ye were both happy and cheerful in that which God has granted you ye were smiling and laughing for this great bounty.
I swear to God the True One that verily the people of the Horizon of Abha are jealous of you for this bestowal, the light of which will shine through centuries and ages.

---

[433] Wargha is an earlier rendering of the name Varqá.

[434] In Persian literature, liver is the spiritual equivalent to the heart as the centre of emotions.

> Then they put the bodies, severed in two, in a hole smoothed over and hidden from the eyes of others until God raised up the son of this Great One to bring forth the crumbling and decayed remains from their radiant tomb. He carried those two holy bodies to the consecrated ground and blessed earth, their lasting resting-place and placed them underneath the earth in order that they may be two radiant signs testifying to a sacrifice in the Cause of God.
> I implore God to illumine this blessed ground with a light radiating from the Kingdom of Abha and to confirm those who make pilgrimages to this holy ground through the grace of his Mercy, supplicating God to pardon and forgive their sins and to admit them into the depths of the sea of His Mercy forever. Upon ye both be Baha and praise throughout the centuries and cycles.
> (Signed) E.E.[435]
> Translated by Mirza Valiollah Khan Wargha
> Teheran, February 23, 1914.

Next to the mausoleum is the grave of the martyr Mullá Áqá Ján. Lilian Kappes was buried next to Varqá and Rúḥu'lláh's resting place. She was an American believer who went to Persia to assist the Bahá'í community. In particular, she was instrumental in establishing the Tarbiyat School for Girls in Tehran. The resting places of such illustrious souls remind us of the words of 'Abdu'l-Bahá:

> Holy places are undoubtedly centres of the outpouring of Divine grace, because on entering the illumined sites associated with martyrs and holy souls, and by observing reverence, both physical and spiritual, one's heart is moved with great tenderness.[436]

---

[435] E.E. are the initials of 'Abdu'l-Bahá in Arabic.

[436] Shoghi Effendi, A Synopsis and Codification of the Kitáb-i-Aqdas, the Most Holy Book of Bahá'u'lláh (Baháí'World Centre, 1973), 93.

XVII – In the Aftermath

This section narrates what happened to the main characters of this story after the martyrdom of Varqá and Rúḥu'lláh. It depicts the path God traced for them according to the merit of their actions because, according to the Bahá'í teachings, justice, human and divine, is sustained by both reward and punishment.[437]

17.1 Ḥájíbu'd-Dawlih

Martha Root wrote that following the death of Varqá and his son[438]

> The Prime Minister was very angry with the Chief of the Court [Ḥájíbu'd-Dawlih] He called him and demanded why he had done this hideous deed. The only answer was: "I thought perhaps Bahá'ís had killed the King and I wanted revenge!" The Prime Minister replied: "You knew the murderer was a Muslim!" That Chief of the Court still lives, a miserable, unhappy, trembling man when the Varqá name is mentioned. He still walks the streets of Tihrán.
>
> Also, the Chief of the great Bakhtáyárí Tribe whose son today has an important place in the government, wishing to hear the truth about this atrocious crime, a few years ago invited that former Chief of the Court to dine in his home. His sons were present and a few other men relatives. They asked him to tell them the whole story about the killing of the Varqá father and son. There was a reason why they wished to hear because the host's own brother had become a Bahá'í years earlier through the teacher, 'Alí Muḥammad Varqá. The former Chief of the Court did tell them everything and it was exactly as the third prisoner had related it. The Bakhtáyárí Chief and his relatives

[437] Bahá'u'lláh, Tablets of Bahá'u'lláh: Revealed after the Kitáb-i-Aqdas, 126.
[438] Root, "White Roses of Persia (Part 4)," 257.

wept, and they were so angry they beat the former Chief of the Court and kicked him out into the street.

17.2 Muẓaffari'd-Dín Sháh

Muẓaffari'd-Dín Sháh reigned between 1896 and 1907. He was familiar with the teachings of the Bahá'í Faith due to his association with Varqá when he was Crown Prince in Azerbaijan. Of all the sons of the late Sháh, he was the most tolerant of the Bahá'í community. One of the highlights of his government was the establishment of the first parliament which was "in accordance with the explicit command of the Most Holy Book [Kitáb-i-Aqdas]", according to 'Abdu'l-Bahá.[439] In that book Bahá'u'lláh wrote that in Tehran "[e]relong will the state of affairs within thee be changed, and the reins of power fall into the hands of the people"[440] and therefore it can be interpreted as a partial fulfillment of that prophecy.

His successor Muḥammad 'Alí-Sháh, however, overturned his father's achievement and reverted to an absolutist monarchy canceling the new constitution and bombarding the parliament on 23 June 1908, an event which precipitated his political downfall. His son Ahmad, was the last Sháh of the Qájár dynasty which ended in 1925. The new Pahlavi dynasty was proclaimed in its stead under the leadership of Reza Sháh (1925-1941). The four shahs to follow Muẓaffari'd-Dín Sháh, however, all died in exile.

17.3 The Prime Minister

Amín us-Sultán, the Prime Minister who brought Varqá, Rúḥu'lláh, Mírzá Ḥusayn Zanjání and Ḥájí Ímám from Zanján to Tehran and put them in the Anbár prison, was dismissed six months later by the new Sháh who sent him into exile. Subsequently re-instated by the

---

[439] Mina Yazdani, "'Abdu'l-Bahá and the Iranian Constitutional Revolution: Embracing Principles While Disapproving Methodologies," The Journal of Baha'i Studies 24, no. 1/2 (2014): 48.
[440] Bahá'u'lláh, The Kitáb-i-Aqdas: The Most Holy Book, 54.

following Sháh between 1898 and 1904, he was assassinated in 1907 in front of the parliament.[441]

17.4 Mas'úd Mírzá

Mas'úd Mírzá, the eldest son of the defunct Sháh and a renowned persecutor of the Bahá'ís in his various provincial governorships, the "Infernal Tree",[442] went into exile in Europe along with his four sons for disaffection with the government. While there, he met 'Abdu'l-Bahá in Geneva:

> In 1911 the Master spent a few quiet days in the French Alps, presumably to rest, before continuing to London. Here took place a remarkable encounter which illustrates the universality of His love, even towards those whose hearts ran hostile to Him and to His Father's Cause. Juliet Thompson tells us the following about this occasion which she herself witnessed:
>
> Monstrously sinned against, too great was He to claim the right to forgive. In His almost off-hand brushing aside of a cruelty, in the ineffable sweetness with which He ignored it, it was as though He said: Forgiveness belongs only to God.
>
> An example of this was His memorable meeting with the royal prince, Zillah Sultan [Mas'úd Mírzá], brother of the new Sháh of Persia, Muẓaffari'd-Dín Sháh.[443] Not alone 'Abdu'l-Bahá, but a great number of His followers, band after band of Bahá'í martyrs, had suffered worse than death at the hands of these two princes. When the downfall of the Sháh, with that of the Sultan of Turkey, set 'Abdu'l-Bahá at liberty, 'Abdu'l-Bahá, beginning His journey through Europe, went first to Thonon-les-Bains, on the Lake of Geneva. The exiled Sháh was then somewhere in Europe; Zillah-Sultan, also in exile with his two

---

[441] Encyclopedia Iranica, s.v. "Amīn-Al-Solṭān," https://iranicaonline.org/articles/atabak-e-azam.

[442] Shoghi Effendi, God Passes By, 232.

[443] Muḥammad 'Alí Sháh succeded his father, Muẓaffari'd-Dín Sháh, to the throne.

sons, had fled to Geneva. Thus 'Abdu'l-Bahá, the exonerated and free, and Zillah Sultan, the fugitive, were almost within a stone's throw of each other.

In the suite of Abdu'l-Bahá was a distinguished European who had visited Persia and there met Zillah Sultan. One day when the European was standing on the balustraded terrace of the hotel in Thonon and 'Abdu'l-Bahá was pacing to and fro at a little distance, Zillah Sultan approached the terrace. 'Abdu'l-Bahá was wearing, as always, the turban, the long white belted robe and long aba of Persia. His hair, according to the ancient custom of the Persian nobility, flowed to His shoulders. Zillah Sultan, after greeting the European, immediately asked:

'"Who is that Persian nobleman?"'

'"Abdu'l-Bahá."

'"Take me to Him."

In describing the scene later, the European said: "If you could have heard the wretch mumbling his miserable excuses!" But 'Abdu'l-Bahá took the prince in His arms. "All that is of the past," He answered, "Never think of it again. Send your two sons to see me. I want to meet your sons."

They came, one at a time. Each spent a day with the Master. The first, though an immature boy, nevertheless showed Him great deference. The second, older and more sensitive, left the room of 'Abdu'l-Bahá, where he had been received alone, weeping uncontrollably. "If only I could be born again," he said, "into any other family than mine."

For not only had many Bahá'ís been martyred during his uncle's reign (upwards of a hundred by his father's instigation), and the life of 'Abdu'l-Bahá threatened again and again, but his grandfather, Naṣiri'd-Dín Sháh , had ordered the execution of the Báb, as well as the torture and death of thousands of Babis.

The young prince was "born again" —a Bahá'í.'"[444]

17.5 The Jalálu'd-Dawlih (Mas'úd Mírzá's son)

Like his father Mas'úd Mírzá, this individual went from disgrace to remorse. Not only had he imprisoned Varqá as the Governor of Yazd but in the ensuing years he was instrumental and supportive of brutal persecutions of the Bahá'í community. For example, in 1891 he was responsible for the massacre known as the "Seven Martyrs of Yazd" and other barbarities in 1903 where, in Hasan Balyuzi's words, "the madness that gripped the fanatics, and the extravagances of individuals bent on securing personal gain, were intentionally not contained."[445] In the midst of this a believer was shot from a cannon by the direct orders of Jalálu'd-Dawlih.[446] According to Shoghi Effendi:

> The rapacious Prince Jalálu'd-Dawlih, branded by the Supreme Pen as "the tyrant of Yazd," was, about a year after the iniquities he had perpetrated, deprived of his post, recalled to Ṭihrán, and forced to return a part of the property he had stolen from his victims.[447]

Sent into exile, in London he sought the presence of 'Abdu'l-Bahá and threw himself at His feet supplicating miserably for forgiveness.[448] Like his father, he died sank in obscurity.

17.6 Ahmad Khán, the Governor of Zanján

---

444 Annamarie Honnold, Vignettes: From the Life of 'Abdu'l-Bahá (George Ronald, 1997), 51.
445 Hasan Balyuzi, 'Abdu'l-Bahá: The Centre of the Covenant of Bahá'u'lláh (Oxford: George Ronald, 1971), 103.
446 White, The Bahá'í World (1979-83), 975-979.
447 Shoghi Effendi, God Passes By, 232.
448 Taherzadeh, The Revelation of Bahá'u'lláh. Vol. 2: Adrianople 1863-68, 361.

After Zanján, Ahmad Khán became Commander of the Royal Bodyguard and Governor-General of Arabistan and at various times governor of Gorgan, Astarabad, Fars, and Tehran as well as Minister of War. However, he fell out of grace, was arrested and was sent into exile to a mountainous region of Iran in 1907, four years before his political assassination in 1911 at the age of 59 years in front of his house.

17.7 Mírzá Ḥusayn Zanjání and Ḥájí Ímám

Mírzá Ḥusayn Zanjání and Ḥájí Ímám were the two other Bahá'ís in the Anbár when Varqá and Rúḥu'lláh were martyred that Ḥájíbu'd-Dawlih could not kill. They were released fourteen weeks later and passed on the story of Varqá and Rúḥu'lláh to the world.

After that tragic afternoon they were sent back to the dungeon where they found that their quilts and covers had been taken away and they were forced to sit directly on the damp floor. However, they were so preoccupied with what had happened that the discomfort was barely noticed. As they had seen the executioner leave the room with a bloody dagger they assumed Varqá had been killed. What then, they wondered, had happened to the child?

The two Bahá'ís related that in the night some guards came in and discussed how they were going to distribute the prisoners' clothes among themselves when they were killed the next day. Mírzá Ḥusayn Zanjání and Ḥájí Ímám were unconcerned about the threat to their own lives. They were only concerned about Rúḥu'lláh. They begged one of the jailors who had been kind to the Bahá'í prisoners to tell them what had happened inside the chamber.

According to Mírzá Ḥusayn Zanjání the day following the martyrdom of Varqá and Rúḥu'lláh, the jailors came to demand their clothes. The jailors thought that both Bahá'ís were going to be executed. They even demanded the prisoners' socks and shoes, saying: "It is your turn to be killed today. If you do not let us have your clothes, your executioners will get them though they belong to us by right, for we have looked after you here in prison".[449] Neither Bahá'í was scared. The only property left to Mírzá Ḥusayn Zanjání and Ḥájí Ímám was some rock sugar and they gave it away to the jailors remarking: "This will give us a little more blood, so that the executioner who cuts our throats will not say the Bahá'ís have any less blood than other people!"[450]

Their visitors to the prison were put on close watch and food could only be delivered to them by the local Bahá'ís after four months.[451] For three consecutive days both were taken to be executed but each time something prevented their martyrdoms.[452]

Mírzá Ḥusayn Zanjání wrote that Rúḥu'lláh appeared to him in a dream. Rúḥu'lláh was smiling, saying: "Mírzá Ḥusayn, did you see how I rode on the neck of the Emperor?"[453] These words were a reference to his last pilgrimage to the Holy Land where 'Abdu'l-Bahá told the child: "Should God will it, He can make Rúḥu'lláh ride on the neck of an emperor to proclaim the Cause of God".[454]

Both believers continued to serve the Cause with courage and determination. Ḥájí Ímám and Mírzá Ḥusayn Zanjání were released fourteen months later and lived to an advanced age. Throughout their lives they recounted the stories of the persecution and execution of the Bahá'ís, and continued to serve the Faith. Mírzá Ḥusayn Zanjání visited 'Abdu'l-Bahá in 1913 and later died as a martyr for the Cause in Russia. Kazem Kazemzadeh wrote:

> The Bahá'ís of Charjuy in Russian Turkistan invited him to visit the town to debate with a particularly violent Mullá who was attacking the Faith. He easily bested the Mullá in argument. At night a number of the Mullá's followers broke into the house and pistolwhipped Mírzá Ḥusayn. He traveled

[449] Faizi, Fire on the Mountain Top, 93.
[450] Faizi, Fire on the Mountain Top, 93.
[451] Faizi, Fire on the Mountain Top, 93.
[452] Faizi, Fire on the Mountain Top, 93.
[453] Balyuzi, Eminent Bahá'ís in the Time of Bahá'u'lláh, 97.
[454] Balyuzi, Eminent Bahá'ís in the Time of Bahá'u'lláh, 97.

to 'Ishqábád, where he died of his wounds.[455]

Ḥájí Ímám died of pneumonia when as an old man in the heart of winter, he was preparing to travel to wash his friend's body for burial. "We promised one another that the one of us who survived the other would perform this last task for his friend'," he said.[456] Ḥájí Ímám died in 'Ishqábád. His life regret was that he could not gain the crown of martyrdom like his three Anbár companions.[457]

17.8 Laqá'íyyih Khánum

Laqá'íyyih Khánum was the second wife of Varqá to whom he married in Zanján after the divorce of his wife Núríyyih Khánum. The wedding took place sometime in 1893-1894 when he was approximately thirty-eight years of age. The divorce was due largely to the mother-in-law's pressure, a very influential lady.

Laqá'íyyih Khánum and Varqá were married for about two years before his martyrdom in 1896.[458] She was also the daughter of Ḥájí Ímám who stayed along with Varqá and Rúḥu'lláh at the Anbár prison. Eventually, father and daughter both moved to 'Ishqábád in Russia (now Turkmenistan) where a new Bahá'í community was blooming away from the tyranny of the Persian establishment. A great deal of information about Varqá and Rúḥu'lláh has come from her own oral narrative.

Laqá'íyyih Khánum remarried to Muḥammad Riḍá Iṣfahání, a distinguished believer resident of 'Ishqábád whose father had previously attained the presence of the Báb and Bahá'u'lláh.[459] [460]

---

[455] Kazemzadeh, Varqá and Rúhu'llah: Deathless in Martyrdom, 44.
[456] Kazemzadeh, Varqá and Rúhu'llah: Deathless in Martyrdom, 44.
[457] Kazemzadeh, Varqá and Rúhu'llah: Deathless in Martyrdom, 44.
[458] Kazemzadeh, Varqá and Rúhu'llah: Deathless in Martyrdom.
[459] Moojan Momen, "The Bahá'í Community of Ashkhabad: Its Social Basis and Importance in Bahá'í History," Cultural Change and Continuity in Central Asia, 280 (1991), https://www.momen.org/relstud/ishqabad.htm.
[460] Firuz Kazemzadeh, "In Memoriam: Kazem Kazemzadeh (1898-1989)," The Bahá'í World (1986-1992), 1998, 945-47.

From Laqá'íyyih Khánum, four children came to the world: Kazem, Ruha, Monnavar and Zia'u'llah.

Their son Kazem Kazemzadeh (1898- 1989)[461] who settled in the United States became the first deputy of the Ḥuqúqu'lláh for the Western Hemisphere in September 1968. Given the need to facilitate the payments of the Persian believers in that country, Kazem Kazemzadeh was appointed to that role by the Trustee of the Ḥuqúqu'lláh Dr 'Alí-Muḥammad Varqá.[462]

Laqá'íyyih Khánum passed away in Iran at an advanced age around 1945-1946. Her granddaughter Marina Banuazizi said, "I remember how sad everyone was at home and how much I missed her".[463] In his memoirs Firuz Kazemzadeh,[464] [465] Kazem Kazemzadeh's son and Laqá'íyyih Khánum's grandson, shared the following remembrances:

> One bright, warm day I stopped by the post office. In my mail box there was a letter from home, telling me that my grandmother, Laqá'íyyih Khánum, had died. Her passing was sudden and mercifully instant. I came out of the post office and sat on the steps, tears running down my cheeks. Nanejan [466], as we called her, meant a great deal to me. She transmitted to me the heroic heritage of early Bahá'í history. She made Mír Jalíl, Umm-i-Ashraf, Abá Baṣír, Siyyid Ashraf, Rúḥu'lláh, Varqá, and Mírzá Ḥusayn Zanjání come to life in my imagination when I was but a child. Her devotion to the Faith, her unusual combination of strength and gentleness, her love for her children and grandchildren, her open mindedness, and her unselfishness left a deep impression on my mind and

---

[461] Kazemzadeh, The Bahá'í World, vol. XX, 945-47.
[462] The Universal House of Justice, The Bahá'í World (1954-1963), vol. XIII (Haifa, Israel: Bahá'í World Centre, 1970).
[463] Personal communication to the author.
[464] October 27, 1924 - May 17, 2017
[465] Bahaipedia, "Firuz Kazemzadeh," last modified 27 July 2020, https://bahaipedia.org/Firuz_Kazemzadeh.
[466] "Dear grandmother" in Persian language.

soul. Decades later the mullahs[467] dealt Nanejan another blow. Their bulldozers leveled her gravestone at the Bahá'í cemetery in Tehran.

According to Monireh Kazemzadeh,

> My father [Firuz Kazemzadeh] spoke often of his grandmother, always with the greatest respect and warmth. He told me how she married Varqá at a young age, how the soldiers/guards who came to seize her husband ripped the earrings out of her ears (I have no written documentation of that story), and how she remained a faithful servant of the Faith — and a devoted mother and grandmother — until her death. She is also the source of my knowledge of Persian cooking, as she taught her daughter-in-law, my grandmother, who then taught her own daughter-in-law, my mother, who passed on the traditions to me —so I feel a very concrete connection to this much loved and admired lady.[468]

Paying tribute to the life of Firuz Kazemzadeh (1924-2017), illustrious descendant of Laqá'íyyih Khánum, the Universal House of Justice wrote at his death in May 2017:

> His valued contributions as a member of the National Spiritual Assembly of the United States over an extended period of time and his pioneering endeavours in the area of external affairs at both national and international levels will long illumine the annals of the Cause. Particularly notable were his activities in defence of the fledging Bahá'í communities in the former Soviet Union, in the latter part of the last century and of the beleaguered Bahá'í community in the Cradle of the Faith[469] [470]

---

467 Muslim priests.
468 Personal communication to the author.
469 The Universal House of Justice, May 2017.
470 National Spiritual Assembly of the Bahá'ís of the United States, "Memorial for Dr. Firuz Kazemzadeh," 22 Aug 2017, https://www.youtube.com/watch?v=CPyRspqT8Os.

17.9 Mírzá Ḥusayn Yazdí

Mírzá Ḥusayn Yazdí was Varqá's eldest brother who visited Bahá'u'lláh in 1879 along with his father Mihdí. He settled as a pioneer of the Faith in the town of Miyándu'áb in the province of 'Á<u>dh</u>irbayján in 1876[471] and married Bíbí Yazdí.[472] Mírzá Ḥusayn Yazdí attained the presence of Bahá'u'lláh in Baghdad twice and remained a staunch teacher of the Faith. This strong believer died in 1915.[473]

17.10 Núríyyih - Varqá's First Wife

According to Barron Harper in his book Lights of Fortitude, "Years later Varqá's first wife was brought to Ṭihrán by 'Azízu'lláh. There she declared her belief in Bahá'u'lláh and became a devoted Bahá'í".[474] In a Tablet, 'Abdu'l-Bahá gave her the title of Amatu'l-Hagh (the maidservant of God). Hand of the Cause Dr 'Alí-Muḥammad Varqá remarked:

> I remember her helping me in my childhood to memorize Bahá'í prayers. She passed away in our home when I was 8 or 9 years old, and she was buried in our family graveyard and finally was transferred to the Bahá'í cemetery in Tihran before its destruction by the mob during the revolution.[475]

17.11 Varqá's Mother-in-law

The maternal grandmother of Rúḥu'lláh continued to live in spiritual darkness. When she learned of the martyrdom of her son-in-law and

---

[471] Momen, The Bahá'í Communities of Iran 1851-1921: The North of Iran, 372.
[472] Source: MyHeritage.com
[473] Source: MyHeritage.com
[474] Barron Deems Harper, Lights of Fortitude: Glimpses into the Lives of the Hands of the Cause of God (Oxford: George Ronald, 2007), 42.
[475] Harper, Lights of Fortitude, 459-60.

grandson in Tehran she invited her friends and relatives to a banquet, entertained by musicians to celebrate their deaths.[476] [477]

17.12 'Abdu'lláh Núrí

The maternal grandfather of Rúḥu'lláh, 'Abdu'lláh Khán settled in Tehran after fleeing Zanján. He eventually divorced his wife due to her opposition. In Tehran, his house was a center for Bahá'í meetings and activities. He met Bahá'u'lláh and was present when His ascension took place in 1892. The year after the martyrdom of Varqá and Rúḥu'lláh, 'Abdu'lláh Khán and his grandson 'Azízu'lláh visited again 'Abdu'l-Bahá in the Holy Land and were received very kindly.[478] He died in 1899 as a firm believer.[479]

17.13 'Azízu'lláh Varqá

Varqá was survived by his two sons 'Azízu'lláh and Valíyu'lláh who served the Cause with the same enthusiasm as their beloved father and brother. He was about fifteen when his father was killed.

Referring to the two brothers 'Abdu'l-Bahá said: "These esteemed people have left us with two remembrances. They have left us two gifts: One is Mírzá 'Azízu'lláh and the other is Mírzá Valíyu'lláh Varqá."[480] They were in their teens when their father was killed. 'Azízu'lláh was educated by the Hand of the Cause Mírzá Ḥasan Adib, as per 'Abdu'l-Bahá's direct instructions. Mírzá Ḥasan Adib was a professional educator. 'Azízu'llah lived in the house of Muḥammad Karím 'Attar, a strong believer from Tehran.[481] In turn, Valíyu'lláh grew up under the care of his uncle Mírzá Ḥusayn Yazdí in Miyándu'áb as outlined in the next section. According to Moojan Momen:

---

[476] Balyuzi, Eminent Bahá'ís in the Time of Bahá'u'lláh, 84.
[477] Darius Shahrokh, Varqá and Son: The Heavenly Doves, 15.
[478] Earl Redman, Visiting 'Abdu'l-Bahá, Volume 1: The West Discover the Master, 1897-1911, 4 (Oxford: George Ronald, 2019).
[479] Momen, The Bahá'í Communities of Iran 1851-1921: The North of Iran, 370.
[480] Star of the West, vol. 3, No. 18 (February 1913), 362-364.
[481] Momen, The Bahá'í Communities of Iran 1851-1921: The North of Iran.

> 'Abdu'l-Bahá instructed that when he was old enough, 'Azízu'lláh Varqá be given sufficient capital to start a shop and business. He set up the Mithaqiyyih Company on Lalihzar Avenue, importing goods from Europe. His shop became a gathering place for young Bahá'ís and for teaching the Bahá'í Faith. After some years this commercial venture failed and Varqá was employed by the Russian Loan and Discount Bank. Since most of the princes and notables of Iran were in debt to this bank and since Varqá was appointed by its manager, E.K. Grube, as the sole liaison between the bank and these private customers, this put Varqá in a very powerful position in Tehran society. During the Constitutional Revolution 'Abdu'l-Bahá sent numerous private messages to Muḥammad 'Alí Sháh through Varqá, urging the Sháh to resolve his differences with Parliament. Varqá accompanied 'Abdu'l-Bahá on the European stages of his western journeys in 1913. By 1925 he had retired to the village of Khániyabad (6 km south of Tehran on the Hamadan road) that he owned.[482]

The US Bahá'í News reports in their January 1932 issue: "The passing of that distinguished member of the Cause, Jenabi Azízullah Khan Vargha, son of the beloved poet Vargha who suffered martyrdom for the Holy Cause, was noted with the deepest sense of grief at his loss."[483]

17.14 Epilogue

Crisis and victory are the systole and diastole of Bahá'í history while at each heartbeat the Faith jumps a leap forward towards the final triumph. "With every fresh tribulation", Bahá'u'lláh says, "He manifested a fuller measure of Thy Cause, and exalted more highly Thy word."[484] The following chapters shows this divine dynamics as the result of Varqá's and Rúḥu'lláh's labours of love. It clearly

---

[482] Momen, The Bahá'í Communities of Iran 1851-1921: The North of Iran, 70.
[483] The National Spiritual Assembly of the Bahá'ís of the United States and Canada, "International News Items," Bahá'í News, January, 1932.
[484] Bahá'u'lláh, Prayers and Meditations, 37.

demonstrates the operation of this vital principle of growth in the lives of the descendants of the great Varqá, particularly in the services of the Hands of the Cause Valíyu'lláh Varqá and Dr 'Alí-Muḥammad Varqá, his son and grandson, respectively, as explored in the next two chapters.

The sense of devotion that Mullá Mihdí instilled in his son Varqá, was in turn passed on to the next generation like a strong family chain built across three centuries. It remind us of 'Abdu'l-Bahá's words in that "... an especial blessing is conferred on some families and some generations."[485]

[485] 'Abdu'l-Bahá, Some Answered Questions (Bahá'í Publishing Trust: Wilmette, Illinois, 1990), 319.

XVIII - Valíyu'lláh Varqá

Valíyu'lláh Varqá was about thirteen years old when he lost his father in the prison of Anbár. He grew up as a devoted Bahá'í, completely dedicated to the needs of the Cause. In 1951, the Guardian appointed him a Hand of the Cause of God. As previously stated, his father, the martyr Varqá, was posthumously designated a Hand of the Cause by 'Abdu'l-Bahá. He is the father of the Hand of the Cause Dr 'Alí-Muḥammad Varqá.

18.1 In Tabríz

Valíyu'lláh Varqá as a child stayed at the home of his maternal grandmother when his father was forced to leave the city of Tabríz. He grew up under her influence and she successfully instilled in him hatred of the Bahá'ís. In his autobiography[486] written at the request of the Spiritual Assembly of Tehran, Mr Varqá wrote that at night he cried sincerely for his father's condition. This continued until he reached the age of 16 years. At that time, his uncle, Ḥusayn, came to Tabríz and arranged for Valíyu'lláh to go live with his family in Míyanduáb. A few years later, under the guidance of this relative, he entered the Bahá'í Faith. Mr Varqá wrote:

> During my stay in Míyanduáb, the late Siyyid Assadu'lláh Qumí visited there and was a guest of my uncle. Feeling that I was extremely anxious to visit the Holy Shrines and the Center of the Covenant, he promised me, when leaving Míyanduáb, that whenever he intended to leave for the Holy Land he would inform me that I might join him at Tabríz. Shortly afterwards I received his message telling me that he was ready to leave. Filled with great enthusiasm for this auspicious journey I did not even inform my uncle of my intended departure, since I thought he would definitely not allow me to make the journey

[486] Bahá'í World Centre, "Váliyu'lláh Varqá 1884—1955," in The Bahá'í World, vol. XIII, 831-4.

because of his great affection for me. I forthwith left for Marághih in company of one of the aged believers, and thence I proceeded to Tabríz. At Tabríz I was summoned by the Local Spiritual Assembly, who, after holding consultation regarding my aim, informed me that they had decided I should go to Ṭihrán to stay with my brother Mírzá 'Azízu'lláh Khán. To persuade them to revise their decision was out of the question and I was therefore obliged to leave for Ṭihrán.[487]

18.2 Studying in Tehran and at the Holy Land

Mr Varqá as a young man settled in Tehran living with his brother 'Azízu'lláh.[488] In the capital he studied at the Tarbiyat School for Boys, a Bahá'í institutional establishment, and the American College of Tehran. According to him, "At the same time I began to study English outside the school and took up a course in Arabic with Bahá'í scholars."[489]

In the year 1909, when Mr Varqá was about twenty-five years old, he reached the presence of 'Abdu'l-Bahá in the Holy Land and since then he served his Master with all diligence. He studied in the American University of Beirut, near 'Akká. Among his life plans was to study further in a university in England. Every summer he was called by 'Abdu'l-Bahá to the Holy Land where he nourished his soul with the blessings of visiting the Blessed Shrines of the Báb and Bahá'u'lláh and being in the constant presence of the Master. "During my stay in Beirut …" he recalled, "I had the opportunity to study the Cause and take teaching courses with other students under the late Ḥájí Mírzá Ḥaydar-'Alí."[490]

---

[487] Bahá'í World Centre, "Váliyu'lláh Varqá 1884—1955," in The Bahá'í World, vol. XIII, 831-4.
[488] Encyclopedia Iranica, s.v. "Wali-Allāh Varqā," http://www.iranicaonline.org/articles/varqa-wali-allah.
[489] Bahá'í World Centre, "Váliyu'lláh Varqá 1884—1955," in The Bahá'í World, vol. XIII, 831-4.
[490] Bahá'í World Centre, "Váliyu'lláh Varqá 1884—1955," 831-4, vol. XIII, The Bahá'í World.

18.3 Settling in Tehran

In the summer of 1909, Mr Varqá returned unexpectedly to Tehran to carry out a specific mission entrusted by 'Abdu'l-Bahá. Mr Varqá also got employment at the court of Muḥammad Sháh.[491]

He married Bahíyyih ʿAṭáʾí[492] who gave birth to ten children. Years later, he would say, "I must express my great appreciation to my wife, who has sincerely collaborated with me since our marriage and who had, in fact, a greater share than myself in training the children in the Bahá'í Spirit."[493] Once, a believer named Jalál Toeg was invited to Bahíyyih Khánum (Mr Varqá's wife and Dr Varqá's mother).

> During the same visit, Bahíyyih Khánum invited Jalál Toeg to retrieve a medium-sized trunk that was hidden away in a storage room that he had to access by ladder. Jalál retrieved the trunk and brought it into the living room. Dr Varqá's mother opened the container and reverently displayed its contents which were neatly folded in square bundles. With a growing sense of awe, the Toeg family viewed sacred relics that had once belonged to the Báb, Bahá'u'lláh and 'Abdu'l-Bahá! They consisted of various articles of clothing and accessories, including robes, slippers, a comb, some writing materials that included reed pens and ink-wells, and a turban which had been sown with gold filigree thread.[494]

Mr Varqá also worked for the Russian Legation and the Turkish Embassy in Tehran as first secretary translator. "At both the Embassies," he observed, "I had made it a condition with them not to require me to do anything concerned with politics. After many years

---

[491] Encyclopedia Iranica, WALI-ALLĀH VARQĀ, 2007, by Iraj Ayman.
[492] d. 1983 in London.
[493] Bahá'í World Centre, "Váliyu'lláh Varqá 1884—1955," in The Bahá'í World, vol. XIII, 834.
[494] Jack McLean, "Divine Simplicity: Remembering the Last Hand of the Cause of God, Dr 'Alí-Muhammad Varqá," 2007, https://jack-mclean.com/essays/divine-simplicity-remembering-the-last-hand-of-the-cause-of-god-dr-ali-muhammad-varqa/.

of service, however, I was asked to do a service which slightly touched on politics, whereupon I tendered my resignation."[495] During those years Mr Varqá served as a member of the Spiritual Assembly of Tehran and several Bahá'í committees.

18.4 Travelling with 'Abdu'l-Bahá

When 'Abdu'l-Bahá visited the West in 1912, Mr Varqá joined His entourage in America as His translator. At that time, he was about twenty-eight years old.

One night in New York on 19 July the Master

> … spoke about the martyrs of the Faith and visited the son of Varqá, the martyr, Mírzá Valíyu'lláh Varqá, who was the recipient of the Master's loving kindness. He then spoke of the martyrdom of Varqá and his son Rúḥu'lláh in a most impressive and dignified manner, paying tribute to and demonstrating His great loyalty to these servants of the threshold of the Blessed Beauty.[496]

Mr Varqá as a young man accompanied the Master on subsequent trips to Great Britain and France. He stayed with the entourage until 9 February 1913 in Paris after which he returned to Iran. During the journey Mr Varqá served as treasurer of the Bahá'í Funds.[497]

On one occasion in New York, 'Abdu'l-Bahá introduced Valíyu'lláh Varqá to the American friends: "He is my son, whatever he says it is true. Believe it".[498] At that time he was about twenty-six years of age and we can imagine the effect that this close association with the Master over several months had on his young life.

---

[495] Bahá'í World Centre, "Váliyu'lláh Varqá 1884—1955," in The Bahá'í World, vol. XIII, 831-4.
[496] Zarqání, Mahmúd's Diary The Diary of Mírzá Mahmúd-i-Zarqání Chronicling `Abdu'l-Bahá's Journey to America, 174.
[497] McLean, Divine Simplicity: Remembering the last Hand of the Cause of God, Dr 'Alí-Muhammad Varqá.
[498] Root, "White Roses of Persia (Part 4)," 258-59.

18.5 At the National Spiritual Assembly and as a Hand of the Cause

In 1934 Mr Varqá was elected to the first National Spiritual Assembly of Iran where he served as chairman several times. He remained a member of that institution until his death in 1955.

At the age of sixty-seven, this pre-eminent brother of Rúḥu'lláh received the designation of being a Hand of the Cause of God from Shoghi Effendi in 1951. He was appointed in the first contingent of Hands of the Cause announced by the Guardian. Like some other members of the National Spiritual Assembly of Iran who were later appointed Hands of the Cause, Valíyu'lláh Varqá continued serving on both institutions, to "continue discharge vital administrative, teaching duties pending assignment of specific functions as need arises", as the beloved Guardian had instructed.[499] Eventually, the Hands were relieved of service on the institutions of the National Spiritual Assembly and focused on their service to the institution of the Hands of the Cause.

18.6 Trustee of the Ḥuqúqu'lláh

Mr Varqá was designated Trustee of Ḥuqúqu'lláh in 1940. The Ḥuqúqu'lláh (In Arabic, "Right of God") is an ordinance enunciated by Bahá'u'lláh in the Kitáb-i-Aqdas. It is a voluntary payment offered to the Center of the Cause. The funds are used to advance the Cause of God, for socio-economic projects or for philanthropic purposes (please see appendices for Dr Varqá's talk about the Ḥuqúqu'lláh).

As indicated above, in 1940 Shoghi Effendi appointed Mr Varqá as Trustee of Ḥuqúqu'lláh following the death of Ḥájí Ghulám Riḍá in 1939. The first Trustee (Amín) of the Huqúq'u'lláh appointed by Bahá'u'lláh was Ḥájí Sháh-Muhammad Manshádi, entitled Amínu'l-Bayán (d. 1881). Upon his death, Ḥájí Amín (1831-1928), was appointed by Bahá'u'lláh as the second Trustee. The third Trustee was

[499] Muhájir, Hand of the Cause of God Furútan, 220.

Ḥájí Ghulám Riḍá (entitled Amín-i-Amín) who died in 1939. The fourth and fifth Trustees were Valíyu'lláh Varqá (1884-1955) and his son Dr 'Alí-Muḥammad Varqá (1912-2007), respectively. [500]

Mr Varqá was sometimes assisted by his son Dr 'Alí-Muḥammad Varqá. "For the last twelve years," Mr Varqá wrote in his autobiography, "I have had the inestimable honor to serve as the Trustee of Ḥuqúqu'lláh, having been appointed by the beloved Guardian, and it is my utmost wish that I may be able during these last days of my life to render befitting service to our Holy Cause and give satisfaction to our beloved Guardian."[501] Mr Varqá resigned from his professional work in order to devote himself to the demands of his role as Trustee of the Ḥuqúqu'lláh. During his time as Trustee, the observance of the Ḥuqúqu'lláh spread widely throughout Iran.[502] Mr Varqá served continuously as the Trustee for fifteen years until his death in 1955.

Mr Varqá was also present with 'Abdu'l-Bahá at the cornerstone laying ceremony of the House of Worship of Chicago in 1912. He again visited the site for the dedication of the Temple in 1953, almost forty-one years ago. In that occasion he was requested to chant the Tablet of Visitation in Arabic.

It is known that the celebrated Tablet of Ahmad came to us through this Hand of the Cause who received it as a gift from one of the members of Ahmad's family. Following Shoghi Effendi's instructions, Mr Varqá donated the Tablet to the National Spiritual Assembly of the Bahá'ís of the United States on the occasion of the dedication of the House of Worship. As Mr Faizi, another Hand of the Cause, wrote "Now the beloved friends of that country are the trustees of this great gift of God to humanity".[503]

---

[501] For Mr Valíyu'lláh Varqá's obituary please see: Bahá'í World, Vol. 13, pp. 831-4. https://bahai.works/Bahá'%C3%AD_World/Volume_13/In_Memoriam
[502] Ramin Khadem, and Fred Badiyan, "Huqúqu'lláh the Right of God," 1995, https://www.youtube.com/watch?v=21TY10KdBMM.
[503] Abu'l-Qásim Faizi, "A Flame of Fire: The Story of the Tablet of Ahmad," Bahá'ís News, April, 1976, 4.

18.7 An Anecdote about Valíyu'lláh Varqá

This story was related by Mr Arvid Yaganegi and took place in the late 1930s in Iran.[504]

> My late grandfather was a Zoroastrian native of Yazd. In his early years he experienced intense religious persecution which continued when he joined the ranks of the Bahá'ís. He had lost his father as young boy and had learned how to guard and protect his own personal safety and of those close to him.
> In his late teens he moved to Teheran to look for entrepreneurial opportunities and attempt to start a business. Mr Valíyu'lláh Varqá had known him and was a mentoring and kind fatherly figure. In his early twenties my grandfather landed on his feet and was a successful trader in a prominent city bazaar in central Teheran supplying building timbers.
>
> The religious persecution and provocation he had known all his life had followed him. A few others that were sadly misinformed about the Bahá'í Faith who frequented the markets, would assemble in the centre of the bazaar and yell out obscenities about the central Figures of the Faith. The young trader who was known to take some umbrage at these displays of disrespect, would invariably intervene by imposing himself on these individuals seeking to correct their behaviour. A short time later these hapless few would be seen announcing their withdrawals of these offensive suggestions, albeit under some duress. Reports of his interventions reached the Spiritual Assembly of the Bahá'ís of Teheran. Mr Varqá assured them that he would keep an eye on this vigorous Baha'i youth and would gently counsel him. With Varqá's loving guidance and support the young man learned over time to overlook the howling of profanities in the markets.

504 Arvid Yaganegi, personal communication to the author.

> There was one more synonymous dramatic episode to play out however. The scene was set on one busy morning of fine weather, two men assembled just outside the timber shop. They started hurling egregious religious vulgarities once more as an audience gathered around the clamour. The intensely chagrined trader emerged from his workshop and once again intervened; and a few minutes later this misinformed pair unequivocally withdrew their ill-mannered claims. The young merchant was enjoying the satisfaction of the outcome, when he looked up at once and saw the radiant appearance of his mentor, Mr Varqá. "Oh no", he thought. The young man's demeanour was filled with remorse as he expressed a willingness to accept any punishment or sanction that Mr Varqa would recommend to the Spiritual Assembly of Teheran.
>
> Mr Varqá helped him to his feet, and reassured that there would be no punishment for today, explaining that when he entered the bazaar, he saw these foolish men conducting themselves with such offense, he looked to the heavens and said, "Oh 'Abdu'l Bahá, may you send someone here to deal with them", and so it was. Mr Varqá went onto say like a wise loving father that the events of this day would remain just between them and that physical intervention was no longer required in the future. A great burden was lifted and these gentle words expressed with a soft heart which had a profound impact my grandfather. The remaining years in the bazaar were without such incidents.

18.8 Travelling as a Hand of the Cause

Mr Varqá traveled to different parts of the world. His obituary describes the magnitude and extent of his travels:

> In 1953 he prepared himself, under the instructions of the Guardian, for participation in the Intercontinental Conferences. He first attended the Kampala Conference and then the Conference in Chicago. During the interval between

the latter and the Conference in Stockholm he was directed by the Guardian to proceed to South America, where he visited the area between Brazil and Santiago in Chile within forty-six days. His mission was to meet the friends and to give the Message to the people. On July 10, 1953, he left for Europe and, after participating in the Stockholm Conference, he visited a large number of cities in Germany by the order of the Guardian. In Hamburg, Frankfurt, Stuttgart, Munich and Esslingen he met many Bahá'í friends and others. In Stuttgart the preliminary signs of his illness began to appear. He stayed in a hospital for a week in Stuttgart and then for a further month in Ulm, where he underwent an operation.

Mr Varqá's request to Shoghi Effendi for a visit to Haifa had been granted for the time when the New Delhi Conference, in which Mr. Varqá was to participate, should have been concluded. He therefore left soon for New Delhi, not waiting to complete the convalescence period, and consequently had a very hard time during the days of the Conference. He then received the Guardian's instructions to proceed to 'Iráq, Egypt and Syria on a teaching mission. He forthwith left New Delhi for 'Iráq. In that country his illness took a serious turn and he suffered extreme pain. He was therefore obliged to stay in the Hazíratu'l-Quds in Baghdad. After a while, when he felt himself slightly better, he left for Cairo, Ismailia, Suez, Port Said, and Alexandria, where he visited the friends and gladdened their hearts by giving them an account of the magnificent results of the Conferences and of the rapid progress of the Cause in the world.

He then left for Turkey, where he visited the towns of Qazi Antap, Iskanderun, Adana and Istanbul, and met the friends. The unexpected cold weather in Turkey that year and Mr Varqá's ill health caused him a great deal of suffering. He now reported to the beloved Guardian an account of his journeys and was then kindly instructed to return to Írán. After his arrival in Ṭihrán the Guardian appointed a time when he could visit the Holy Land. This visit to the Holy Shrines and to the beloved Guardian, which lasted about two weeks, inspired him with a new life and revitalized him for still further activities. He was then instructed by Shoghi Effendi to proceed to Germany so as to join the Hands of the Cause and at the same time to complete the course of his medical treatment. From there, on the Guardian's instructions, he departed for Austria and stayed in Vienna for some time, where he started teaching the Cause and giving public addresses to large crowds of searchers for truth. He then returned to Írán.

In March 1955 he felt very severe pain which made him extremely uneasy. He therefore left for Europe again for medical treatment, visiting first Paris and then Italy. While receiving treatment he did not forget his teaching mission whenever he found an opportunity. He then proceeded to Germany and went to a hospital in Tübingen where for forty-one days he passed the last part of his brilliant life. Even during these last days he did not neglect his teaching duty. Whenever he felt a mitigation of pain and suffering he called to his bedside both friends and seekers of truth and spoke to them of the Teachings. But the light of his life was steadily fading, and it was on Saturday, November 12, 1955, that he passed away and joined the Concourse on High. He was a drop that fell in the Great Ocean, a beam of light that attained to the luminous Sun.[505]

18.9 Tributes to Hand of the Cause Valíyu'lláh Varqá

As a Hand of the Cause Mr Varqá was distinguished. Hasan Sabri who met him at the 1953 Intercontinental Conference in Kampala said: "The first thing that struck me about him was his total and complete humility. He was a very humble person, very dignified, very outstanding, very impressive as a personality but very humble."[506]

---

[505] For his obituary see: Bahá'í World, Vol. 13, pp. 831-4. https://bahai.works/Bahá'%C3%AD_World/Volume_13/In_Memoriam

[506] Khadem, and Badiyan, Huqúqu'lláh The Right of God, 1995. See Bibliography.

Mr Varqá was the English interpreter for the Hand of the Cause Martha Root at her visit to Tehran in Naw Rúz 1930. He was described as a "wonderful soul … an excellent interpreter, for which the spiritual perception and marvelous spirit he could convey the true meaning of her words with accuracy and fluency." [507]

Shoghi Effendi said once that among the company of the Hands of the Cause, Valíyu'lláh Varqá was "outstanding". [508] When he died in Germany travel teaching and the news reached Shoghi Effendi, he exclaimed: "He was the finest man we had."[509] And to the friends gathered at Mr Varqá's funeral Shoghi Effendi wrote:

> The Bahá'ís could not have a better example before them of nobility and faithfulness than this distinguished Hand of the Cause; and it is a blessing for the German friends that their country should have received his dust. The Guardian urges you all to follow in the footsteps of this beloved Hand, and to redouble your efforts to achieve the goals of the World Crusade apportioned to the German believers. He assures you all of his prayers for your success…[510]

Once Dr 'Alí-Muḥammad Varqá, Valíyu'lláh's son, was asked why Shoghi Effendi had appointed his father a Hand of the Cause. His response was: "Because Shoghi Effendi recognized in him this capacity, devotion and sincerity. From him there was a feeling of nothingness. He devoted his life, mind and health to the Faith. The Faith for him was above all."[511]

---

[507] Luṭfu'lláh Ḥakím. "The Divine Traces in Persia," The Star of the West, vol. 21, no. 3, (June 1930), 94.
[508] Javidukht Khadem, Zikrullah Khadem, the Itinerant Hand of the Cause of God (Wilmette, Illinois: Bahá'í Publishing Trust, 1990), 222.
[509] Rabbani, The Priceless Pearl, 176.
[510] Bahá'í World Centre, "Váliyu'lláh Varqá 1884—1955," in The Bahá'í World, vol. XIII, 831-4.
[511] McLean, Divine Simplicity: Remembering the last Hand of the Cause of God, Dr 'Alí-Muhammad Varqá, 2007.

And about the humility of the Hands of the Cause as a unique characteristic of service in the Bahá'í Faith, let us bear in mind these words once said by 'Abdu'l-Bahá:

> The Hands of the Cause are such blessed souls that the evidences of their sanctity and spirituality will be felt in the hearts of people. Their influence must be such that the souls may be carried away by their goodly character, their pure motives, their justice and fairness, that individuals may be enamoured of their praiseworthy character and their virtuous attributes, and that people may turn their faces towards them for their qualities and resplendent signs. "Hand of the Cause" is not a title which can be given to anybody. Neither is it a position to be handed down to whomsoever may desire it... The more any soul becomes self-effacing, the more confirmed will he be in the service of the Cause of God; and the more humble, the nearer will he be to Him.[512]

---

[512] Taherzadeh, The Revelation of Bahá'u'lláh. Vol 4: Mazra'ih & Bahji 1877-92, 285.

XIX - Dr 'Alí-Muḥammad Varqá

On his father's death in 1955, Dr 'Alí-Muḥammad Varqá was appointed a Hand of the Cause of God and Trustee of the Ḥuqúqu'lláh. In those capacities, he participated in the consultations focused on developing various new Bahá'í institutions such as the Continental Boards of Counsellors, the International Teaching Centre and the Office of Ḥuqúqu'lláh. He travelled around the world visiting and encouraging Bahá'í communities. He bore the same name as his grandfather — 'Alí Muḥammad Varqá. As an educator and academic by profession, Dr Varqá also contributed to the advancement and socio-economic development of Iran.

He travelled around the world visiting and encouraging Bahá'í communities, faithfully obeying the obligations entrusted to the Hands of the Cause in the beloved Master's Will and Testament to "diffuse the Divine Fragrances, to edify the souls of men, to promote learning," and, of course, "to improve the character of all men".[513]

19.1 'Abdu'l-Bahá Blesses Dr Varqá's Photograph as a Child

There is a beautiful story about Valíyu'lláh Varqá while in America serving as a translator to 'Abdu'l-Bahá. One day he received a picture of his first-born, Dr 'Alí Muḥammad Varqá. According to the latter:

> When I was born in Iran, my father [Valíyu'lláh Varqá] was in the company of the beloved Master in the United States. The news reached him that in Tehran a son was born to his wife. He knew that his child was born but he was not able to see me. He asked my uncle ['Azízu'lláh Varqá] to send a picture of me to

[513] 'Abdu'l-Bahá, The Will and Testament of 'Abdu'l-Bahá (Wilmette, Illinois: Bahá'í Publishing Trust, 1990), 13.

> him. I was six months old when my uncle took me in his lap and took a picture, and sent it to my father.[514]

One of the believers named Áqá Mírzá Asadu'lláh Qumí showed the photograph to 'Abdu'l-Bahá Who wrote on the two arms of the child the words "Yad" (*Hand*, in Arabic) and "Mu'ayyad" (*Confirmed* or *successful*, in Arabic). At the top of the photograph, the Master wrote "Ya Bahá'u'l-Abhá" (O Thou Glory of the Most Glorious).

Since this event occurred in 1912, the family kept the photograph private until one day when was shown to the members of the National Spiritual Assembly of Iran at Dr Varqá's residence in Tehran. It happened that his mother showed the picture to the guests telling them the circumstances of 'Abdu'l-Bahá's writing on it. The Hand of the Cause Mr Furútan was present at the meeting who later wrote an article in the Bahá'í News. As secretary of the National Spiritual Assembly of Iran, Mr Furútan sent this historical photograph to the beloved Guardian. Since the photograph was kept private with the family for forty-five years since 1912, Shoghi Effendi apparently became aware of its existence around a year before his death in November 1957 whereas Dr Varqá's appointment as a Hand of the Cause took place about two years earlier in November 1955. [515] [516]

There is another anecdote from Dr Varqá's childhood, narrated by Allan Waters:

> Dr Varqá once shared a precious memory of when, as a child in his father's house in Ṭihrán, he met the second Trustee of Ḥuqúqu'lláh, Ḥájí Amín, and his assistant Jináb-i-Ḥájí

---

[514] 'Alí Muhammad Varqá, "Hand of the Cause Dr. Varqá and His Baby Picture When Seen by 'Abdu'l-Bahá While in America," November 19, 2016, http://thebabhistory.blogspot.com/2016/11/hand-of-cause-dr-varqa-and-his-baby.html.

[515] Harper, Lights of Fortitude: Glimpses into the Lives of the Hands of the Cause of God, 351.

[516] Hand of the Cause Dr Varqá's Statement on Childhood Photograph. Available at: https://iranian.com/2009/04/14/childhood-photo-of-dr-varqa

Ghulam-Riḍá. "I was maybe nine or ten years old", he related, "I knew that Ḥájí Amín collected the money, the contribution to Ḥuqúqu'lláh, and sent it to 'Abdu'l-Bahá. Therefore, I looked in my savings box and I found three pennies, and I went to Ḥájí Amín and I offered these three pennies to him." At that moment, in that house, although none could have guessed it, four of the five eventual Trustees of Ḥuqúqu'lláh were present".[517]

19.2 Services in the Cradle of the Faith

Dr 'Alí-Muḥammad Varqá was the first child in the marriage of Valíyu'lláh and Bahíyyih Varqá. The exact date of the birth of Dr Varqá is unknown; so when a date had to be determined the first of January was chosen.[518] Up until the letter half of the 1920s there were no birth certificates and identification cards in Iran. [519] People used to keep their date of birth in family books or on a volume of the Writings which sometimes went missing. In addition, in Islamic countries the celebration of birthdays used to be discouraged as it was seen as an act of self-centredness. Another Hand of the Cause that chose 1 January as a date-of-birth was Zikru'lláh Khádem because it was easy to memorize.[520]

The child grew up in the midst of a staunch Bahá'í family which had yielded two glorious martyrs, his grandfather Varqá and his uncle Rúḥu'lláh. When he became a young boy, he joined the Tarbíyat School for Boys which was founded and managed by the Bahá'í community. At the Tarbíyat Schools he was able to mingle with youth from other Baha'i families who later became prominent in the service to the Faith, like himself.

---

[517] Allan Waters, Ḥuqúqu'lláh, the Right of God (Victoria, Australia: Bahá'í Publications Australia, 2012), 7-10.
[518] Allan Waters' personal communication to the author.
[519] Boris Handal, The Khamsis: A Cradle of True Gold, xviii (IngramSpark, 2020). https://books.google.com.au/books?id=7PuazQEACAAJ.
[520] Riaz Khadem, Prelude to the Guardianship, 245 (Oxford: George Ronald, 2014).

Since his younger years he served in several committees and helped as a teacher of Bahá'í children's classes.[521] For example, in 1941 the National Youth Committee was formed by three youths that later would become Hands of the Cause: Dr Varqá, Mr Zikru'lláh Khádem and Mr Abu'l-Qásim Faizí. In that committee also were a future member of the Universal House of Justice Mr 'Alí Nakhjavání, and a future Continental Counsellor in Africa, Dr Míhdí Samandarí.

His secondary education was completed at the Dár ul-Funún Institute after which he undertook his obligatory military service as 3rd lieutenant (sotván sevvom) in the field of artillery. By the end of his military service in 1935 Dr Varqá was married to Rawhaniyyih Muhtadi.[522] The marriage had three daughters: Elahe, Nadieh and Faraneh.

Settling in other cities was ideal to bring the Faith to other latitudes. Dr Varqá was able to take school teaching positions first in Tehran and later in the interior of the country working for the Ministry of Education.[523] [524] It is noteworthy that Dr Varqá is listed as a teaching staff at the Tarbíyat School (History and Geography, 7th Grade).[525] This may have happened between his secondary school graduation and 1934 when Tarbiyat School was closed by the government. By that time Dr Varqá was about 22 years old.

In 1940, when he was twenty-six years old, "with much difficulty received a transfer to the capital to help his father who had been appointed by Shoghi Effendi as the Trustee of Ḥuqúqu'lláh in the same year[526] and also to pursue university studies.

---

[521] Hugh C Adamson, Historical Dictionary of the Bahá'í Faith, 488 (Scarecrow Press, 2006).

[522] d. 2001 in Montreal, Quebec.

[523] Baharieh Rouhani Ma'ani, "The Evolution of the Institution of Ḥuqúqu'lláh," in the Institution of Ḥuqúqu'lláh Newsletter, issue 61, 10, January 1996.

[524] Iraj Ayman, "Varqā, 'Ali-Moḥammad," in Encyclopædia Iranica, ed. Ehsan Yarshater (in press), in press.

[525] Soli Shahvar, The Forgotten Schools: The Baha'is and Modern Education in Iran, 1899–1934 (Taylor & Francis, 2013), 156.

[526] Baharieh Rouhani Ma'ani, "The Evolution of the Institution of Ḥuqúqu'lláh," in the Institution of Ḥuqúqu'lláh Newsletter, issue 61, 10, January 1996.

19.3 Academic Achievements

Dr Varqá gained excellence in the fields of school and university education. At the Teachers Training College of the University of Tehran, known as Danesh Saraye Ali (House of Higher Knowledge) he obtained an undergraduate degree in history. Furthermore, he completed another undergraduate degree in Economics from the Faculty of Law at the same University.[527] At the same time, he taught part-time at the Teachers Training College while being in charge of its secretariat.

When Dr Varqá was 34 years old, in 1946, one year after the end of World War II, a scholarship was granted to him by the Iranian government to pursue a doctorate at the faculty of literature and human sciences at the Sorbonne University. Due to the oil bonanza and the Pahlavi regime strong emphasis on modernizing the country during the middle of the last century, thousands of Iranian students obtained government scholarships to study overseas on the condition that upon their return, they would contribute to the socioeconomic development of the country that was under way.[528] Four years later, he graduated with a thesis in the field of geomorphology entitled Problème de l'hydrolique Agricole et de l'irrigation en l'Iran.[529] The findings from his seminal study on Iranian irrigational practices have been subsequently cited by various academics.[530] [531] [532]

---

[527] Abdu'l-Ali Alaii, "Ali-Moḥammad Varqā, Šarḥ-E Ḥāl-E Ayādi-E Amr Allāh Ba Qalam-E Ḵodešān," in Moʾassassa-Ye Ayādi-Ye Amr Allāh (Tehran: 1973).
[528] Andrew Scott Cooper, "The Fall of Heaven: The Pahlavis and the Final Days of Imperial Iran " The Middle East Journal 71, no. 1 (2017).
[529] Vargha, Ali Mohammad. "Le problème de l'hydraulique agricole et de l'irrigation en Iran", Paris-Sorbonne, Thèse, Paris, 1949.
[530] Ronnie Tooyak Tingook, "Numerical Simulation of the Base-Level Buffers and Buttresses Conceptual Model of Fluvial Systems" (University of Texas Arlington, 2012), http://hdl.handle.net/10106/11049.
[531] Henri Goblot, Les Qanats: Une Technique D'acquisition De L'eau (De Gruyter, 1979).
[532] Johannes Humlum, Underjordiske Vandingskanaler Kareze, Qanat, Foggara, vol. 16 (Geografisk Institut, 1965).

With his doctoral degree in hand, Dr Varqá returned to Iran in 1950 and was appointed assistant professor at the University of Tabríz. After a number of years, he moved to the University of Tehran's Department of Geology. Such impressive educational credentials were further augmented when, while retaining his position at the University of Tehran, he was invited to serve as a professor of Physical Geography and Geomorphology at the newly-restructured Teachers Training College which had become the University of Teacher Education (Daneshgah-e Tarbiat-e Mo'allem). At that institution, Dr Varqá created the Department of Geology, developed the curriculum of teaching and learning resources, and became its head until his retirement in 1977 at the age of 65 years.

His contributions to the fields of teaching and research certainly assisted with the socio-economic of Iran. Even long after his retirement Dr Varqá was promoting scholarship in his field. "I was fortunate to spend some brief moments with him while serving in the Holy Land in 1996 and 1997", wrote Dr Ron Tingook. "I had tea with him once along with my coworker at his home, and when he learned that I wanted to pursue [a PhD in] geology he was very encouraging … Having the honor to reference his technical work in my technical evaluation was my primary driver."[533]

Dr Varqá continued assisting his father in the administration of the Ḥuqúqu'lláh, in which the number of those who were observing this sacred law was increasing at a high rate in Iran. Likewise, he continued serving the Faith actively on various local and national committees.[534]

As a former academic, Dr Varqá always maintained a keen interest in educational matters. For instance, from the World Centre, Dr Varqá led an International Education Committee in Iran for a period of time. The committee was appointed by the Universal House of Justice. Initially it was an idea proposed by the Hand of the Cause of God Dr Rahmatu'lláh Muhájir aimed at enhancing the education of children

---

[533] Dr Ron Tingook, personal communication to the author.
[534] Adamson, Historical Dictionary of the Bahá'í Faith, 489, 2006.

in the developing countries.[535] The project involved the participation of Iranian Bahá'í educators in 21 African countries during the Five Year Plan (1974-1979) of the Universal House of Justice. To carry out this, a special International Education Fund was created in Iran. Its capital remained a trust fund under the careful stewardship of the Universal House of Justice.[536]

19.4 Dr Varqá's Appointment

On 15 November 1955, on the occasion of Valíyu'lláh Varqá's passing, the Guardian sent a six-sentence cable to the National Spiritual Assembly of Iran:

> Profoundly grieved by loss of outstanding Hand of Cause of God, exemplary Trustee of Ḥuqúqu'lláh, distinguished representative of most venerable community of Bahá'í world, worthy son, brother of twin immortal martyrs of the Faith, dearly beloved disciple of Center of the Covenant.
>
> Shining record of his services extending over half century enriched the annals of Heroic and Formative Ages of Bahá'í Dispensation.
>
> His reward in Abhá Kingdom is inestimable. Advise you to erect on my behalf befitting monument at his grave.
>
> His mantle as Trustee of funds of Ḥuqúq now falls on 'Alí-Muḥammad his son.
>
> Instruct Rawhani Ṭihrán to arrange befitting memorial gatherings in capital and provinces to honor memory of mighty pillar in cradle of Faith of Bahá'u'lláh.

---

[535] Muhájir, Dr Muhájir: Hand of the Cause of God, Knight of Bahá'u'lláh, 251.
[536] Muhájir, Dr Muhájir: Hand of the Cause of God, Knight of Bahá'u'lláh, 251.

> Newly appointed Trustee of Ḥuqúq is now elevated to rank of Hand of Cause.[537]

In particular, the fourth and sixth lines particularly later shocked Dr 'Alí-Muḥammad Varqá, the son of the Hand of the Cause Valíyu'lláh Varqá. Mr Furútan, as secretary of the National Spiritual Assembly, had received the aforementioned cable from the Guardian and was in charge of delivering the news to Dr Alí-Muḥammad Varqá. Upon receiving the cable, Mr Furútan went immediately to Dr Varqá.[538]

In her book *Hand of the Cause of God Furútan*, Iran Furútan Muhájir relates the following story on how Dr Varqá heard of his designation as a Hand of the Cause:

> ... [It] was Mr. Furútan who had to convey this message to Dr. Varqá. In the memorial meeting for Hand of the Cause Valíyu'lláh Varqá, after prayers had been chanted Mr. Furútan read the message for the congregation. He had finished reading the first part when Dr. Varqá stood up and left the hall. He was overwhelmed with the news that that he was now appointed Trustee of the Huqúq. Mr. Furútan went after him and found him in the corridor weeping. He related, "I hugged him and consoled him and said, 'I have news for you. Wait until you hear it; that is when you will really weep.' I then read the rest of the message of the beloved Guardian to him." [539]

According to Mrs Muhájir, "These events testify to the humility of the Hands of the Cause. None of them ever believed they were worthy of this august station." [540]

---

[537] Shoghi Effendi, Messages to the Bahá'í World: 1950–1957 (Wilmette, Illinois: US Bahá'í Publishing Trust, 1971), 173-74.

[538] Bahá'í Perspective, "Appointment of the Hands of the Cause," 2015, https://www.youtube.com/watch?v=peW4QAaB7Ts. The transcription has been edited to facilitate understanding of the context.

[539] Muhájir, Hand of the Cause of God Furútan, 220.

[540] Muhájir, Hand of the Cause of God Furútan, 220.

The untimely death of the Guardian in November 1957 was a devastating blow to Dr Varqá as well as to the other Hands. Dr Varqá attended the funeral in London and from there he travelled to the Holy Land for the Conclave of the Hands of the Cause. One of the first tasks the Hands undertook was to establish whether the Guardian had left a will and testament. The Hands of the Cause among themselves appointed nine members to search Shoghi Effendi's office to see whether he left a will and a testament.

An official statement issued by the Hands of the Holy Land concluded that such a document was non-existent.

> This morning immediately after 9:00 a.m. we, the five Hands of the Cause assigned to service at the World Centre of the Faith, Rúhíyyih Khánum, Mason Remey, Amelia E. Collins, Ugo Giachery, and Leroy Ioas as well as Hands of the Cause Ḥasan Balyuzi, a member of the Afnán family, Mr. Horace Holley, representing the believers of the Western Hemisphere, Músá Banání; representing the believers of the African continent, and Dr 'Alí-Muḥammad Varqá Trustee of the beloved Guardian, representing also the Asian continent, (totaling to the number of Bahá) have met, in order to open the Guardian's safe and desk [and] search for a Will and Testament if one was executed by Shoghi Effendi.[541]

Dr Varqá later said of that 19 November 1957 morning:

> Amatu'l-Bahá delivered us the keys of the safe and asked us "you are free to go everywhere and investigate if you can find a will and testament". I remember, we were probably two or three hours in that room. The other Hands were waiting in Bahjí … We looked everywhere, everywhere—we didn't find anything.[542]

---

[541] Rụhíyyih Rabbani, The Ministry of the Custodians 1957–1963 (Haifa, Israel 1992), 27.
[542] BahaiVideos, "The Hands of the Cause," last modified 30 July 2020, 2008, https://www.youtube.com/watch?v=vlmq7CCj_hE.

A pilgrim recalled a meeting with Dr Varqá in his office at the Bahá'í World Centre where he commented about that historical day:

> Dr Varqá told us how, after the passing of the beloved Guardian, the Hands of the Cause gathered in Haifa appointed nine of them to search the Guardian's office, which had been sealed by Amatu'l-Bahá Rúhíyyih Khánum, in order to find out whether he had left any testament. Dr Varqá recounted his surprise and admiration at the frugality of the office. Tears filled his eyes as he described Shoghi Effendi's desk whose top had a crack running through it from side to side.[543]

On 25 November 1957, the Hands of the Cause formed from among themselves a body of nine members as Custodians of the Bahá'í World Centre in order "to carry on from this Centre the provisions of the World Bahá'í Crusade and to discharge there our responsibility of protecting and propagating the Faith of Bahá'u'lláh".[544] Dr Varqá did not form part of this body but acted as a substitute Custodian at various times when one of the permanent members was away, until the Universal House of Justice was elected in 1963.

In the intervening years between the passing of Shoghi Effendi in 1957 and the establishment of the Universal House of Justice in 1963, "the Hands of the Cause directed the affairs of the Faith in their capacity as Chief Stewards of Bahá'u'lláh's embryonic World Commonwealth."[545]

In an extraordinary statement in the Kitáb-i-Aqdas where Baha'u'llah foretells a possible discontinuity in the Aghsán's[546] being the Centre of the Faith (i.e., 'Abdu'l-Bahá and Shoghi Effendi) that might take place before the establishment of the Universal House of Justice, He places the responsibility of managing the material assets of the Faith on what we now understand was a reference to the ministry of the Hands of the Cause:

---

[543] Enrique Sanchez Jr, personal communication to the author.
[544] Rabbani, The Ministry of the Custodians 1957–1963, 31.
[545] Bahá'u'lláh, The Kitáb-i-Aqdas: The Most Holy Book, note 183.
[546] Bahá'u'lláh's direct male descendants.

> Endowments dedicated to charity revert to God, the Revealer of Signs. None hath the right to dispose of them without leave from Him Who is the Dawning-place of Revelation. After Him, this authority shall pass to the Aghsán, and after them to the House of Justice—should it be established in the world by then—that they may use these endowments for the benefit of the Places which have been exalted in this Cause, and for whatsoever hath been enjoined upon them by Him Who is the God of might and power. Otherwise, the endowments shall revert to the people of Bahá who speak not except by His leave and judge not save in accordance with what God hath decreed in this Tablet—lo, they are the champions of victory betwixt heaven and earth—that they may use them in the manner that hath been laid down in the Book by God, the Mighty, the Bountiful.[547]

As Custodians of the Faith, they also managed the Ḥuqúqu'lláh, whose Trustee, Dr 'Alí-Muḥammad Varqá, had been appointed by the Guardian of the Faith in 1955. During the ministry of the Custodians, Dr Varqá lived in Ṭihrán, Iran. He submitted regular reports to the Custodians and, according to their instructions and disbursed the amounts he received for the Ḥuqúq.[548] Normally, Dr Varqá dedicated his summer university breaks to travel and to visiting Bahá'í communities in Iran and abroad.

Dr Varqá was present during the First International Convention in 1963 when the Universal House of Justice was elected. Subsequent to this historic event, he also attended the first Bahá'í World Congress in London which celebrated the centenary of the Declaration of Bahá'u'lláh, as well as the victorious consummation of the beloved Guardian world-encircling Crusade—a Crusade inaugurated by Shoghi Effendi a decade earlier. During the joyful occasion of the Congress, Dr Varqá was joined by eleven other Hands of the Cause,

---

547 Bahá'u'lláh, The Kitáb-i-Aqdas: The Most Holy Book, 34-35.

548 Baharieh Rouhani Ma'ani, "The Evolution of the Institution of Ḥuqúqu'lláh," in the Institution of Ḥuqúqu'lláh Newsletter, issue 61, 2, January 1996.

who had brought to the space the "nearness of the Guardian's spirit and his presence",[549] and the nine members of the newly-elected Supreme Body. Adding to this was the attendance of six thousand or so believers from all corners of the globe who rejoiced in the monumental developments of the Faith of Bahá'u'lláh—at the time, signifying the largest gathering of Bahá'ís ever witnessed.

In testimony to the extraordinary work of the Hands, the Universal House of Justice remarked in a message dated 30 April 1963 addressed to the First Bahá'í World Congress:

> The paeans of joy and gratitude, of love and adoration which we now raise to the throne of Bahá'u'lláh would be inadequate, and the celebrations of this Most Great Jubilee in which, as promised by our beloved Guardian, we are now engaged, would be marred were no tribute paid at this time to the Hands of the Cause of God. For they share the victory with their beloved commander, he who raised them up and appointed them. They kept the ship on its course and brought it safe to port. The Universal House of Justice, with pride and love, recalls on this supreme occasion its profound admiration for the heroic work which they have accomplished. We do not wish to dwell on the appalling dangers which faced the infant Cause when it was suddenly deprived of our beloved Shoghi Effendi, but rather to acknowledge with all the love and gratitude of our hearts the reality of the sacrifice, the labor, the self-discipline, the superb stewardship of the Hands of the Cause of God.[550]

19.5 An Important Mission

An interesting coincidence between Bahá'u'lláh's and Varqá's family is that both originated in the province of Núr. 'Abdu'lláh Núrí, Varqá's father-in-law and Rúḥu'lláh's grandfather, was also

---

[549] Beatrice Ashton, "The Most Great Jubilee," The Baha'i World (1963-1968), 1974, 59.

[550] Message of the Universal House of Justice dated 30 April 1963 to the First Bahá'í World Congress held in London.

contemporary of Bahá'u'lláh having visited Him in the Holy Land sometime between 1890 and 1891. He was also present on the solemn occasion of the Ascension of Bahá'u'lláh in 1892.

Mírzá Buzurg, Bahá'u'lláh's father and a Persian aristocrat who served as a minister to the Sháh, had passed away in Tehran in 1839. However, nobody knows when Bahá'u'lláh's mother, Khadíjih Khánum, passed away nor where she is buried.[551]

Mírzá Buzurg's body was taken to the city of Najaf in Iraq which was considered a holy city as it was the place where the Iman 'Alí, cousin and son-in-law of Prophet Muḥammad, was buried. For this reason, Najaf is the third holiest spot in Islam Shí'ih, the major religion in Iran. The first and second holiest spots are Mecca and the Mosque of al-Aqsa in Jerusalem, respectively. The latter, according to Shí'ih followers, is the place from where Prophet Muḥammad "flew" up to the heavens.

As Najaf was considered a holy place, Shí'ih followers long to be buried there, a tradition that still continues to this day. The cemetery is called Wadi al-Salam meaning the "Valley of Peace". Literally thousands of corpses were, and still are, transported on mule from Iran, sometimes in very unhygienic conditions. It is considered the largest cemetery in the world and contains the remains of approximately five million people spread over 900 hectares. Approximately 50,000 bodies are interred there every year.

But nobody knew exactly where in that vast cemetery Mírzá Buzurg was buried. Shoghi Effendi made the identification of the location of his remains a goal of the Ten Year Crusade for the Iranian community. A corollary to this goal was the transfer of the remains to the Bahá'í cemetery of Baghdad. Such a task was indeed painstaking and laborious as after more than a century the inscriptions on many tombstones had faded and graves were damaged by weather and lack of care. Mr Rawḥání, an Iranian believer who spoke Arabic, was given

[551] Baharieh Rouhani Ma'ani, Leaves of the Twin Divine Trees, 80-81 (George Ronald Publisher, 2008).

the hallowed task to shoulder. It took three years to find the grave and, of course, involved arduous research. He later commented:

> In 1954 we decided to go pioneering and arranged our affairs so as to leave as soon as possible. Suddenly we received a request from the National Assembly for me to go to Tehran. I went there immediately and met with Hand of the Cause Furútan. He asked me to a meeting at 8:00 p.m. at Hand of the Cause Dr Varqá's home. At the appointed time I went there. They told me: the beloved Guardian has requested that you leave for Iraq to search for the remains of the father of the Blessed Beauty and the mother of the Báb[552] and to transfer them to the Ḥazíratu'l-Quds. When I mentioned that I was preparing to go pioneering, they said that the instruction of the Guardian had priority. The National Assembly then wrote me a letter to this effect. After receiving this letter I left for Iraq.[553]

According to volume XIII of *The Bahá'í World*:

> In July, 1957 the sacred remains of Mírzá Buzurg, the father of Bahá'u'lláh, were identified and removed to a Bahá'í cemetery. On July 27 of that year, Hands of the Cause 'Alí Akbar Furútan, Shu'a'u'llah 'Alá'í and 'Alí Muḥammad Varqá arrived from Ṭihrán to join Hand of the Cause Tarázu'lláh Samandari in paying homage, on behalf of the Guardian, to the memory of that "blessed and highly revered personage."[554]

19.6 His Travels around the World

In the same year, Dr Varqá, representing the beloved Guardian attended the inaugural convention of the first National Spiritual

---

[552] Baharieh Rouhani Ma'ani notes: "She was buried in either Najaf or Karbilá. The exact place of her interment will be made public at an appropriate time in the future and her remains will be transferred to the Bahá'í cemetery of Baghdad, fulfilment of Shoghi Effendi's wishes, which he set as a goal of the Ten Year Plan (1953-63)" (p. 24).

[553] Muhájir, Hand of the Cause of God Furútan, 288.

[554] The Universal House of Justice, The Bahá'í World (1954-1963), 297.

Assembly of Argentina, Bolivia, Chile, Uruguay and Paraguay. Bahá'í News reported on that historical and luminous Convention which included a visit to the resting-place of May Maxwell (1870-1940),[555] Amatu'l-Bahá Rúhíyyih Khánum's mother, and an early pioneer to South America.

> Bahá'í history will record the first pilgrimage of the believers of the five countries accompanying the Hand of the Cause, Dr. Varqá, to the Tomb of May Maxwell "living in solitary glory in the southern outpost of the Western Hemisphere," whose Tomb, as promised by Shoghi Effendi "will become the historic center of pioneer Bahá'í activity." The event took place on the first day of Riḍván April 21, as the friends gathered in the tranquil cemetery outside the village of Quilmés to pay homage to the radiant martyr who fills a special niche in the hearts of all South American believers. The "Tablet of Visitation" was chanted in Persian by the Hand of the Cause, followed by its recitation for the first time in the Spanish language at this sacred spot.
>
> Unforgettable, too, will be the joyous Riḍván Festival, held on the evening of April 21, as Dr Varqá gave a new awareness of the meaning of this sacred festival, recalling the first Riḍván when the great Declaration was made, and the annual celebration of this event as the only holy period in which Bahá'í forces are united in formulating plans for action in the year ahead… Then the Hand of the Cause, Dr Varqá, lighted a candle from the Tomb of Bahá'u'lláh, symbolically shedding illumination on the assemblage during the election of the Convention officers. This was followed by the anointing of the friends by Dr Varqá, using four flasks of attar of roses sent by the beloved Guardian for this purpose.

---

[555] Marion Holley, "May Maxwell (in Memoriam)," in The Baha'i World (1938-1940), ed. The National Spiritual Assembly of the Bahá'ís of the United States and Canada, vol. VIII, 631-642 (Wilmette, Illinois: Bahá'í Publishing Trust, 1942).

> Dr Varqá then read the Guardian's Convention Message to the four Latin-American Conventions.[556] [557]

Because Dr Varqá was the only Hand of the Cause fluent in French, he was assigned majority of the work pertaining to French-speaking communities in Europe, Central America and the Caribbean and Africa. His work included strengthening the National Spiritual Assembly of France when, in 1960, three years after Shoghi Effendi's passing, most members were expelled from the Cause for supporting Mason Remey's claims to the Guardianship. The National Spiritual Assembly was dissolved by the Hands of the Cause and a new national body was formed in 1962. Dr Varqá spent fifteen days consulting and strengthening that institution and the community in their firmness to the Covenant.[558]

Dr Varqá was the official representative of the Bahá'í World Centre at several inaugural national conventions. For instance, in 1958 Dr Varqá represented the Hands of the Cause at the Bahá'í Intercontinental Conference in Jakarta and Singapore. Likewise, he was the Hands' official representative for the inaugural convention of Belgium (1962) and Luxembourg (1962). Furthermore, Dr Varqá represented the Universal House of Justice at the first national conventions of Central Africa (Congo and Gabon) (1971), Jordan (1975), French Antilles (1977), Mauritania (1978), Windwards Islands (1981), Martinique (1984), French Guiana (1984), St Lucia (1983), Czechoslovakia (April 1991), Greenland (May 1992) and Sicily (1995). He also served as the representative of the House of Justice on two other instances; these were the two conventions which formed the Regional Spiritual Assemblies of Ukraine, Belarus and Moldova (May 1992) and Slovenia and Croatia (May 1994). As a Hand of the Cause he travelled extensively —at times, making lengthy

---

[556] Ellen Sims, "Argentina, Bolivia, Chile, Uruguay and Paraguay Form National Assembly in Buenos Aires," Bahá'í News, June, 1957, 9-10.

[557] The four new Latin-American National Spiritual Assemblies were (a) Argentina, Chile, Uruguay, Paraguay and Bolivia; (b) Brasil, Peru, Colombia, Ecuador and Venezuela; (c) Greater Antilles and (d) Mexico and the Central-American republics.

[558] Rabbani, The Ministry of the Custodians 1957–1963, 371.

trips— throughout the globe to assist local and national communities and to participate in innumerable summer schools and conferences that spanned sixty different countries around the world.[559] [560]

Dr Varqá's contribution to the development of the institution of the Continental Boards of Counsellors[561] and the International Teaching Centre[562] were also foremost among his major accomplishments. Dr Ayman, a former Continental Counsellor, notes:

> In participating in consultations with the Universal House of Justice, Dr Varqá contributed to the process that created the institution of the Continental Boards of Counsellors, fostered the development of the administrative institutions of the Bahá'í Faith, and the establishment and evolution of the International Teaching Centre, based in Haifa …[563]

19.7 The Islamic Revolution of Iran

During the closing months of 1978 and the beginning of 1979 Dr Varqá was visiting European countries when the Islamic revolution broke out in Iran. A campaign of persecution, harassment, imprisonment, killing, and confiscation which continues to this day, was waged against the Bahá'ís in the Cradle of the Faith.

It was obvious that his life was going to be in danger if he returned to Iran. At that time he was visiting Luxembourg and received advice from the Bahá'í World Centre not to travel back to Iran.[564] According to Barron Harper:

---

559 Adamson, Historical Dictionary of the Bahá'í Faith, 2006, 489.

560 Ayman, "Varqā, 'Ali-Moḥammad," in Encyclopædia Iranica.

561 The Universal House of Justice announced the establishment of the Continental Board of Counselors to all National Spiritual Assemblies on 21 June 1968, as a new development of the Administrative Order of Bahá'u'lláh.

562 The institution of the International Teaching Centre was created by the Universal House of Justice in 1973 with all the seventeen living Hands of the Cause as ex officio members along with three Counselors.

563 Dr Iraj Ayman. Personal communication to the author.

564 Adamson, Historical Dictionary of the Bahá'í Faith, 2006, 489.

> While Dr Varqá was visiting Bahá'í communities in Europe in 1978, he received a message from the National Spiritual Assembly of Iran advising him to delay his return home, as the government had determined to impose a heavy duty on the Bahá'í properties and endowments that had been held in the name of Shoghi Effendi. The National Assembly believed that if Dr Varqá, who was the representative of the owners of Bahá'í property and the Trustee of Ḥuqúqu'lláh, was not in the country, the Assembly might better negotiate with the government to reduce the tax. Thus, with the approval of the Universal House of Justice, he remained in Europe to perform other services. When the Iranian Revolution occurred in 1979, the situation for the Bahá'ís worsened and Dr Varqá never returned to Iran. He was accepted as a refugee in Canada, where he lived for a number of years before being called to service in the Holy Land by the Universal House of Justice.[565]

This turbulent period in the history of the Faith was the catalyst for Persian believers leaving Iran in the face of mounting persecutions. Across several gatherings in 1980, and now living in the West, Dr. Varqá called on hundreds of these believers who had fled Iran and settled in North America to pioneer overseas. The cables from the National Spiritual Assembly of the United States to the Universal House of Justice reflect the galvanizing spirit of those meetings held at the beginning of 1980:

> TWO HUNDRED AND FIFTY PERSIAN FRIENDS GATHERED SAN DIEGO CENTER 24 FEBRUARY PRESENCE HAND CAUSE VARQÁ DEEPLY GRIEVED PASSING DEAR HAND CAUSE BALYUZI. OFFER HEARTFELT SUBMISSION SUPREME INSTITUTION. FIFTY BELIEVERS DETERMINED RESPOND FILL PIONEERING TRAVEL TEACHING GOALS. OTHERS HOPEFUL MOVE LATER. BESEECH PRAYERS HOLY SHRINES BESTOWAL CONFIRMATION SUCCESS.
> (From a cablegram received 26 February 1980)

---

[565] Harper, Lights of Certitude, 354.

> FOURTEEN HUNDRED PERSIAN BELIEVERS GATHERED SANTA MONICA CALIFORNIA 24 FEBRUARY PRESENCE HAND CAUSE VARQÁ COUNSELORS KHAMSI SALMANPUR AND AYMAN TWO NATIONAL SPIRITUAL ASSEMBLY MEMBERS AND AUXILIARY BOARD MEMBER JALIL MAHMOUDI. SPIRIT DEDICATION INTENSE. COUNSELORS REMAINED LOS ANGELES FOLLOWING TWO DAYS TO CONSULT WITH PROSPECTIVE PIONEERS ... (From a cablegram received 2 March 1980)[566]

The Hand of the Cause Dr Varqá eventually settled in Montreal, Canada, spending his time between home and Haifa particularly since 1992. In 1996 he transferred his residence to Haifa.

19.8 The Office of Ḥuqúqu'lláh

In January 1992, the Hand of the Cause also initiated a Ḥuqúqu'lláh Newsletter that was distributed to all Deputy Trustees, their representatives and all National Spiritual Assemblies all over the world. In his first issue Dr Varqá "expressed his hope that this publication will become a vehicle for communication among the friends and education in the Right of God, that it will strengthen the relationship between the institution of Ḥuqúqu'lláh and other institutions of the Faith".[567] An appendix of this book contains one of Dr Varqá's talks where he expounds on the importance of the sacred law of Ḥuqúqu'lláh.

At the request of the Universal House in Justice, in the summer of 1997, Dr Varqá undertook a trip to Europe and North America where he spoke at length and elaborated on the law of Ḥuqúqu'lláh. At the age of eighty-five, the Hand of the Cause addressed hundreds of believers in Barcelona (Spain), Frankfurt (Germany) and in various American cities such as New York, Dallas, Chicago and Los Angeles

---

[566] Handal, The Khamsis: A Cradle of True Gold, 201-02.
[567] Waters, Ḥuqúqu'lláh, The Right of God, 136.

as well as in Vancouver, Canada. These activities were followed by meetings in Bahá'í communities in Italy and the United Kingdom. Thousands of friends congregated in those gatherings eager to listen to the Hand of the Cause. Dr Varqá said:

> Following a meeting that I had with the House of Justice last January, I received instructions from that Supreme Body to come to the United States and meet with the American friends in order to draw their attention to the exigencies and needs of the Faith at this critical time in the history of mankind, during which the existing orders are breaking down, giving way to the emergence of a new paradigm based on the love and spiritual values presented by Bahá'u'lláh to mankind.[568]

After returning to Iran following the completion of his studies in Paris in 1950, Dr Varqá had served in various administrative capacities within the Bahá'í community up until his appointment as a Hand of the Cause five years later. In particular, he dedicated time to assist his father Valíyu'lláh Varqá in his role as Trustee of the Ḥuqúqu'lláh. As the new Trustee of the Ḥuqúqu'lláh, Dr Varqá continued his father's role with exemplary dedication and unstinting vitality.

At Riḍván 1991, the House of Justice made the law of Ḥuqúqu'lláh universally applicable. "All are lovingly called to observe it", was the exhortation of the Supreme Body.[569] Already in 1984 the delegates to the National Convention of the United States had signed a roll to the Universal House of Justice requesting for this law of God to be applied to all believers in their country. [570]Although previously the law of Ḥuqúqu'lláh was not applicable to the Western believers, a number of them followed it out of their own heart. It is known that the first

---

[568] Waters, Ḥuqúqu'lláh, The Right of God, 173.

[569] Message of the Universal House of Justice to the Bahá'ís of the World, Riḍván 1991.

[570] Letter of the Univeral House of Justice to the National Spiritual Assembly of the Bahá'ís of the United States dated 6 August 1984.

Western believer to observe the law was Thomas Breakwell (1872–1902). He was also the first Englishman to become a Bahá'í.[571]

In the years preceding its momentus announcement, the House of Justice focused on educating the Bahá'í world in the law of the Ḥuqúqu'lláh, an objective that was made an explicit goal of the Six Year Plan (1986–1992).

As indicated above, at Riḍván 1991, the House of Justice made the law of Ḥuqúqu'lláh universally applicable. On that announcement, the Universal House of Justice wrote to Dr Varqá:

> On occasion worldwide application Law Ḥuqúqu'lláh coinciding opening Holy Year, we extend to you our heartfelt congratulations and deepest gratitude for your self-sacrificing labours exerted over so many years and for the exalted standard you have set for all those who will serve in this institution in the centuries to come.[572]

On the Day of the Covenant, 26 November 1991, the Universal House of Justice announced the establishment of the Office of Ḥuqúqu'lláh under the direction of the Chief Trustee of Ḥuqúqu'lláh, Dr Varqá[573] "in anticipation of the worldwide application of the Law of Ḥuqúqu'lláh next Riḍván [1992]."[574] Allan Waters explains that "Bahá'u'lláh affirmed that future rulings regarding the implementation of the law of Ḥuqúqu'lláh would be enacted by the Universal House of Justice. As the enactment of these details was left until the establishment of the House of Justice, Shoghi Effendi was not required to develop and refine the structure and functioning of the institution of Ḥuqúqu'lláh during his lifetime."[575]

---

[571] Rajwantee Lakshiman-Lepain, The Life of Thomas Breakwell, 3 (London: Bahá'í Publishing Trust, 1998).
[572] Waters, Ḥuqúqu'lláh, The Right of God, 140.
[573] The Office of Ḥuqúqu'lláh was created in November 1991 by the Universal House of Justice.
[574] Message of the Universal House of Justice to the Bahá'ís of the World, 27 November 1991.
[575] Waters, Ḥuqúqu'lláh, The Right of God, 7-10.

"And when in Riḍván 1992 the law of Ḥuqúqu'lláh became a universally binding obligation," wrote Allan Waters, "Dr Varqá realised one of his most ardent hopes and cherished desires—that all believers would have the privilege and bounty of obeying this law and offering the Right of God."[576]

Signifying a further development in the institution of Ḥuqúqu'lláh, this Office was charged with dealing with all the affairs related to this important institution and law. The Office was also made responsible for the functioning of the network of Regional and National Boards of Ḥuqúqu'lláh throughout the world and for providing guidance about the application and implementation of this sacred law.

The first boards, formed with Deputies and Representatives, were created in 1987 in the United States, Canada, Asia and Europe. The first conference for these officers took place in Haifa in January 1987. A second conference on the Ḥuqúqu'lláh was held at Landegg Academy in August 1991 while the third conference followed in New York in November 1992.[577]

Following these developments a three-member International Board of Trustees of Ḥuqúqu'lláh[578] was created in 2005 to guide and supervise the work of Regional and National Boards of Trustees of Ḥuqúqu'lláh around the world.

With the appointment of the International Board of Trustees in 2005, Dr Varqá, then ninety-three years old, was relieved from the heavy burden of directly managing the Office of Ḥuqúqu'lláh, although he was kept informed of developments on a regular basis.

In 2005, the Hand of the Cause reached fifty years in his appointment as a Trustee by Shoghi Effendi. The Universal House of Justice wrote to him the following words recognising his brilliant contribution.

---

576 Waters, Ḥuqúqu'lláh, The Right of God, 7-10.

577 Waters, Ḥuqúqu'lláh, The Right of God, 138.

578 Message of the Universal House of Justice to the Bahá'ís of the World, Riḍván 2005.

> Under your admirable stewardship the institution of Ḥuqúqu'lláh has developed from a phase when only Eastern believers were required to observe the mighty law on which it is founded to the current stage of worldwide observance. Among the notable accomplishments during this process were the launching of a worldwide programme for the education of the believers in the law of Ḥuqúqu'lláh, the formation of a network of Boards of Trustees in many parts of the world, the establishment of the Office of Ḥuqúqu'lláh in the Holy Land, and the convening of a series of international Ḥuqúqu'lláh conferences.
>
> Our gratitude to you is beyond expression in words. Through your consecration to the performance of the duties assigned to you by Shoghi Effendi, you have made a contribution to the development of the World Order of Bahá'u'lláh which will be remembered throughout the Dispensation, as the law of Ḥuqúqu'lláh exerts its beneficent influence on the growth and flourishing of a world civilization.[579]

19.9 A Source of Love

Dr Varqá left a lasting impression on all sort of believers, whether they were local Bahá'ís, pioneers, pilgrims or staff members at the World Centre of the Faith in the Holy Land.

In his travels around the world, Dr. Varqá was an unceasing flow of encouragement and wisdom to believers' hearts. Every place he went, the friends were exhilarated by his visits. He touched the very core of people's beings, reaching them with pure love and unalloyed affection. A believer recalled his impression of Dr Varqá's character: "gentle kindliness, the humane understanding, the compassion and the loving-kindness of this man".[580]

---

[579] Waters, Ḥuqúqu'lláh, The Right of God, 7-10.
[580] McLean, Divine Simplicity: Remembering the last Hand of the Cause of God, Dr 'Alí-Muhammad Varqá, 2007.

"When Dr Varqá Hand of the Cause", a believer wrote, "heard that we were pioneers from the Cayman Islands, he invited us to his house that evening. I was so happy to see the beloved professor of my sister, who we adored. We spent that evening with Dr. and Mrs. Varqá and a few Bahá'í friends. It was a memorable milestone in our blessed life." [581]

His presence at a summer school, according to the Bahá'í News published in 1970, "contributed widely to awaken the enthusiasm of the friends".[582] A participant at a Peace Conference wrote that Dr Varqá "showered his young audience with universal love and visibly increased their love of learning about the Faith and the solution it offers for the ills of humanity."[583] Further, a believer, newly enrolled at this time, commented: "From the moment I set my eyes on him, I was dumb-struck. I couldn't speak at all, not even when being introduced. I felt a very strong but quiet power that emanated from him. This was something that I had never really felt before from anyone. I would say he seemed the most humble person I have ever met."[584]

"Mr. Varqá was long awaited by the hundreds of youth at the conference", said another Bahá'í. "He reflected so much love through his piercing and luminous eyes and with his radiant smile he made our hearts to rejoice. Everyone wanted a photo with him and regardless of him being fatigued, Mr. Varqá allowed hundreds of photos to be taken with so much generosity, patience and love. He conveyed a calm and serene disposition typical of those who live in radiant acquiescence. He dedicated all his time to us without giving himself a space to rest.

---

[581] Shahla Behroozi Gillbanks, Footprints in the Sand of Time: Memories of a Maidservant (Sandy, Bedfordshire: The Afnan Library Trust, 2019), 247. http://www.afnanlibrary.org/wp-content/uploads/2019/05/Footprints-in-the-Sands-of-Time-c.pdf.

[582] National Spiritual Assembly of the Bahá'ís of the United States, "Schools in Belgium," Bahá'í News, June, 1970, 16.

[583] Bahá'í World Centre, "The Work and Travels of the Hands of the Cause," The Bahá'í World (1986-1992), 1998, 638.

[584] McLean, Divine Simplicity: Remembering the last Hand of the Cause of God, Dr 'Alí-Muhammad Varqá, 2007.

His presence was majestic and upright like a king but wearing a crown of humility."[585]

Dr Varqá had a special love for pilgrims. A believer attending pilgrimage remarked: "Dear Dr. Varqá, so pure and sweet—so frail but luminous. He is remarkable continuing to offer this incredible service to pilgrims, to make them feel so welcome and cared for and loved. …we are so fortunate to have this precious opportunity to be in his presence, to feel his selfless love and his enormous dedication to this great faith of God. No easy retirement for him. He serves in all the ways he can to his last days."[586]Another pilgrim wrote:

> In 2005 my wife, my mother-in-law, and I went on pilgrimage to the Holy Land. One afternoon the guide informed us that Dr Varqá wanted to receive the friends from the Latin American pilgrimage group at his office. To our surprise and emotion, he received us with great humility and much warmth thanking us for taking the time. The eight or nine of us were so excited in his presence that we uttered nothing but thanks. He told us of his love and admiration for the Bahá'ís of Latin America and his happiness that we had been able to make the pilgrimage… We left his office inspired and moved, aware of how fortunate we were. [587]

Even until the last months of his life, Dr Varqá's continued to look personally after the pilgrims in the Holy Land. "My own last memory of Dr. Varqá was on May 27th of this year (2007)", Géza Farkas wrote. "Since one of his great joys was to have seen during his lifetime the Bahá'í Faith spread all over the world, he loved after his addresses to the pilgrims assembled in Haifa to hear prayers chanted, sung, and recited in their native languages. Among many others, even though I am Canadian, I recited a prayer in my mother tongue of Hungarian.

---

[585] Oscar Rojas, personal communication.
[586] McLean, Divine Simplicity: Remembering the last Hand of the Cause of God, Dr 'Alí-Muhammad Varqá, 2007.
[587] Enrique Sanchez Jr, personal communication to the author.

All of us did so with added fervour to the beaming face of our beloved Dr. Varqá."[588]

"The experience of being in his presence is enshrined in my soul forever", recalls a youth who used to drive him every day to a conference venue. "Dr Varqá would tell us not to spend time overthinking unimportant matters. He told us a story about this: 'That there was a very knowledgeable and renowned professor, and he was once asked whether at night he kept his beard over or under the blanket. The poor professor couldn't sleep at all that night!'"[589] Likewise, a Latin American Bahá'í who attended the same conference commented: "Something that impressed me most about him was that he exhibited in his demeanor a combination of two apparently incompatible characteristics: authority and humility".[590]

Believers serving at the World Centre remember Dr Varqá fondly. "For I and my family who, in spite of our unworthiness," wrote a former staff member, "had the honor and bounty of serving that beloved and chosen of Bahá —The Trustee/Chief Trustee of Ḥuqúqu'lláh, The Hand of the Cause of God, Dr Varqá. He was a most loving, gentle, kind, generous, thoughtful and noble spiritual being that we had the honor of crossing his path in our lives, for every moment of which we will remain eternally grateful. Just being in his joyful presence was inspiring and uplifting."[591]

In drawing on her vivid memories, Gloria Sadeghi Mogharabi shared:

> I had the honor and privilege of being in his presence almost every day while serving at the Bahá'í World Centre. In Dr. Varqá's eyes, you could see a depthless ocean of love and kindness. He was my dearest friend and confidante. I remember that every time I would visit him, he would joke that the storm (toofan) had arrived. My heart would fill with joy when he showered me with his love. Dr. Varqá truly had an

[588] Géza Farkas, 2007, at http://thegezafracas.blogspot.com, with permission.
[589] Dr Farid Tebyani, personal communication to the author.
[590] Dr Omar Brdarevic, personal communication to the author.
[591] Personal communication to the author.

> immense sense of humor, a benevolent and generous heart, and a glorious spirit. He will be greatly missed.[592]

Dr Janet Khan, a member of the Research Office of the Bahá'í World Centre, draws attention towards particular aspects of his noble character: "On reflection, Dr. Varqá impressed me as being a very quiet, sweet-natured, humble and highly perceptive man. In spite of age and declining health, he remained totally dedicated to the work of the Cause until the last days of his life."[593] "Dr Varqá", said Michael Day, another former staff member, "seemed to me to radiate loving kindness and serenity".[594] Allan Waters provided further insight about Dr Varqá's spiritual qualities and attributes:

> He brought a nobility of spirit to his daily undertakings, and he did this with the utmost humility. He possessed a gentleness and a dignity, and those privileged to spend time in his presence, whether believers or not, knew that there was someone with a magnetic responsibility, someone who also carried an important mantle of responsibility.[595]

19.10 The End of a Chapter in Bahá'í History

Dr Varqá was the last-living and longest-serving Hand of the Cause and Trustee of the Ḥuqúqu'lláh. He served in these capacities for 52 years. Out of the 42 Hands appointed by Shoghi Effendi (including ten posthumously), he was the only one never able to meet the Guardian. Shoghi Effendi appointed Dr Varqá two years before his untimely death. According to Jack McLean:

> Dr Varqá had more than once mentioned that he did not anticipate that Shoghi Effendi would leave this life at age 60, with the torch of his many, prodigious accomplishments burnt out by three and half decades of incessant, superhuman labour.

---

[592] Gloria Sadeghi Mogharabi, personal communication to the author.
[593] Dr Janet Khan, personal communication to the author.
[594] Michael Day, personal communication to the author.
[595] Waters, Ḥuqúqu'lláh, The Right of God, 8-9.

> No doubt he looked forward to meeting his Guardian in this world, but destiny was to decree otherwise.[596]

Dr Varqá served with the same degree of consecration as his illustrious father and grandfather —all three of them members of the sacred Institution of the Hands of the Cause of God.

Until the very last breaths of his earthly existence he was engaged in correspondence with a large number of friends and institutions throughout the worldwide community. Dr Varqá passed away on 22 September 2017 at the age of 95, just a few weeks before the fiftieth anniversary of the passing of the beloved Guardian. He was buried in the hallowed grounds of the Bahá'í cemetery in Haifa. In a letter dated 23 September 2007, the Supreme Body addressed the Bahá'ís of the world:

> In the early hours of last night, revered, greatly admired, well-loved Hand of the Cause of God Dr 'Alí-Muḥammad Varqá departed this earthly plane after a period of outstanding, consecrated service to the Blessed Beauty that spanned many decades.
>
> With grieving hearts we bid farewell to the last of that noble company, the Chief Stewards of Bahá'u'lláh's embryonic World Commonwealth, into which he is now gathered in realms of deathless delight and joy. The fervor of his love for the teaching work inspired countless believers across the globe, whether at the events he attended as the representative of the Guardian or of the Universal House of Justice, or in his extensive travels to promote the goals of the Master's Divine Plan. In such activities he contributed mightily to the progress of the Ten Year Crusade and subsequent global teaching plans. Until his final days, he was leonine in his determination to protect the Faith. He wore with marked distinction the mantle of Trustee of Ḥuqúqu'lláh that fell to him from the shoulders

---

[596] McLean, Divine Simplicity: Remembering the last Hand of the Cause of God, Dr 'Alí-Muhammad Varqá, 2007.

> of his illustrious father, impressing a record of imperishable achievement on the annals of the Formative Age—achievement which has set a pattern that secures important features for the operation into the future of that divinely ordained institution. Throughout the many years of his valiant endeavor to maintain the integrity of the two offices of so high a rank to which he was simultaneously elevated, his manner was imbued with a luminous gentleness, a genuine kindliness and a natural dignity which combined to reflect the character of a saintly personality. For these exemplary traits he will ever be remembered. Our heartfelt sympathy reaches out to the members of his dear family in their sad loss, which is shared by the entire Bahá'í community. With deeply held trust in the bounties of the Gracious Lord, we pray at the Sacred Threshold for the progress of his resplendent soul throughout the divine worlds."[597]

On the occasion of the Day of the Covenant in 2007, the House of Justice poignantly called to mind the following: "How sobering, indeed, it is to realize that Dr Varqá's departure brought to an end the remarkable stewardship of an institution whose legacy is unparalleled in religious history! … The passing of Dr Varqá marks both the end of a chapter of Bahá'í history and the beginning of a new stage in the unfolding of that Order."[598] That he was and will continue to be "well-loved" by the lovers of the Most Great Beauty is a sure testimony to his life lived in utmost faithfulness to the Cause of God.

Indeed, as 'Abdu'l-Bahá foretold, Dr Varqá was a *Yad* and *Mu'ayyad*, a *Confirmed* and *Hand* of the Cause of God.[599]

---

[597] Waters, Ḥuqúqu'lláh, The Right of God, 2012, 7-10.
[598] Message of the Universal House of Justice dated 27 November 2007. Source: Bahá'í Reference Library.
[599] Harper, Lights of Fortitude, 2007, 351.

Figure 37: Varqá, Rúḥu'lláh, Mírzá Ḥusayn Zanjání and Ḥájí Ímám Zanjání chained to each other in the Anbár prison from left to right.

Figure 38: The mausoleum of Varqá and Rúḥu'lláh in Tehran.

Figure 39: Muẓaffari'd-Dín Sháh (reigned 1896–1907).

Figure 40: Rúḥu'lláh's surviving brothers: Mírzá Valíyu'lláh Varqá (left) and Mírzá 'Azízu'lláh Varqá (right), in Tehran in 1908.

Figure 41:'Abdu'l-Bahá in Dublin, New Hampshire, in 1912. Valíyu'lláh Varqá is second from the right. Source: National Bahá'í Archives, United States.

Figure 42: Valíyu'lláh Varqá as a young man.

Figure 43: First National Spiritual Assembly of Iran formed in 1934. The future Hands of the Cause Shu'á'u'lláh 'Alá'í and Valíyu'lláh Varqá are seated first and second from the left, respectively.

Figure 44: Bahá'is of Lima welcoming Hand of the Cause Valíyu'lláh Varqá in Lima, Peru, August 1953.

Figure 45: Hand of the Cause and Trustee of the Ḥuqúqu'lláh Valíyu'lláh Varqá.

Figure 46: Members of the first Spiritual Assembly of Tehran (1897). Mírzá 'Azízu'lláh Varqá is seated in the middle of the front row holding the Greatest Name. On the middle row three of the four Hands of the Cause are seated: (from left to right) Mírzá Ḥasan-i-Adíb, Ibn-i- Aṣdaq, Ḥájí Mullá Akbar (Ḥájí Akhund). The covered faces are those of Covenant-breakers. Courtesy: George Ronald Oxford.

Figure 47. Childhood photograph of Dr Varqá on which 'Abdu'l-Bahá wrote "Hand", "Confirmed" and "Yá Bahá u'l-Abhá" (O Thou Glory of the Most Glorious).

Figure 48: Members of Iran's National Youth Committee in 98 BE. Seated from right to left: Mr 'Alí-Muḥammad Varqá (later Hand of the Cause), Mr 'Alí Nakhjavání, Mrs Rúḥangiz Mutivayyih, Dr Míhdí Samandarí and Mr Muḥammad Yazdání. Standing from right to left: Mr 'Abdu'lláh Misbáh, unknown, Mr Salim Nunu, Mr Zikru'lláh Khádem (later Hand of the Cause) and Mr Abu'l-Qásim Faizi (later Hand of the Cause).

Figure 49: Hand of the Cause Dr 'Alí-Muḥammad Varqá (front row, second right) and members of the first National Spiritual Assembly of Congo and Gabon (1971). Courtesy: Bahá'í World Centre.

Figure 50: Dr Varqá attending the 1985 International Bahá'í Youth Conference in Lima. The author is on the left.

Figure 51: Hand of the Cause of God and Trustee of the Ḥuqúqu'lláh Dr 'Alí-Muḥammad Varqá. Courtesy: Bahá'í World Centre.

Figure 52: 1985 International Bahá'í Youth Conference, Lima, Peru.

Figure 53: Gathered on the steps of the Seat of the Universal House of Justice on Mount Carmel, Haifa, Israel are members of the Continental Boards of Counsellors together with members of the Universal House of Justice, the International Teaching Centre, and, at front, centre, the Hand of the Cause of God Dr 'Alí-Muḥammad Varqá, December 2005. Courtesy: Bahá'í World Centre.

Figure 54: Hand of the Cause Dr Varqá with members of the Universal House of Justice, 2007. Courtesy: Bahá'í World Centre.

XX - Final Reflections

Like us who live every day and make an effort to do something for our Faith, with purity of motive and not caring much about the predictability of the result, Varqá and Rúḥu'lláh pressed ahead every hour with single-minded commitment, regardless of how obscure and uncertain the next stage in their life was and how meagre the outcome would be. If two single traits can be attributed to them, bravery and resilience would be the author's preferred choice because the stories reveal that even in the most dangerous circumstances, no trace of fear or hesitation can be found in their actions. The courage to assert their Faith at any cost in such an aggressive and dangerous milieu is probably the most salient of the various take-home messages that their story has left to posterity.

Depending on the perspective of the reader, the story of Varqá and Rúḥu'lláh can be construed as the journey of a father and a son, the saga of an adult and a child, the tale of maturity and innocence, the chronicle between a mentor and his mentee, or the depiction of intrepidity and radiance. Neither the universal history nor the ancient mythology represents a progenitor and offspring immolating themselves, facing each other, and defying the executioners with love. This is a drama weaving the mortal and the immortal, a stage that only Providence could have created to show these two perennial sides to us. Nobody deserved to die in such tragic circumstances. Both walked toward death with admirable stoicism while at the same time embracing happily their passage to eternity. This is the sublimity of Varqá's and Rúḥu'lláh's narrative, that such uniqueness has not ever been registered or even thought about, taking the form of a legend. Their story has been told throughout the world in many languages and will continue to go around as far as faith, heroism and nobility are sought by the human heart.

We all have something of Varqá and Rúḥu'lláh. Like looking at ourselves in a mirror, their existence tells us something of what we are, but more importantly of what parts of us can be improved upon. Both protagonists are exemplary models of a Bahá'í life for adults, youth and children. For the adult, here is a well-educated man that used his knowledge to disseminate the Cause of Bahá'u'lláh to both the rich and the poor, to prince and the commoner, to the scholar and to the illiterate, in freedom or in prison. Varqá is also the archetype of the father that aims raising such an accomplished son like Rúḥu'lláh. Reading into his life there is so much spiritual richness, meaning and resilience for us to learn and emulate in our lives. One wonders whether Varqá is an early fulfillment of Bahá'u'lláh's promise of "calling into being of a new race of men"?[600]

Rúḥu'lláh was a child whose exceptional abilities exceeded his own age and whose character drew the interest of any observer or audience. The concept of adolescence is unfortunately often associated to its etymology deriving meaning from the Latin word *adolescere,* meaning "be lacking of". Here is an adolescent whose disposition and capacities challenge contemporary schools of thinking regarding this period of development[601] which in general, assert that youth are in a stage of development short of the necessary qualities to work as adults.[602] "While global trends project an image of those in their adolescence as problematic, lost in the throes of tumultuous physical and emotional change, unresponsive and self-consumed," as the Universal House of Justice writes, [603] Rúḥu'lláh's personality rises in contrast to those historically deep-sitting psychological and social assumptions. Here is an adolescent who acts more like a protagonist rather than a bystander, who is characterized by altruistic motives, a strong spiritual perception, a keen sense of justice and a desire to contribute to the

---

[600] Shoghi Effendi, The Advent of Divine Justice (Wilmette, Illinois: Bahá'í Publishing Trust, 1990), 16.

[601] Sona Farid-Arbab, "Advancing in Bahá'í-Inspired Education," The Journal of Bahá'í Studies 26, no. 4, 71 (2016).

[602] Boris Handal, Mobile Makes Learning Free: Building Conceptual, Professional and School Capacity, 80 (Charlotte, NC: Information Age Publishing, 2015).

[603] The Universal House of Justice, Riḍván 2010 Message. Source: Bahá'í Reference Library.

construction of a better world. The hero of our story questions the status quo and does something about it, contributing publicly to a discourse which was only the divines and courtiers realm. People were naturally drawn to his talent like the Governor who once remarked: "This child's strange power of argument is a miracle in itself".[604]

Varqá's and Rúḥu'lláh's story reminds us that evil, cruelty and fanaticism are among the lowest of human passions, real and difficult to eradicate from our environment and will perhaps come up again and again in history. Although not necessarily part of our spiritual DNA this dark side of creation is ready to appear when ignorance supplants enlightenment, when religion becomes a cause for malevolence, when an establishment turns wrong and masses blindly follow the tyrant. Traces of light suddenly turn up in the story but alas, are rejected violently because in the kingdom of gloominess and dreariness there is no space for sunlight. Clarity is a threat to obscurity as much as justice is a menace to self-righteousness and farcical hypocrisy. That is the power of our story, a magnificent duet embodying angelic virtues, valiantly opening a window of grace in a country whose spiritual sky only supported clouds and fog, where love had almost ceased to exist.

How disappointed both Varqá and Rúḥu'lláh might have felt looking at the degradation of their country, observing their countrymen under the influence of a religious system that was obsolete and bankrupt. They had endeavoured to open the eyes of their fellow nationals to the Light which they had witnessed and willingly sacrificed their very lives so that the lives of others may receive divine illumination. Varqá and Rúḥu'lláh and the other personages of this account had publicly and with superhuman courage, tried to present the beauty of the teachings of Bahá'u'lláh, and demonstrate how precious a treasure these principles and teachings were, but, alas, little place for spiritual beauty was found in people's hearts. The establishment itself had become so entrenched in their man-made dogmas with a desperation to usurp political power, that the notion of a new Day of God was plainly discarded from their orthodox and corrupt agendas.

---

[604] Faizi, Fire on the Mountain Top, 80.

Paraphrasing the Gospels, the letter of the law had supplanted its spirit and what was left was only hatred and superstition, all calling to mind Bahá'u'lláh's words condemning the perfidy of the religious leaders of His time:

> O YE THAT ARE FOOLISH, YET HAVE A NAME TO BE WISE! Wherefore do ye wear the guise of shepherds, when inwardly ye have become wolves, intent upon My flock? Ye are even as the star, which riseth ere the dawn, and which, though it seem radiant and luminous, leadeth the wayfarers of My city astray into the paths of perdition.[605]

> O YE SEEMING FAIR YET INWARDLY FOUL! Ye are like clear but bitter water, which to outward seeming is crystal pure but of which, when tested by the divine Assayer, not a drop is accepted. Yea, the sun beam falls alike upon the dust and the mirror, yet differ they in reflection even as doth the star from the earth: nay, immeasurable is the difference![606]

How much has Iran changed since the time Varqás had to flee Yazd? The evidence shows that although time has changed the mindset has not, unfortunately. Under the tacit consent of the top government leadership, Bahá'ís are systematically harassed, imprisoned for their beliefs, even tortured and worst, killed. Their homes are pillaged, their civil rights denied and their freedom to practice their religion denied, not even having their natural entitlement to bury their dead. As in Qájárs time they have to pay large amounts of money, a legal extortion, to be released from jail facing a judiciary which is just a mask for oppression, with no place to lodge an appeal. With no separation between church and state, God's name is still invoked to justify atrocities and injustice against a religious minority which only wishes the betterment of the country. Rotten as sin and pervasive as a cancer, as in 150 years ago, the system oppresses without mercy not only the strong like Varqá but also the vulnerable, the elderly, the women or the children like the new Rúḥu'lláhs. A re-invented state-

[605] Bahá'u'lláh, The Hidden Words, 30.
[606] Bahá'u'lláh, The Hidden Words, 30.

based diabolic monsters is out there unrestrained roaming the streets, never satisfied with the blood and money of the innocent, and disguised in sanctimony and self-righteousness. "Lay not aside the fear of God, O ye the learned of the world", is Bahá'u'lláh's dire forewarning to the Shí'ih ecclesiasts. "How long will ye persist in your injustice?"[607] And again:

> O OPPRESSORS ON EARTH! Withdraw your hands from tyranny, for I have pledged Myself not to forgive any man's injustice. This is My covenant which I have irrevocably decreed in the preserved tablet and sealed with My seal. [608]

To the Bahá'í women playing what is often seen as an unassuming role, unnoticeable in the narrative but always laboring ceaselessly in the background, this account pays special homage. We see the women either relentlessly caught between the loyalty to the husband believer and the fanatic pressure of her extended kinfolk, and yet coming up triumphantly within the fold of the Faith. Or as the admirable mother urging her son not to recant his faith despite death threats that proved to be true. Here is the wife confronting the guards coming to arrest the husband and get her earrings torn out of her ears for such a brave stance. She is also the fearless woman who in order to provide food and clean clothes to the Bahá'í prisoners coming interstate disguised herself as the sister in order to access the gaols. Or the lady that behind the veil and the curtain declares her faith to the travel teacher stating that this is the Message that she has waiting for all her life and therefore she is ready to embrace it. The heroic figure of Táhirih also comes in the narrative as an example of courage and firmness. The prudish literary customs of those times did not allow observing women's domestic lives let alone putting them on paper. Navid Jamali writes that "referring to women's names was forbidden by common laws".[609] "The houses did not even have windows opening upon the

---

[607] Bahá'u'lláh, Gleanings from the Writings of Bahá'u'lláh, 98.
[608] Bahá'u'lláh, The Hidden Words, 44.
[609] Navid Jamali, "The Lost Links: An Introduction to the Matrilineal Genealogy of the Qajar Dynasty," https://www.academia.edu/37455230/The_Lost_Links_An_Introduction_to_the_Matrilineal_Genealogy_of_the_Qajar_Dynasty.

outside world", explains 'Abdu'l-Bahá.[610] It is against this this backdrop that they played the role of the family back bone even when the man was away visiting Bahá'í groups and individuals, or in jail, leaving her and the children alone and vulnerable without much support from the extended family and facing a hostile and reproving environment. As 'Abdu'l-Bahá brings to our attention, "Among the miracles which distinguish this sacred dispensation is this, that women have evinced a greater boldness than men when enlisted in the ranks of the Faith."[611]

In their exploits, Varqá and Rúḥu'lláh sensed that every movement of them was guided by the Divine Will, conveying a powerful message to the public. "One does not know what is hidden behind the veil of the future." Varqá said, when from the prison and on horseback the group was paraded in chains and stocks, "Whatever it may be, it will redound to the victory of the Cause. We do not know, but He Who is the Master of Providence knows".[612] Every move they made was a step into uncertainty, taking them near the clutches of the enemy. Their destiny took them randomly to various scenarios, teaching in restricted environments such as the heir prince's royal cortege and an influential regional governor's court, where they engaged with the high nobility, prominent bureaucrats and leading ecclesiastics. Without planning Varqá was able to explain the Faith to the most powerful —and cruelest— of the Sháh's sons. Through our two heroes the sovereign himself had the inestimable privilege of seeing the portrait of the Blessed Báb, a powerful opportunity for him to change his behaviour, just days before his assassination by a revolutionary in 1896.

Varqá belonged to a network of a few travel teachers who had taken upon themselves the mission of visiting the nascent rural and urban Bahá'í groups, building communities, deepening and strengthening the believers, sharing news and, in plain words, joining the dots. No printed books were available and therefore they disseminated the

---

[610] Bahá'í World Centre, The Compilation of Compilations, vol. II, 365.
[611] Bahá'í World Centre, The Compilation of Compilations, vol. II, 403.
[612] Balyuzi, Eminent Bahá'ís in the Time of Bahá'u'lláh, 89-90.

Tablets by copying them by hand and circulated them, overtly and covertly, from home to home, from village to village, from city to city. They presented the face of the Faith to the authorities, succored the terrorized believers under attack and provided an element of leadership without any formal appointment except a sense of self-abnegation. Those travel teachers like Varqá, maintained contact with Bahá'u'lláh through correspondence, acting as channels of guidance for both isolated believers and groups. The believers referred to them as "mubaligh" meaning a religious teacher, preacher or instructor. Travelling to the Holy Land back and forth allowed them to gain spiritual sustenance to continue their self-imposed missions of propagating and protecting the Faith at a time when there were no Bahá'í administrative institutions to represent them and the Manifestation Himself being the direct Head of the Faith was living in 'Akká, Palestine. It was like an unnoticeable circulatory system continuously irrigating believers and groups and keeping them connected to their Faith. It was not strange then that personalities like Varqá were the prime target of both government and ecclesiastic antagonists.

As the invisible spectator of this epic, the reader from a unique ubiquitous position will see our two personages travelling across the dusty Persian roads, conversing with people about the new Faith, sometimes comfortable within a family environment, or sometimes being arrested by arbitrary governors and put under chains and stocks. Heroes can become so in just one moment but the journey to gain sainthood is much longer. How wonderful is therefore watching them grow in their path of service, gaining knowledge and dispositions and getting more skilled in the art of teaching, until finally become worthy of their immortal crown. Two elements are highly visible on that journey supporting their spiritual journey: service and connection to the Divine through prayer and reading the Writings no matter how scarce these were available. In the process of refining and modelling their spirits both gave the best of them till eventually Varqá became the prototype of an Apostle of Bahá'u'lláh and Rúḥu'lláh turned into a true angel.

How can we explain the willingness of Varqá and Rúḥu'lláh to sacrifice their lives? The only explanation is that they firmly believed that there was hope for humanity and that their sacrifice was necessary to resurrect this hope. Not the hope for change that revolutions, class struggles and wars have demagogically promised to enact. They understood with absolute faith that change can be brought about through love and never by means of strife and contention. Although they knew that the journey they had undertaken would result in the loss of their lives, because blood was the currency of ecclesiastics, government and populace, Varqá and Rúḥu'lláh submitted themselves to their destiny with the belief that their deaths would still make a difference in the world. The light of Varqá's and Rúḥu'lláh's legacy "will shine through centuries and ages",[613] 'Abdu'l-Bahá foretold.

The most immediate impact took place when the Faith received an early mention in *The Times* —the most prestigious newspaper of the nineteenth century. Five days after their martyrdom, in that media, the Bahá'ís were also falsely accused of assassinating the sovereign. As a result, the newspaper published a lengthy clarifying article by the famous British orientalist Professor E.G. Browne portraying the Bahá'í community as a people "living lawfully and peaceably" and informing that the "late Sháh himself seems latterly to have recognised the inoffensive character of the sect". [614] About the same incident a dispatch from the French Ambassador in Tehran to the Foreign Affairs minister in Paris reported that "The Bábis absolutely repudiate violence as a means of action, depending entirely on persuasion and on the purity of their doctrines, which are, in fact much superior to those of Islam".[615] Indeed, a universal proclamation of the Faith.

Varqá's face on the photograph at the Tehran prison, although cruelly restrained in fetters and chains, captures magnificently his deep and penetrating look into the future, a dignified and noble composure, a subtle smile of complacency and a defiant sight to the system. Death

---

[613] Lovejoy, Dwight Barstow Collection, 219.
[614] Momen, The Bábí and Bahá'í Religions 1844-1944: Some Contemporary Western Accounts, 361.
[615] Momen, The Bábí and Bahá'í Religions 1844-1944: Some Contemporary Western Accounts, 361.

was not going to take away from him the most valuable possession he treasured — an immeasurable love for Bahá'u'lláh and 'Abdu'l-Bahá. In turn, Rúḥu'lláh's body language appears to reflect self-confidence and calmness, leaning slightly towards his father as re-assured by his company, reading well the harsh realities of a prison but not feeling scared by them. Too much maturity for a minor in his early teens, at an age where children are well looked after by both parents and society, and would normally be sitting in a classroom, playing with his peers or being loved in the warmth and safety of the family home. As the poet Hatcher talked about that photograph:

> [S]tring side by side
> like waiting game
> they gaze through
> that magic windows
> into my eyes right now
> into my most hidden heart;
> this is for you,
> they are saying ...[616]

Everything changes in this world. In the 1920s a modern prison was opened in Tehran and the Anbár fell into disuse and was destroyed. On the same spot the main civil registry office was erected. From becoming a place of death, the Anbár reappeared to history as a space to celebrate birth and marriage and therefore life and its renewal. The Anbár contour is not surrounded any more by the royal palace complex but is now subsumed into the noisy urban development of central Tehran. However, the memory of the Anbár dungeon will remain like a scar staying forever in the Iranian memory to remind future generations of their troubled past. Its former space lies now as a monument to the Qájár tyranny in the middle of a growing city called by Bahá'u'lláh as the "Mother of the World":

> How vast the number of those men and women, those victims of tyranny, that have, within thy walls, laid down their lives in the path of God, and been buried beneath thy dust with such

[616] Hatcher, in Response to the Revelation: Poetry by Bahá'ís, 15-17.

> cruelty as to cause every honored servant of God to bemoan their plight. [617] … How vast the number of those sanctified beings, those symbols of certitude, who, in their great love for thee, have laid down their lives and sacrificed their all for thy sake! Joy be to thee, and blissfulness to them that inhabit thee. [618]

> O Land of Tá! He Who is the Lord of Names remembereth thee in His glorious station. Thou wert the Day Spring of the Cause of God, the fountain of His Revelation, the manifestation of His Most Great Name—a Name that hath caused the hearts and souls of men to tremble.[619]

Varqá and Náṣiri'd-Dín Sháh passed to the other life within a few hours of each other but went to different destinations. While Varqá was known as one of the most prominent Bahá'í leaders, Náṣiri'd-Dín Sháh had become the most powerful opponent to the nascent religion. In Varqá's passing we found a glorious legacy but Náṣiri'd-Dín Sháh's death opened a political can of worms. Far from being abased by their chains and fetters, Varqá and Rúḥu'lláh —his second youngest son— became exalted in human history and from prison they were liberated directly to immortality. However, history's judgement on Náṣiri'd-Dín Sháh was not kind to him nor for his "five-decade-long, disastrous reign"[620] and for the domino effect that took place after his fall. The Qájár dynasty went soon into a rapid descent leading to its extinction before the end of the next thirty years. The succeeding Sháh was forced to establish a parliament for the first time ten years later after the tragic 1 May 1896 but it proved too-little-too-late as the dynasty's fate was already sealed with the last two Qájár monarchs dying in exile. The Bahá'í community, however, went from strength to strength. The following year the first Spiritual Assembly of Tehran was created under 'Abdu'l-Bahá's supervisión of which 'Azízu'lláh Khán —Varqá's oldest son— was one of its members. In turn, the

---

[617] Bahá'u'lláh, Gleanings from the Writings of Bahá'u'lláh, 120-21.
[618] Bahá'u'lláh, Gleanings from the Writings of Bahá'u'lláh, 109.
[619] Bahá'u'lláh, Gleanings from the Writings of Bahá'u'lláh, 120-21.
[620] Hasan Balyuzi, Bahá'u'lláh, the King of Glory (Oxford: GeorgeRonald, 1980), Bahá'u'lláh, the King of Glory, 1980, 69.

Bahá'í community grew at a rapid pace establishing schools, centres and more spiritual assemblies throughout the country, leading to the election of the National Spiritual Assembly in 1934 under a new dynasty, with Valíyu'lláh Khán —Varqá's third son— one of its founding members.

Indeed, although posthumously appointed by 'Abdu'l-Bahá, as outlined in this book, Varqá during his life had naturally and inadvertently performed the roles of a Hand of the Cause of God whose duties were "to diffuse the Divine Fragrances, to edify the souls of men, to promote learning, to improve the character of all men and to be, at all times and under all conditions, sanctified and detached from earthly things".[621] To crown such a legacy of service, as described in this book, Varqá is known to be the only Hand of the Cause in the Cradle of the Faith to be killed, attaining martyrdom.

Mr Valíyu'lláh Varqá and his son Dr 'Alí-Muḥammad Varqá were also elevated by the beloved Guardian, one after another, to the rank of Chief Trustee of the Ḥuqúqu'lláh, in 1940 and 1955 respectively. Enunciated in the Kitáb-i-Aqdas this sacred law provides the financial means to be "expended for the diffusion of the Fragrances of God and the exaltation of His Word, for benevolent pursuits and for the common weal".[622] As such, the Ḥuqúqu'lláh is an instrument for the re-distribution of wealth, contributing towards the sustenance of socio-economic projects and for philanthropic endeavours. To Mr Valíyu'lláh Varqá was delegated the task of the administration and diffusion of this "essential spiritual obligation"[623] throughout Iran, guided by the Guardian whereas his son devoted much of his efforts to extend the application of the law to the entire Bahá'í world under the guidance of the Universal House of Justice who once wrote to Dr Varqá. "... you have made a contribution to the World Order of Bahá'u'lláh which will be remembered throughout the Dispensation",[624] a blessing from which the whole world is now benefitting.

621 'Abdu'l-Bahá, The Will and Testament of 'Abdu'l-Bahá, 10.
622 'Abdu'l-Bahá, The Will and Testament of 'Abdu'l-Bahá, 15.
623 Waters, Ḥuqúqu'lláh, The Right of God, 75.
624 Waters, Ḥuqúqu'lláh, The Right of God, 99.

Dr Varqá was the last of the Hands of the Cause of God, bringing to conclusion an institution that had lasted 120 years, spanning three centuries from 1887 with the appointment of Ibn-i-Asdaq[625] as the first Hand until Dr Varqá's passing in 2007. Bahá'u'lláh, 'Abdu'l-Bahá and Shoghi Effendi appointed four, four and forty-two Hands, respectively, during their lifetime. The year 1957 witnessed the passing of the beloved Guardian, an event that put the leadership of the Cause on the shoulders of the 27 remaining living Hands until the election of the Universal House of Justice in 1963. "They kept the ship on its course and brought it safe to port"[626], remarked the Universal House of Justice. In the same year the supreme institution determined that it was not possible for them to appoint more Hands of the Cause as this was the Guardian's prerogative set out by 'Abdu'l-Bahá's Will. Upon his death, Dr Varqá therefore became the "last of that noble company, the Chief Stewards of Bahá'u'lláh's embryonic World Commonwealth", [627] which "brought to an end the remarkable stewardship of an institution whose legacy is unparalleled in religious history!", wrote the Universal House of Justice on the Day of the Covenant in 2007. The Supreme Body also wrote, "The passing of Dr Varqá marks both the end of a chapter of Bahá'í history and the beginning of a new stage in the unfolding of that Order."[628]

The three Hands of the Cause in the Varqá family jointly visited a large number of Bahá'í communities in the Americas, Europe, Africa and Asia bringing encouragement and wisdom to believers' hearts. There is nothing more befitting to close this account, remembering these three Hands, than calling to mind Bahá'u'lláh's words of praise to the Hands of the Cause of God contained in the *Lawḥ-i-Dunyá* (Tablet of the World):

---

[625] Balyuzi, Eminent Bahá'ís in the Time of Bahá'u'lláh, 83.
[626] National Spiritual Assembly of the Bahá'ís of the United States, Wellspring of Guidance: Messages from the Universal House of Justice, 1963-1968 (Wilmette, Illinois: Bahá'í Publishing Trust, 1970), 2.
[627] Waters, Ḥuqúqu'lláh, The Right of God, 7-10.
[628] Message of the Universal House of Justice dated 27 November 2007. Source: Bahá'í Reference Library.

Light and glory, greeting and praise be upon the Hands of His Cause, through whom the light of fortitude hath shone forth and the truth hath been established that the authority to choose rests with God, the Powerful, the Mighty, the Unconstrained, through whom the ocean of bounty hath surged and the fragrance of the gracious favours of God, the Lord of mankind, hath been diffused. We beseech Him—exalted is He—to shield them through the power of His hosts, to protect them through the potency of His dominion and to aid them through His indomitable strength which prevaileth over all created things. Sovereignty is God's, the Creator of the heavens and the Lord of the Kingdom of Names.[629]

[629] Bahá'u'lláh, Tablets of Bahá'u'lláh: Revealed after the Kitáb-i-Aqdas, 83.

Appendix I: A Tribute to Dr 'Alí-Muḥammad Varqá by Shahbaz Fatheazam

In an age of simmering dissent and deteriorating civic discourse, humility is not only scorned but eyed with cold contempt. To be louder and higher is inculpable, even encouraged and admired. To be slick, earthly minded and loquacious is the skeleton of the proud fleshed out into a plethora of vainness. This is the archetypal trait of our modern hero casting its mist of fascination over all, corrupting even what is in itself incorruptible. Humility, on the other hand, succumbs to the cheerlessness of us merely being ourselves but which can, in fact, lead to greatness. A perfect example is the figure of the late Hand of the Cause of God, 'Alí Muḥammad Varqá. In his meekness we found strength and in his simplicity a brilliant proof that in such a state identity is not torn away but is given generous and inviting contours of humanity. The meekness of Jináb-i-Varqá was compelling teaching everyone to regard ego as adversary to allow us to operate more effectively under God's rule. But he went beyond. He turned lowliness into a religious virtue – loving everyone unconditionally and receiving each with disarming simplicity. Such a disposition never diminished him, rather it led him into the opposite direction, to eminence and to hidden troves of knowledge. (Is not virtue human power)? He exemplified to perfection the trust Bahá'u'lláh bestowed upon His Hands of the Cause, *'...through whom...truth hath been established'.*[630] Indeed, Dr. Varqá showed to love truth more than himself.

Glued to his humility, or as a manifestation thereof, was his 'douceur' or tenderness. Spinoza reflects upon this. This 'God-intoxicated' philosopher writes that a wise man acts 'courteously and kindly' ['humaniter et benigne'].[631] A sublime maxim which everyone saw

[630] Bahá'u'lláh, Tablets of Bahá'u'lláh: Revealed after the Kitáb-i-Aqdas, 83.
[631] Ethics, Part IV, Proposition XXXVII, Note 1.

in Dr. Varqá's demeanor at all times. Never loud or talkative, he was not taciturn or reserved. More the astute observer and listener, he immensely enjoyed the company of friends and believers and would join in the conversation with his inimitable gentle manners. So gentle, in fact, that even when laughing he would cover his mouth with his hand so as not to be misconstrued as a betrayal of dignity or to slight those involved in any way and even to muffle sound. He possessed a subdued joviality (his was never the sour religion) which was charming, and his beating heart brimmed God's grace on his noble and radiant face. And while he emanated pure love it was never to possess, but to vouchsafe unto others that which should be possessed - true poverty and absolute nothingness.[632]

As an example of his self-effacement, Dr. Varqá once requested Shafiqeh Khánum, then serving at the World Centre together with her husband Hushmand Fatheazam, a very special favor which she later said as perhaps the most cherished memories of him. At the night of the Ascension of 'Abdu'l-Bahá it is customary for the World Centre staff to visit the room in which He passed peacefully into the next world at his home in 7 Haparsim Street in Haifa, in the early hours of November 28, 1921. The hour of visitation to the Bahá'í public begins from 9 p.m. until 11 p.m. for all to visit the sparsely furnished room and which is now a place of pilgrimage. At the appointed hour, the room at the Master's House is then closed for the friends to assemble in the Concourse of the building of the Universal House of Justice for reading and prayers before visiting the Holy Shrine on Mount Carmel where He lies.[633] That special evening Dr. Varqá calls on Shafiqeh Khánum with a request. He told her that he never felt comfortable arriving at the House of 'Abdu'l-Bahá for the evening visitation because whenever he appeared, the friends present would immediately withdraw and allow him complete privacy in the chamber for him to conduct his prayers in perfect solitude. He never

[632] Bahá'u'lláh defines this as "dying from self and the living in God, the being poor in self and rich in the Desired One". See "The Seven Valleys and the Four Valleys", Wilmette, 1991, page 65.
[633] Since January, 2020, work has begun on a chosen site near the Riḍván garden in 'Akká to raise a befitting Shrine that would be the final resting place for the sacred remains of 'Abdu'l-Bahá.

felt at ease with the commotion that would occur whenever he would arrive aside from the fact that he considered it most unfair to disrupt the meditation of others. He asked whether Shafiqeh Khánum would not avail herself to drive him sooner to the House of the Master that special remembrance night, in the earlier part of the evening, at dusk, so that he may pay his respects prior to the general public arriving. This, of course, was arranged and they both arrived at the Holy Site, empty, and approached the room of the Master. They entered, greeted only by the flickering shy candlelight beside the headrest. Jináb-i-Varqá then set aside his walking cane and with some difficulty kneeled by the side of the Master's bed, kissed the edge, and remained nestled on the floor with his feet tucked beside him. He then asked Shafiqeh Khánum to chant a prayer. While she did so he laid his head on the side of the bed with shut eyes as though soul meeting soul, tremulous, devout, clasped to cause '….a hundred veils to fall…to see beyond seeing itself'.[634] Dr. 'Alí-Muḥammad Varqá passed away a few years later in September 22, 2007, buried in the Bahá'í cemetery in Haifa, the longest surviving Hand of the Cause of God, and the last to join his fellow 'Chief Stewards'[635] in the realms beyond.

No language is able to explain how great souls manage to capture and remain enthralled with Absolute Love which is ever-present and which underpins all movement in the universe. A radical unity was personified that solemn night in the prostrated figure before the bedstead but though intensely private, this invisible power is not personal but universal which hits and changes lives. The life of Dr. Varqá had changed before it had begun – the procession of spiritual splendor and color began with his forefather, the Apostle of Bahá'u'lláh, Mírzá 'Alí Muḥammad Varqá, the poet martyr, his young uncle, Rúḥu'lláh also a martyr, his own distinguished father, Valíyu'lláh Varqá, appointed Hand of the Cause late in his life and earlier made Trustee of Ḥuqúqu'lláh by the beloved Guardian – all ancestral, noble figures touched by Absolute Love. And their anointed

---

634 Rumi, Diwan-e Shams-e Tabriz.

635 In a message penned just weeks before his passing, Shoghi Effendi referred to the Hands of the Cause of God as "the Chief Stewards of Bahá'u'lláh's embryonic World Commonwealth" (Bahá'u'lláh, The Kitáb-i-Aqdas: The Most Holy Book, note 183)

mantle chosen to be spread on the awaiting shoulders of the eldest son, 'Alí Muḥammad Varqá, which he wore to perfection, unboastfully. Despite his stellar accomplishments in educational attainment and academic achievement and his contribution to the modernization of Irán, gentle humility was the soul subduing creed Dr. Varqá followed to the very end allowing his entire being to mix in its ray. Together with the other Hands, in unison, one and all, he was the epitome of the prayer revealed in their name: 'Sovereignty is God's…'[636] Hush to all meaner thoughts!

[636] Bahá'u'lláh, Tablets of Bahá'u'lláh: Revealed after the Kitáb-i-Aqdas, 83.

Appendix II: Ḥuqúqu'lláh (The Right of God) – A Talk by the Hand of the Cause Dr 'Alí-Muḥammad Varqá[637]

Dearly Loved Friends,

At the inception of the Six Year Plan of the Universal House of Justice, which coincided with dramatic changes in many aspects of society, a new arena for rapid development of the Faith of God has been attained and the purpose and aim of Bahá'u'lláh's Revelation have been unveiled before the very eyes of Government Authorities, Heads of States and Scholars who were not even aware of its existence.

At this rightful time the Universal House of Justice has emphasized the importance of acquiring knowledge of the laws and ordinances revealed by Bahá'u'lláh, and adopted the translation of the most Holy Book, the Kitáb-i-Aqdas, into English as one of the sublime goals of this new plan.

Among the commandments and decrees revealed in this sacred Book is the law of Ḥuqúqu'lláh, previously applicable only to the friends in the East. The Western friends became aware of this law with the dissemination of the compilation of the Holy text and the Sacred writings prepared by the Research Department of the Universal House of Justice.

Ḥuqúqu'lláh is an Arabic word composed of two words, "Ḥuqúq" meaning "Rights" and "Alláh" meaning "God". Therefore, Ḥuqúqu'lláh means "The Rights of God", a part of the individual's possessions and income offered at the Threshold of the Lord.

---

[637] Talk delivered at the Sixth International Bahá'í Convention, Haifa, May 1, 1988.

In a Tablet addressed to Jináb-i-Zayn referring to Ḥuqúqu'lláh, Bahá'u'lláh states that the progress and the promulgation of the Faith of God, depend on material means, therefore, the expansion and the advancement of God's Revelation and the establishment of a new order and a new world civilization cannot be achieved without material means.

The embryo of this sacred law was established, by the Beloved Báb in the Bayán where, for the first time, the word Ḥuqúqu'lláh was mentioned by Him. Bahá'u'lláh brought some modifications in its contents and accepted it as one of the executive ordinances of His Revelation.

Although Ḥuqúqu'lláh is one of the most significant laws of the Kitáb-i-Aqdas, we should not take the word "Law" in its rigid and literal meaning, defined in the encyclopedia as "the obligatory rule promoted by a sovereign authority". It is not a law which is enforced with pressure, but rather a spiritual obligation based on the love of the believer who is eager to obey the will of his Beloved. In this ordinance there is no room for pressure or intimidation. Obedience is a reflection of the highest degree of love and ardent desire.

Ḥuqúqu'lláh, by its special and unique characteristic, combines might and humility, power and humbleness. It is one of the fundamental ordinances of the Bahá'í Faith, like prayer and fasting. Its importance has been manifested by these words of Bahá'u'lláh:

"Say: O people, the first duty is to recognize the one true God — magnified be His glory — the second is to show forth constancy in His Cause and, after these, one's duty is to purify one's riches and earthly possessions according to that which is prescribed by God...." (The Compilation of Compilations, vol. 1, Ḥuqúqu'lláh)

By studying the writings revealed by Bahá'u'lláh and 'Abdu'l-Bahá regarding , Ḥuqúqu'lláh four essential points emerge:

First, in the Kitáb-i-Aqdas, Bahá'u'lláh states:

"Should a person acquire one hundred mithqals of gold, nineteen mithqals thereof belong unto God, the Creator of earth and heaven. Take heed, O people, lest ye deprive yourselves of this great bounty...."

'Abdu'l-Bahá emphasizes that Ḥuqúqu'lláh is payable on whatever is left over after deducting the yearly expenses.

The payment of Ḥuqúqu'lláh is based on the calculation of the value of one's income in respect of the gold unit. Whenever the annual income of the individual, after the deduction of his complete year's expenses, reaches nineteen mithqals of gold value, (equivalent to 2.22456 ounces or 69.19112 grams), 19% of this amount is the Right of God and should be submitted to the Focal Point of the Faith. The calculation of sustaining means of livelihood which are exempted from Ḥuqúqu'lláh depends on the spiritual maturity of every believer and his innermost conscience. No criterion can be established for this purpose, for it varies according to the living conditions and social status of each believer, and the degree of his spiritual attachment and material detachment.

The second point is that the payment of the Right of God is like a magnet, which attracts divine blessings and confirmation. It is the mainspring of God's mercy and compassion. Bahá'u'lláh, in His writings, showers His limitless benediction upon those who observe this law.

Again, in the Kitáb-i-Aqdas, the Pen of Glory decrees:

"...and whoso fulfilleth the things he hath been commanded, divine blessings will descend upon him from the heaven of the bounty of his Lord, the Bestower, the Bountiful, the Most Generous, the Ancient of Days...."

In another Tablet we read:

"They that have kept their promises, fulfilled their obligations, redeemed their pledges and vows, rendered the Trust of God and His

Right unto Him — these are numbered among the inmates of the all-highest Paradise...." (Bahá'u'lláh, The Compilation of Compilations, vol. 1, Ḥuqúqu'lláh)

In a Tablet revealed by 'Abdu'l-Bahá, we find:

"Those who have observed this weighty ordinance have received heavenly blessings and in both worlds their faces have shone radiantly and their nostrils perfumed by the sweet savours of God's tender mercy...." (The Compilation of Compilations, vol. 1, Ḥuqúqu'lláh)

The third factor is that just as the payment of Ḥuqúqu'lláh would attract divine bounty and blessings, its negligence or failure causes deprivation and is interpreted as tantamount to treachery to a Fund rightfully belonging to God.

This Fund is to be spent on whatever is of benefit for the promulgation of the Faith under the complete and absolute decision of the authority "to which all must turn." ('Abdu'l-Bahá, The Compilation of Compilations, vol. 1, Ḥuqúqu'lláh) Only this authority and none other, not even the donor, has the right to interfere in its management.

In the Kitáb-i-Aqdas, the Pen of Glory warns those who neglect the payment of Ḥuqúqu'lláh:

"O people! Act not treacherously in the matter of Ḥuqúqu'lláh and dispose not of it, except by His leave...."

And He continues:

"Whoso dealeth dishonestly with God will in justice be exposed, and whoso fulfilleth the things he hath been commanded, divine blessings will descend upon him from the heaven of the bounty of his Lord, the Bestower, the Bountiful, the Most Generous, the Ancient of Days...." (ibid)

Therefore, withholding the payment of Ḥuqúqu'lláh or spending it on other concerns, no matter how charitable their nature, would be interpreted as misappropriation of the fund belonging to God, and an act of dishonesty. Any donation for charity and beneficent purposes such as contributions to the various funds should be made after the contributor is free of his debt to God.

And finally, God Almighty has decreed that the payment of the Right of God is conducive to prosperity, and assists the progress of the human soul in the spiritual realms of the Everlasting world.

Bahá'u'lláh says:

"...the treasures laid up by kings and queens are not worthy of mention, nor will they be acceptable in the presence of God. However, a grain of mustard offered by His loved ones will be extolled in the exalted court of His holiness and invested with the ornament of His acceptance...." (Bahá'u'lláh, The Compilation of Compilations, vol. 1, Ḥuqúqu'lláh)

The high station of Ḥuqúqu'lláh and its exceptional rank among the commandments of Bahá'u'lláh is endowed with great veneration and respect.

'Abdu'l-Bahá, referring to the words of Bahá'u'lláh says:

"...the utmost honesty hath to be observed in matters related to the Ḥuqúq. The Institution of Ḥuqúq is sacred." (Bahá'u'lláh, The Compilation of Compilations, vol. 1, Ḥuqúqu'lláh)

In order to respect its sanctity, Bahá'u'lláh strongly forbids soliciting Ḥuqúqu'lláh. No individual or institution is authorized to demand it. Whenever it is necessary to bring the importance of this obligation to the attention of the believers, it should be mentioned as a general reminder. Spiritual maturity must stir the conscience of the believers and, nothing else. In a Tablet addressed to Haji Amín the second Trustee of Ḥuqúqu'lláh, Bahá'u'lláh says:

“No one should demand the Ḥuqúqu’lláh. Its payment should depend on the volition of the individuals themselves... (Bahá’u’lláh, The Compilation of Compilations, vol. 1, Ḥuqúqu’lláh)

And again:

“...Ye may relinquish the whole world but must not allow the detraction of even one jot or tittle from the dignity of the Cause of God. Jináb-i-Amín —upon him be My glory— must also refrain from mentioning this matter, for it is entirely dependent upon the willingness of the individuals themselves. They are well acquainted with the commandment of God and are familiar with that which was revealed in the Book. Let him who wisheth observe it, and led him who wisheth ignore it....” (Bahá’u’lláh, The Compilation of Compilations, vol. 1, Ḥuqúqu’lláh)

The concept of Ḥuqúqu’lláh is an evolutionary process subject to great changes, dependent on our spiritual growth, and our deepening of the Holy writings.

Most of the friends believe Ḥuqúqu’lláh is a way for fund raising, and its aim is to strengthen the material potential of the Faith. Indeed the payment of Ḥuqúqu’lláh contributes to a large extent to the needs of the Cause. It is an important instrument for building and strengthening the structure of the edifice of the World Order of Bahá’u’lláh, and when it is fully established there will be an ever-flowing source of revenue at the disposal of the Focal Point of the Cause of God to promote the Faith and to meet the growing needs of establishing a new world order. But, in fact, the purpose and aim of Ḥuqúqu’lláh is far beyond that and much greater and more spiritual than we imagine.

In 1978/79, following the Iranian upheaval, when the most important source of revenue of the Faith stopped functioning, I asked the Universal House of Justice if it was time for the implementation of Ḥuqúqu’lláh in some of the Western countries. The Universal House of Justice replied that Ḥuqúqu’lláh is a very important law, and its implementation needs time and consultation in the future. At the time, I could not comprehend the wisdom of what had been stated. It was after studying the Holy writings with more depth, that I have realized that Ḥuqúqu'lláh which could be interpreted as the material aspect of the Covenant of God, in reality is a spiritual and learning process, a way of strengthening the link of love and dedication between man and God, and its implementation needs studying and deepening.

Bahá'u'lláh in the Kitáb-i-Aqdas says:

"Indeed there lie concealed in this command, mysteries and benefits which are beyond the comprehension of anyone save God, the All-Knowing, the All-Informed...."

Therefore, we cannot expect to comprehend the essence and the wisdom hidden in this sacred law. They are kept in the treasury of God's knowledge and are related to the evolution and progress of the human soul in the world of God. What we can conceive by our human understanding is that the payment of Ḥuqúqu'lláh is the sign of our love and obedience, a proof of our firmness and steadfastness and a symbol of our trustworthiness in the Covenant of Bahá'u'lláh. It creates and develops our spiritual quality which leads us towards perfection; it harmonizes and balances our material endeavour, protects us from excessive desire which is born in our human nature, and when unleashed turns into a preventive element for our spiritual growth.

It is important to note that although there is some similarity between Ḥuqúqu'lláh and the other donations, and that all are the marvelous fruits of love, enthusiasm and devotion of the believers to the Faith, there are four major differences between them:

1. The payment of Ḥuqúqu'lláh has priority over all other contributions because it belongs to God. The contribution of the believers to the funds should be made from their possessions and not from what belongs to the Lord.

2. The payment of Ḥuqúqu'lláh according to the explicit text of the Kitáb-i-Aqdas is an obligation subject to specific laws and ordinances, whereas other donations are not considered as a law. They are rather

an indication of the sacrifice, generosity, detachment and magnanimity of the contributor to meet the needs of the administration of the Cause.

3. Ḥuqúqu'lláh is determined precisely on accurate calculation, whereas there are no rules related to the frequency or the amount of the contribution to the funds.

4. The disposal of the Ḥuqúqu'lláh is left solely to the Focal Point of the Faith, and none other, whereas the disposal of the other contributions can depend on the purpose for which the contribution has been earmarked.

Undoubtedly, the awareness of the friends about Ḥuqúqu'lláh will raise many questions, including those related to its calculation and the appraisal of that part of one's belongings which is subject to exemption. One should consider that what is revealed in the Kitáb-i-Aqdas about Ḥuqúqu'lláh is only the fundamental basis of this injunction, and the approach of the Blessed Beauty is confined to these guiding lines and general principles. He has not set any special rules or legislation. In all His writings related to this matter, God's self-sufficiency and independence of all things has been manifested, and the fragrance of His compassion, generosity and mercy is inhaled. According to the letter written in 1878 by His secretary to an early believer, for the first time the acceptance of Ḥuqúqu'lláh was granted to those Persian friends who had the desire to contribute, therefore, during five years after the revelation of the law, Bahá'u'lláh did not accept Ḥuqúqu'lláh and on many occasions the offering of the friends was returned to them. It could be assumed that since He, Himself, as the Central Figure of His Revelation, is the only recipient of Ḥuqúqu'lláh, He did not want to go into details, but left them, in conformity to the Will of God, to the Universal House of Justice, the Body which has the power to enact laws that are not precisely given in the Book.

When the Kitáb-i-Aqdas reached Iran and as the friends became aware of its contents, a consultative body, which could be the nucleus of our actual Local Spiritual Assemblies, was formed in Tihran. In their minutes we notice that the dissemination of the knowledge of Ḥuqúqu'lláh was one of the goals set by that body 101 years ago.

The growing eagerness of the believers for the execution of God's injunction led them to ask Bahá'u'lláh for elucidation regarding Ḥuqúqu'lláh and this was given to them in various Tablets. The most important guidance was revealed —in response to Jináb-i-Zayn's request— as an annex to the Kitáb-i-Aqdas in the form of questions and answers. More guidance from the Beloved Master, the Guardian, and in recent decades from the Universal House of Justice has shed light on Ḥuqúqu'lláh which we can find in the compilation issued by the World Centre.

With the increasing awareness of the Bahá'ís and the fast growing complexity of the social and economic system of society, the Bahá'í community will witness the establishment of rules and guidance on Ḥuqúqu'lláh by the Supreme Authority of the Faith. Meanwhile, according to the Universal House of Justice's letter of March 1, 1984, in the absence of explicit text and Holy writings on Ḥuqúqu'lláh, the friends are free to honour the obligation of Ḥuqúqu'lláh based on their own judgement and conscience.

Indeed, while the establishment of rules and directions can explain the different aspects of Ḥuqúqu'lláh, the ideal functioning and efficiency of these legislations depend on the spiritual advancement of the friends and their deepening in the Holy Writings.

That is why the Universal House of Justice has, as one of its major goals of the Six Year Plan, adopted the education of Ḥuqúqu'lláh as a priority, preparing the way for the implementation of the law of God in the Bahá'í world, and has asked the fervent collaboration of the major institutions of the Faith, such as the National Spiritual Assemblies and the Continental Boards of Counsellors to share this important task with the Institution of Ḥuqúqu'lláh in promoting the education of God's injunction to the Bahá'í community at large. During the last two years, some of the National Spiritual Assemblies —in particular the National Spiritual Assemblies of the United States and Canada and a few others in other parts of the world— offered remarkable assistance for this sublime goal and it is hoped many more will join in the future to assist with this task. As a result of the effort of such National Spiritual Assemblies, a number of Western friends are contributing to Ḥuqúqu'lláh even before its formal implementation. This leads us to hope that education on this subject will become more widespread and that, by the end of the Six Year Plan, the Bahá'í world will have attained a higher level of flourishing spiritual advancement.

Bibliography

'Abdu'l-Bahá. *Some Answered Questions*. Bahá'í Publishing Trust: Wilmette, Illinois, 1990.

'Abdu'l-Bahá. *Tablets of Abdul-Baha Abbas*. Chicago: Baha'i Publishing Society, 1909-19.

'Abdu'l-Bahá. *Memorials of the Faithful*. Wilmette, IL: Bahá'í Publishing Trust, 1971.

'Abdu'l-Bahá. *The Will and Testament of 'Abdu'l-Bahá*. Wilmette, Illinois: Bahá'í Publishing Trust, 1990.

'Azíz'u'lláh Azízí. *Crown of Glory: Memoirs of Jináb-i-'Azíz'u'lláh Azízí*. Iran: Bahá'í Publishing Trust, 1976. https://bahai-library.com/pdf/a/azizi_crown_glory.pdf.

Abdu'l-Ali Alaii. "Ali-Moḥammad Varqā, Šarḥ-E Ḥāl-E Ayādi-E Amr Allāh Ba Qalam-E Ḵodešān." In *Mo'assassa-Ye Ayādi-Ye Amr Allāh*. Tehran, 1973.

Abrahamian, Ervand. *Tortured Confessions: Prisons and Public Recantations in Modern Iran*: University of California Press, 1999.

Adamson, Hugh C. *Historical Dictionary of the Bahá'í Faith*: Scarecrow Press, 2006.

Afroukhteh, Youness. *Memories of Nine Years in 'Akká*: Translated by R. Masrour. Oxford: George Ronald, 2003.

Amanat, Abbas. *Pivot of the Universe: Nasir Al-Din Shah Qajar and the Iranian Monarchy, 1831-1896*: Univ of California Press, 1997.

Ashton, Beatrice. "The Most Great Jubilee." *The Baha'i World (1963-1968)*1974.

Ayman, Iraj. "Varqā, 'Ali-Moḥammad." In *Encyclopædia Iranica*. Edited by Ehsan Yarshater, in press.

Ayman, Iraj. *Encyclopedia Iranica.* online edition, 2007. http://www.iranicaonline.org/articles/varqa-wali-allah.

Ayman, Iraj *Encyclopædia Iranica*, 2017. http://www.iranicaonline.org/articles/varqa-ali-mohammad.

Báb, The. *Selections from the Writings of the Báb*: Bahá'í World Centre, 1978.

Bahá'í Chronicles. "Ḥájí Mullá Mihdí-i-Yazdí Aka Ḥájí Mullá Mihdí-i-'Atrí." 31 October 2015. Accessed 20 May 2020. https://bahaichronicles.org/ḥaji-mulla-mihdiy-i-yazdi/.

Bahá'u'lláh. *Epistle to the Son of the Wolf.* Wilmette, Illinois: Bahá'í Publishing Trust, 1988.

Bahá'u'lláh. *Gleanings from the Writings of Bahá'u'lláh*. Translated by Shoghi Effendi. London: Bahá'í Publishing Trust, 1978.

Bahá'u'lláh. *The Kitáb-i-Aqdas: The Most Holy Book.* Wilmette, Illinois: Bahá'í Publishing Trust, 1993.

Bahá'u'lláh. *The Kitáb-i-Íqán: The Book of Certitude*. Wilmette, IL: Bahá'í Publishing Trust, 1989.

Bahá'u'lláh. *Tablets of Bahá'u'lláh: Revealed after the Kitáb-i-Aqdas.* Wilmette, Illinois: Bahá'i Publishing Trust, 1988.

Bahá'í Perspective. "Appointment of the Hands of the Cause." 2015. https://www.youtube.com/watch?v=peW4QAaB7Ts.

Bahá'í World Centre. *The Compilation of Compilations*. Vol. I. Maryborough, Victoria: Bahá'í Publications Australia, 2000.

Bahá'í World Centre. *The Compilation of Compilations*. Vol. II. Maryborough, Victoria: Bahá'í Publications Australia, 2000.

Bahá'í World Centre. "Váliyu'lláh Varqá 1884—1955." In *The Bahá'í World*. Vol. XIII. Haifa, Israel: Bahá'í World Centre, 1970.

Bahá'í World Centre. "The Work and Travels of the Hands of the Cause." *The Bahá'í World (1986-1992)* 1998.

Bahá'u'lláh. *The Hidden Words*. Translated by Shoghi Effendi. Wilmette, Ilinois: Bahá'í Publishing Trust, 1985.

Bahá'u'lláh. *The Seven Valleys and the Four Valleys*. Wilmette, Illinois: Bahá'í Publishing Trust, 1991.

Bahá'u'lláh. *The Summons of the Lord of Hosts*. Haifa, Israel: Bahá'í World Centre, 2002.

Bahá'u'lláh, The Báb, and 'Abdu'l-Bahá. *"A Selection of Prayers Revealed by Bahá'u'lláh, the Báb, and 'Abdu'l-Bahá"*. Wilmette, Illinois: Bahá'i Publishing Trust, 2002.

Bahaipedia. "Firuz Kazemzadeh." Last modified 27 July 2020. https://bahaipedia.org/Firuz_Kazemzadeh.

BahaiVideos. "The Hands of the Cause." Last modified 30 July 2020, 2008.
https://www.youtube.com/watch?v=vlmq7CCj_hE.

Bahá'u'lláh. *Gems of Divine Mysteries*. Haifa, Israel: Bahá'í World Centre, 2002.

Bahá'u'lláh. *Prayers and Meditations*: Bahá'í Publishing Trust, 1978.

Balyuzi, Hasan. *'Abdu'l-Bahá: The Centre of the Covenant of Bahá'u'lláh*. Oxford: George Ronald, 1971.

Balyuzi, Hasan. *Bahá'u'lláh, the King of Glory*. Oxford: GeorgeRonald, 1980.

Balyuzi, Hasan. *Eminent Bahá'ís in the Time of Bahá'u'lláh*. Oxford: George Ronald, 1986.

Behroozi Gillbanks, Shahla. *Footprints in the Sand of Time: Memories of a Maidservant*. Sandy, Bedfordshire: The Afnan Library Trust, 2019. http://www.afnanlibrary.org/wp-content/uploads/2019/05/Footprints-in-the-Sands-of-Time-c.pdf.

Buck, Christopher, and Youli A Ioannesyan. "The 1893 Russian Publication of Bahá'u'lláh's Last Will and Testament: An Academic Attestation of 'Abdu'l-Bahá's Successorship." *Bahá'í Studies Review* 19, no. 1 (2013): 3-44.

Calmard, J. *Encyclopedia Iranica*, 1987. https://iranicaonline.org/articles/atabak-e-azam.

Chase, Thornton. *In Galilee*: Kalimat Press, 1985.

Cooper, Andrew Scott. "The Fall of Heaven: The Pahlavis and the Final Days of Imperial Iran ", *The Middle East Journal* 71, no. 1 (2017): 155-56.

Faizi, Abu'l-Qásim "A Flame of Fire: The Story of the Tablet of Ahmad." *Bahá'ís News*, April, 1976.

Faizi, Gloria. *Fire on the Mountain Top*. New Delhi, India: Bahá'í Publishing Trust, 1973.

Farid-Arbab, Sona. "Advancing in Bahá'í-Inspired Education." *The Journal of Bahá'í Studies* 26, no. 4 (2016): 59.

Fattahzadeh, Rahman. "Mohammad Hassan Khan Etemad Al-Saltanah." Computer Research Center of Islamic Sciences. 2014. http://farabiasl.ir/portal/72-محمدحسن%E2%80%8C-خان%E2%80%8C-(اعتمادالسلطنه)%E2%80%8C.html.

Gail, Marzieh. Six Lessons on Islam (Wilmette, Ill.: Bahá'í Pub. Trust, 1973).

Garis, Mable R. *Martha Root: Lioness at the Threshold*. Wilmette: Ill: Bahá'í Publishing Trust, 1983.

Goblot, Henri. *Les Qanats: Une Technique D'acquisition De L'eau*: De Gruyter, 1979.

Griffiths, J. "The British Role within Qajar Dynastic Succession." University of Manchester, 2011.

Ḥakím, Luṭfu'lláh. "The Divine Traces in Persia." The Bahá'í Magazine, the Star of the West, June, 1930.

Hamadání, Mīrzá Yahyá 'Amídu'l-Atibbá "Memoirs of a Bahá'í in Rasht: 1889–1903." *Bahá'í Studies Review* 18, no. 1 (2012): 127-51.

Handal, Boris. *El Concurso En Lo Alto*. Lima: PROPACEB, 1985.

Handal, Boris. *Eve Nicklin: She of the Brave Heart*. Charleston, South Carolina: CreateSpace, 2011.

Handal, Boris. *The Khamsis: A Cradle of True Gold*: IngramSpark, 2020. https://books.google.com.au/books?id=7PuazQEACAAJ.

Handal, Boris. *Mírzá Mihdí: The Purest Branch*. Oxford: George Ronald, 2017.

Handal, Boris. *Mobile Makes Learning Free: Building Conceptual, Professional and School Capacity*. Charlotte, NC: Information Age Publishing, 2015.

Handal, Boris. *A Trilogy of Consecration: The Courier, the Historian and the Missionary*: IngramSparks, 2020.

Harper, Barron Deems. *Lights of Fortitude: Glimpses into the Lives of the Hands of the Cause of God*. Oxford: George Ronald, 2007.

Hatcher, John S. "A Sense of History." In *Response to the Revelation: Poetry by Bahá'ís*. Ontario: The Canadian Association for Studies on the Bahá'í Faith, 1980.

Hatcher, John S. , and Amrollah Hemmat. *Reunion with the Beloved: Poetry and Martyrdom*. Hong Kong: Juxta Publishing Limited, 2004.

Holley, Marion. "May Maxwell (in Memoriam)." In *The Baha'i World (1938-1940)*. Edited by The National Spiritual Assembly of the Bahá'ís of the United States and Canada. Vol. VIII. Wilmette, Illinois: Bahá'í Publishing Trust, 1942.

Honnold, Annamarie. *Vignettes: From the Life of 'Abdu'l-Bahá*: George Ronald, 1997.

Humlum, Johannes. *Underjordiske Vandingskanaler Kareze, Qanat, Foggara*. Vol. 16: Geografisk Institut, 1965.

Iranian Cultural Heritage, Handicrafts and Tourism Organization. *Nomination of Golestan Palace for Inscription on the World Heritage List*. Tehran, 2012. https://whc.unesco.org/uploads/nominations/1422.pdf.

Iranian Review. Contemporary History. 2016. http://www.iranreview.org/content/Documents/Assassination-of-Nasser-al-Din-Shah.htm.

Jamali, Navid. "The Lost Links: An Introduction to the Matrilineal Genealogy of the Qajar Dynasty." https://www.academia.edu/37455230/The_Lost_Links_An_Introduction_to_the_Matrilineal_Genealogy_of_the_Qajar_Dynasty.

Jasion, Jan Teofil *'Abdu'l-Bahá in France 1911-1913*. Paris: Editions Bahá'íes France, 2017.

Kasra, Niloofar. "Haj Ali Khan Hajib Al-Dawlah." *Institute of Iranian Contemporary Historical Studies News*2015. http://www.iichs.ir/News-619/اعتمادالسلطنه-اول---حاج%E2%80%8Cعلی%E2%80%8Cخان-حاجب%E2%80%8Cالدوله/?id=619.

Kazemzadeh, Firuz. "In Memoriam: Kazem Kazemzadeh (1898-1989)." *The Bahá'í World (1986-1992)*, 1998.

Kazemzadeh, Kazem. "Varqá and Rúhu'llah: Deathless in Martyrdom." *World Order*Winter 1974-1975.

Khadem, Javidukht. *Zikrullah Khadem, the Itinerant Hand of the Cause of God*. Wilmette, Illinois: Bahá'í Publishing Trust, 1990.

Khadem, Ramin, and Fred Badiyan. "Huqúqu'lláh the Right of God." 1995. https://www.youtube.com/watch?v=21TY10KdBMM.

Khadem, Riaz. *Prelude to the Guardianship*. Oxford: George Ronald, 2014.

Khazaei, Yaghoub. "An Analysis of the Pre-Modern and Modern Prison Structure Case Study: Tehran's Anbár and Qasr Prisons." *Journal of Historical Researches* 10, no. 38 (2018).

Koochi, Mohammad Reza Rezaeian, Ghadir Najafzadeh Shavaki, and Sajad Moradi. "Analysis of Some Punishment Practices Based on Legal-Historical Principles of Iranian Society: Qajar Dynasty Case Study." *Journal of History Culture and Art Research* 6, no. 2 (2017): 647-54.

Lakshiman-Lepain, Rajwantee. *The Life of Thomas Breakwell.* London: Bahá'í Publishing Trust, 1998.

Lambden, Stephen "The Sinaitic Mysteries: Notes on Moses/Sinai Motifs in Bahá'í Scripture." In *Studies in Honour of the Late Hasan M. Balyuzi.* edited by Moojan Momen. Los Angeles: Kalimat Press, 1988.

Lovejoy, Thellie. *Dwight Barstow Collection.* 2005.

Ma'ani, Baharieh Rouhani. *Leaves of the Twin Divine Trees*: George Ronald Publisher, 2008.

Masumian, Bijan, and Adib Masumian. "The Báb in the World of Images." *Bahá'í Studies Review* 19, no. 1 (2013): 171-90.

McGlinn, Sen. "The Leiden List of the Writings of Bahá'u'lláh." 1997. https://www.h-net.org/~bahai/notes/bhtabs.htm.

McLean, Jack. "Divine Simplicity: Remembering the Last Hand of the Cause of God, Dr 'Alí-Muhammad Varqá." 2007. https://jack-mclean.com/essays/divine-simplicity-remembering-the-last-hand-of-the-cause-of-god-dr-ali-muhammad-varqa/.

Mírzá Abu'l-Faḍl-i-Gulpáygání. *Bahá'í Proofs*. New York: J.W. Pratt & Co, 1902.

https://bahai-library.com/gulpaygani_bahai_proofs.

Momen, Moojan. *The Bábí and Bahá'í Religions 1844-1944: Some Contemporary Western Accounts*. Oxford: George Ronald, 1981.

Momen, Moojan. *Bahá'í Communities of Iran*. Vol. II. Oxford: George Ronald, in press.

Momen, Moojan. *The Bahá'í Communities of Iran 1851-1921: The North of Iran*. Vol. I. Oxford: George Ronald, 2015.

Momen, Moojan. "The Bahá'í Community of Ashkhabad: Its Social Basis and Importance in Bahá'í History." *Cultural Change and Continuity in Central Asia* (1991): 278-305. https://www.momen.org/relstud/ishqabad.htm.

Momen, Moojan. "Persecution and Resilience: A History of the Baha'i Religion in Qajar Isfahan." *Journal of religious history* 36, no. 4 (2012): 471-85.

Momen, Moojan. "Relativism: A Basis for Bahá'í Metaphysics." *Studies in Honor of the Late Hasan M. Balyuzi* (1988): 185-217.

Muhájir, Í.F. *Hand of the Cause of God Furútan*: Bahá'í Publishing Trust, 2017.

Muhájir, Írán Furútan. *Dr Muhájir: Hand of the Cause of God, Knight of Bahá'u'lláh*. London: Bahá'í Publishing Trust, 1992.

Muhájir, Raḥmatu'lláh. "The Legacy of the Martyrs." 2020. https://bahai.works/Audio:Rahmatu'llah_Muhajir/About_the_legacy_of_the_martyrs.

Nabíl-i-A'zam. *The Dawn-Breakers: Nabíl's Narrative of the Early Days of the Bahá'í Revelation*. Wilmette, IL: Bahá'í Publishing Trust, 1970.

National Spiritual Assembly of the Bahá'ís of the United States. "Memorial for Dr. Firuz Kazemzadeh." 22 Aug 2017. https://www.youtube.com/watch?v=CPyRspqT8Os.

Olsen, Birgit Anette, Thomas Olander, and Kristian Kristiansen. *Tracing the Indo-Europeans: New Evidence from Archaeology and Historical Linguistics*: Oxbow Books, 2019.

Quinn, Sholeh A. "The Genesis of the Bábí-Bahá'í Faiths in Shíráz and Fárs: By Mírzá Habíb'u'lláh Afnán (Tr. And Annotated by Ahang Rabbani)(Leiden: Brill, 2008. 404 Pages.)." *American Journal of Islam and Society* 27, no. 2 (2010): 107-09.

Rabbani, Ahang. *Witnesses to Bábí and Bahá'í History*. Vol. 5. *Ponder Thou Upon the Martyrdom of Hájí Muhammad-Ridá: Nineteen Historical Accounts*, edited by Ahang Rabbani, 2007. https://bahai-library.com/pdf/r/rabbani_martyrdom_haji_muhammad-rida.pdf.

Rabbani, Rụhíyyih. *The Ministry of the Custodians 1957–1963*. Haifa, Israel, 1992.

Rabbani, Rụhíyyih. *The Priceless Pearl*: London: Bahá'í Pub. Trust, 1969.

Redman, Earl. *Visiting 'Abdu'l-Bahá, Volume 1: The West Discover the Master, 1897-1911*. Oxford: George Ronald, 2019.

Root, Martha. "The Only Pictures of the Báb." *Bahá'í Magazine, The Star of the West*, May, 1930.

Root, Martha. "White Roses of Persia (Part 1)." *Star of the West, vol. 23, issue 6*, June, 1932.

Root, Martha. "White Roses of Persia (Part 2)." *Star of the West, vol. 23, issue 6*, September, 1932.

Root, Martha. "White Roses of Persia (Part 3)." *Star of the West, vol. 23, issue 7*, October, 1932.

Root, Martha. "White Roses of Persia (Part 4)." *Star of the West, vol. 23, issue 8*, November, 1932.

Rouhani Ma'ani, Baharieh "The Evolution of Ḥuqúqu'lláh." January 1996.

Ruhe, David S. *Door of Hope: A Century of the Bahá'í Faith in the Holy Land*: George Ronald, 1983.

Ryman, Danièle. "Aromatherapy Bible." 2016. Accessed 30 August 2020. http://aromatherapybible.com/rose/.

Safizadeh, Fereydoun. "Shahsavan in the Grip of Development." *Cultural Survival Quarterly Magazine*, March, 1984. https://www.culturalsurvival.org/publications/cultural-survival-quarterly/shahsavan-grip-development.

Savi, Julio, and Faezeh Mardani. "The Mathnaví by Rúhu'lláh Varqá, the Martyr: A Few Notes on Its Historical Context and Poetical Content." *Lights of Irfan* 9 (2018): 269-84. http://irfancolloquia.org/pdf/lights19_savi_mardani_ruhullah.pdf.

Shah Mirza Mohammad Khan Amin Khaqan. "Execution of Mirza Reza Kermani." 2013.

http://navideshahed.com/en/news/312363/execution-of-mirza-reza-kermani.

Shahvar, Soli. *The Forgotten Schools: The Baha'is and Modern Education in Iran, 1899–1934*. Taylor & Francis, 2013.

Shahrokh, Darius. ed., *The Mystery of Sacrifice*, 1992. https://bahai-library.com/wttp/PDF/The%20Mystery%20of%20Martyrdom.pdf.

Shahrokh, Darius. *Varqá and Son: The Heavenly Doves*, 1992. https://bahai-library.com/shahrokh_varqa_son.

Shoghi Effendi. *The Advent of Divine Justice*. Wilmette, Illinois: Bahá'í Publishing Trust, 1990.

Shoghi Effendi. *The Dispensation of Bahá'u'lláh*. Wilmette, ILL: Bahá'í Publishing Trust, 1991.

Shoghi Effendi. *God Passes By*. Wilmette, IL: Bahá'í Publishing Trust, ed. 1979.

Shoghi Effendi. *Messages to the Bahá'í World: 1950–1957*. Wilmette, Illinois: US Bahá'í Publishing Trust, 1971.

Shoghi Effendi. "Pillars of the Faith." *The Bahá'í World,* 1930.

Shoghi Effendi. *The Promised Day Has Come*. Wimette, Illinois: Bahá'í Publishing Trust, 1980.

Shoghi Effendi. *Messages to America. Wilmette: Bahá'í Publishing Trust, 1947.*

Shoghi Effendi. *A Synopsis and Codification of the Kitáb-i-Aqdas, the Most Holy Book of Bahá'u'lláh*: Bahá'í World Centre, 1973.

Shoghi Effendi. *The Unfolding Destiny of the British Bahá'í Community*. London: Bahá'í Publishing Trust, 1981.

Sims, Ellen. "Argentina, Bolivia, Chile, Uruguay and Paraguay Form National Assembly in Buenos Aires." *Bahá'í News*, June, 1957.

Star of the West. "Martyrs and Prisoners in Persia 1896 ", 17 May 1912.
Star of the West. "Abdul-Baha Introduces Mirza Wargha to the New York Friends." February, 1913.

National Spiritual Assembly of the Bahá'ís of the United States. "Schools in Belgium." *Bahá'í News*, June, 1970.

National Spiritual Assembly of the Bahá'ís of the United States. *Wellspring of Guidance: Messages from the Universal House of Justice, 1963-1968*. Wilmette, Illinois: Bahá'í Publishing Trust, 1970.

Stiles-Maneck, S. "Wisdom and Dissimulation: The Use and Meaning of Hikmat in the Bahá'í Writings and History." *Bahá'í Studies Review* 6 (1996): 11-23.

Sulaymání, 'Azízu'lláh. *Masábíh-i-Hidáyat*. Vol. 1. Tehran, 1947-1976.

Taherzadeh, Adib. *The Covenant of Bahá'u'lláh*. Oxford: George Ronald, 1992.

Taherzadeh, Adib. *The Revelation of Bahá'u'lláh. Vol 4: Mazra'ih & Bahji 1877-92*. Vol. 4. Oxford: George Ronald, 1988.

Taherzadeh, Adib. *The Revelation of Bahá'u'lláh. Vol. 1: Baghdad 1853-63*. Vol. 1980. 2 vols. Oxford: George Ronald, 1974.

Taherzadeh, Adib. *The Revelation of Bahá'u'lláh. Vol. 2: Adrianople 1863-68*. Vol. 2. Oxford: George Ronald, 1987.

Tapper, Richard. "Black Sheep, White Sheep and Red-Heads: A Historical Sketch of the Shāhsavan of Āzarbāijān." *Iran* 4, no. 1 (1966): 61-84.

The Báb. *Selections from the Writings of the Báb*. Haifa: Bahá'í World Centre, 1976.

The National Spiritual Assembly of the Bahá'ís of the United States and Canada. *Bahá'í News*, June, 1934.

The National Spiritual Assembly of the Bahá'ís of the United States and Canada. "International News Items." *Bahá'í News*, January, 1932.

The Universal House of Justice. *The Bahá'í World (1954-1963)*. Vol. XIII. Haifa, Israel: Bahá'í World Centre, 1970.

The Universal House of Justice. "In Memoriam: Valíyu'lláh Varqá." *The Bahá'í World (1954-1963)*, 1970.

Thompson, Juliet. *The Diary of Juliet Thompson*: Kalimát Press, 1983. https://bahai-library.com/thompson_diary&chapter=4.

Tingook, Ronnie Tooyak. "Numerical Simulation of the Base-Level Buffers and Buttresses Conceptual Model of Fluvial Systems." University of Texas Arlington, 2012. http://hdl.handle.net/10106/11049.

Tiven, Benjamin. "Hossain Amanat." *Bidoun*Spring 2013. https://bidoun.org/articles/hossein-amanat.

Towshend, George. "Three Kinds of Martyrdom." *The Bahá'í World*, 1956.

Varqá, 'Alí Muhammad. "Hand of the Cause Dr. Varqá and His Baby Picture When Seen by 'Abdu'l-Bahá While in America." November 19, 2016. http://thebabhistory.blogspot.com/2016/11/hand-of-cause-dr-varqa-and-his-baby.html.

Waters, Allan. *Ḥuqúqu'lláh, the Right of God.* Victoria, Australia: Bahá'í Publications Australia, 2012.

White, Roger. "Bahá'u'lláh and the Fourth Estate." *The Bahá'í World (1979-1983)* 1986. https://bahai-library.com/pdf/w/white_bw18_bahaullah_press.pdf.

Yazdani, Mina. "'Abdu'l-Bahá and the Iranian Constitutional Revolution: Embracing Principles While Disapproving Methodologies." *The Journal of Baha'i Studies* 24, no. 1/2 (2014): 47.

Yule, Henry. *The Travels of Marco Polo*: Cambridge University Press, 2010.

Zarqání, Mahmúd. *Mahmúd's Diary the Diary of Mírzá Mahmúd-i-Zarqání Chronicling `Abdu'l-Bahá's Journey to America.* Translated by Mohi Sobhani with the assistance of Shirley Macias. Oxford: George Ronald, 1998.

Ziaei, Misagh. "The Lawh-i-Tibb (Tablet to the Physician)–Beyond Health Maxims." *The Journal of Bahá'í Studies* 29, no. 3 (2019): 67-100.

Index of Names

'Abdu'l-Bahá, i, v, vii, viii, xix, 21, 22, 23, 24, 32, 34, 41, 42, 50, 54, 61, 62, 71, 72, 73, 74, 77, 79, 80, 82, 83, 84, 104, 113, 114, 118, 119, 124, 143, 151, 153, 154, 158, 182, 206, 207, 209, 214, 215, 217, 220, 221, 222, 224, 228, 229, 230, 233, 234, 235, 237,243, 244, 246, 253, 275, 279, 291, 293, 294, 296, 297, 304
'Abdu'lláh Núrí, 39, 40, 47, 54, 68, 84, 85, 103, 104, 115, 119, 229, 255
'Akká, 34, 41, 42, 46, 48, 54, 56, 64, 72, 74, 79, 80, 84, 85, 86, 87, 97, 98, 100, 102, 143, 146, 157, 233, 292
'Alá'u'd-Dawlih, 76, 117, 193
'Azízu'lláh Varqá, 47, 48, 76, 77, 84, 86, 87, 90, 104, 105, 115, 119, 180, 214, 228, 229, 230, 233, 274, 278, 295
'Azízu'lláh'Varqá, 107, 108
'Ishqábád, 124, 225
Ahmad Khán, 117, 118, 119, 120, 122, 123, 128, 130, 131, 171, 222, 223
Anbar, 294
Aṭrí, 41
Baghdad, 30, 41, 42, 43, 228, 240, 256, 257
Bahá'u'lláh, v, vii, xii, xix, 21, 24, 41, 42, 43, 44, 45, 47, 48, 49, 54, 56, 61, 62, 64, 78, 84, 85, 86, 87, 102, 109, 110, 111, 113, 117, 121, 123, 139, 142, 143, 144, 148, 157, 158, 186, 189, 208, 215, 225, 228, 229, 233, 234, 236, 250, 253, 255, 256, 257, 258, 260, 264, 266, 271, 287, 288, 290, 292, 294, 296, 297, 303, 310
Bahá'u'lláh, 30
Bahíyyih Khánum, 77
Bahjí, vi, vii, 72, 84, 85, 87, 90, 99, 215, 252
Bíbí Túbá, 31, 65
Dr 'Alí-Muhammad Varqá, v, vi, vii, viii, ix, 226, 228, 231, 232, 234, 237, 242, 244, 245, 246, 247, 248, 249, 250, 251, 252, 253, 254, 257, 258, 259, 260, 261, 262, 263, 264, 265, 266, 267, 268, 269, 270, 271, 272, 279, 281, 282, 284, 285, 296, 297, 303
Ḥájí Ímám, 115, 120, 121, 132, 160, 166, 171, 172, 182, 201, 205, 206, 208, 210, 212, 213, 219, 223, 224, 225
Ḥájíbu'd-Dawlih, 150, 172, 173, 174, 175, 177, 185,

186, 189, 190, 191, 198, 205, 206, 218
Ḥuqúqu'lláh, vi, ix, xix, 50, 178, 226, 236, 244, 245, 247, 249, 250, 254, 261, 262, 263, 264, 265, 266, 269, 270, 271, 277, 282, 296, 303, 309
Isfahán, 21, 37, 63, 64, 67, 68, 69, 70, 84, 118, 147
Jalálu'd-Dawlih, 222
Kámrán Mírzá, 37, 194
Kitáb-i-Aqdas, xix, 61, 62, 82, 219, 236, 253, 296, 303, 309, 310
Laqá'íyyih Khánum, 115, 132, 192, 225, 226, 227
Mas'úd Mírzá, 22, 37, 63, 64, 67, 68, 69, 70, 118, 174, 195, 220, 222
Mírzá Ḥasan Yazdí, 31
Mírzá Ḥusayn Yazdí, 30, 31, 33, 35, 41, 47, 93, 96, 228, 229
Mírzá Ḥusayn Zanjání, 117, 121, 123, 124, 125, 131, 132, 160, 161, 163, 164, 165, 169, 171, 172, 183, 201, 205, 206, 208, 210, 211, 212, 213, 219, 223, 224, 226
Mullá Mihdí, 27, 29, 30, 31, 32, 33, 34, 35, 36, 40, 41, 42
Muẓaffari'd-Dín Sháh, 37, 38, 94, 118, 219, 220, 274
Naṣiri'd-Dín Sháh, 37, 38, 39, 63, 124, 132, 161, 171, 172, 177, 186, 196, 197, 221
Núríyyih, 40, 47, 225, 228
Rúḥu'lláh, v, viii, x, xii, 23, 24, 25, 47, 48, 49, 65, 66, 71, 72, 73, 74, 75, 76, 77, 78, 79, 80, 81, 82, 84, 86, 90, 95, 102, 103, 104, 105, 107, 108, 111, 113, 114, 115, 117, 120, 121, 122, 123, 124, 129, 132, 133, 150, 160, 161, 163, 164, 166, 167, 169, 171, 172, 175, 177, 178, 180, 181, 182, 183, 186, 190, 191, 201, 203, 204, 205, 206, 207, 208, 209, 210, 211, 212, 213, 214, 216, 217, 218, 219, 223, 224, 225, 226, 228, 229, 235, 236, 255, 273, 274, 286, 287, 288, 291, 293, 294, 295
Shoghi Effendi, v, vii, xi, xix, 21, 22, 24, 38, 139, 144, 145, 146, 174, 222, 232, 236, 237, 239, 240, 241, 242, 247, 250, 251, 252, 253, 254, 255, 256, 257, 258, 259, 261, 264, 265, 266, 270, 271, 296, 297, 311
Síyáh-Chál, 177, 182
Tabríz, 34, 35, 36, 38, 39, 41, 47, 49, 50, 51, 54, 61, 63, 70, 84, 92, 94, 95, 96, 102, 103, 104, 105, 106, 108, 173, 189, 232, 249
Tehran, xi, 21, 23, 37, 47, 89, 103, 104, 105, 115, 118, 119, 121, 124, 129, 131, 140, 145, 149, 160, 164,

165, 168, 169, 170, 171, 172, 176, 178, 181, 184, 189, 190, 194, 201, 205, 211, 217, 219, 223, 227, 229, 230, 232, 233, 234, 242, 247, 248, 249, 256, 257, 273, 274, 278, 293, 295
The Báb, vii, xix, 25, 29, 30, 31, 33, 37, 43, 45, 50, 51, 52, 53, 54, 79, 94, 108, 117, 121, 138, 140, 142, 144, 145, 172, 184, 185, 186, 222, 225, 233, 234, 257, 291, 304
Umm-i-Ashraf, 108, 109, 111, 115, 226
Valíyu'lláh Varqá, vi, vii, 47, 53, 73, 106, 215, 229, 232, 233, 234, 235, 236, 237, 239, 240, 241, 242, 250, 251, 263, 274, 275, 276, 277, 296
Varqá, v, vii, viii, ix, xi, 21, 22, 23, 24, 25, 27, 31, 33, 35, 37, 38, 39, 40, 41, 42, 43, 44, 45, 46, 47, 48, 49, 50, 52, 53, 54, 55, 56, 57, 61, 62, 63, 65, 67, 68, 69, 70, 71, 72, 73, 75, 76, 84, 85, 88, 89, 90, 95, 96, 102, 103, 104, 105, 107, 108, 113, 114, 115, 117, 118, 119, 120, 121, 122, 123, 124, 125, 126, 127, 128, 129, 130, 131, 132, 133, 135, 136, 146, 150, 151, 153, 154, 155, 156, 157, 158, 160, 161, 162, 163, 164, 165, 166, 167, 168, 169, 170, 171, 172, 175, 177, 178, 180, 181, 183, 184, 185, 186, 190, 191, 201, 204, 205, 206, 207, 210, 211, 212, 213, 214, 215, 216, 217, 218, 219, 223, 225, 226, 228, 229, 232, 235, 236, 246, 253, 255, 273, 280, 286, 287, 288, 289, 291, 293, 295, 296
Yazd, 21, 27, 28, 29, 30, 31, 33, 34, 35, 37, 63, 64, 67, 68, 69, 76, 91, 222, 289
Zanján, 21, 47, 76, 101, 104, 105, 107, 108, 109, 110, 114, 115, 117, 118, 119, 120, 121, 122, 123, 124, 131, 132, 160, 162, 163, 164, 165, 169, 171, 182, 184, 189, 190, 211, 219, 223, 225, 229

www.ingramcontent.com/pod-product-compliance
Lightning Source LLC
Chambersburg PA
CBHW070247010526
44107CB00056B/2375
9780648901457